UNBUILT
MASTERWORKS
OF THE 21st CENTURY

UNBUILT MASTERWORKS
OF THE 21st CENTURY

Inspirational Architecture
for the Digital Age

WILL JONES

With 900 illustrations, 747 in color

Dedication
To my wife Stephanie, for unending support and constant delight.

Acknowledgements
I would like to thank Lucas Dietrich, Cat Glover, Avni Patel and Cameron Laux
for their great work in making this book possible. My gratitude also goes to all
of the architects and their press teams who worked with me to enable such a diverse
and interesting array of projects to be included; thank you.

On the cover
Front: Ciudad del Motor, Spain by UN Studio (computer rendering)
Back: Changsha Culture Park, China by MAD (computer rendering)

First published in 2009 in hardcover in the United States of America by
Thames & Hudson Inc., 500 Fifth Avenue, New York, New York 10110

thamesandhudsonusa.com

Library of Congress Catalog Card Number 2008911983

ISBN 978-0-500-34254-1

Printed and bound in China by SNP Leefung Printers Limited

CONTENTS

INTRODUCTION

Zaha Hadid is today one of the world's most celebrated architects. Her unique designs are feted by governments, sheikhs, museums and corporate magnates alike; and yet, to date she has seen only around ten of her schemes built. After setting up practice in 1980, Hadid had to wait thirteen years for the completion of her first building, the Vitra Fire Station in Germany. Even after that, work didn't come any easier and she was forced to support her architectural endeavours with teaching work and product design.

So, what of Hadid's unrealized designs, or the innumerable other schemes conceived by architects the world over that didn't make it any further than the drawing board? *Unbuilt Masterworks of the 21st Century* sets out to display some of the most creative works from architects around the world that never came to fruition. They vary dramatically in terms of size and scope, ranging from footbridges to masterplans for cities; libraries to skyscrapers; and houses to hotels and museums. The architects chosen represent some of the largest and most forward thinking in the world, new small firms, plus those of a singularly unique design style. They are a heterogeneous group but one that has in common a back catalogue of brilliant designs that never saw the light of day.

This collection of unbuilt masterworks is a library of brilliant and challenging ideas, all of which are totally viable. And so, the question must be why didn't these projects get built? The reasons are many and varied and competition entries are a good place to start. Here alone is a vast collection of unrealized schemes. For instance, the Grand Egyptian Museum in Cairo competition in 2002 drew over three hundred entries from practices all around the globe. Only one scheme could win. Similarly, the competition for the repopulation of the World Trade Center site, following the events of 11 September 2001, drew massive attention. Again, there could be only one winner. However, in this particular case even the triumphant scheme, a twisting shard-like tower by Daniel Libeskind, will not be built true to its original design; such are the whims of the site owner and the drastic changes made to the design since the announcement of Libeskind's victory.

Finance is another great stumbling block. The length of time it takes to design a large building is in most cases counted in months and years. In that intervening time, architects and their clients may find that the cost of land, materials or labour soars to a level not previously envisaged. What once was a viable scheme now becomes a money guzzling monster best killed off before it completely engulfs the person or organization paying for its design and construction.

Similarly, architectural projects fall foul of personality clashes, restrictive planning dictats or government intervention. London is a fine example of a city strangled by political and heritage organizations, each with its own agenda when it comes to the erection of new large buildings. Every project has to run the gauntlet of both planning and political decision-makers, who judge its merit on aspects as varied as the impact it has on sight lines of St Paul's Cathedral or the building's ability to produce a percentage of its own power. Designs are passed between the Mayor's Office, English Heritage, the Office of the Deputy Prime Minister, a Borough planning authority and seemingly almost anyone else wishing to have a say. The media also gets involved, powerful players sway public opinion and what was once an original inspirational design is often changed beyond recognition. In the midst of all this wrangling, the designer, developer and client, get dragged from pillar to post and until more often than not one of them grows tired of the whole charade and pulls out. Almost always this means the end of the project.

However, many would argue that the numerous laws and regulations now imposed on buildings in the UK are put there for a reason. Do they stifle the creativity of architects wishing to build there? Or, do they serve a valuable purpose, weeding out the less than rigorously planned schemes? The answer lies not in Britain or Europe but in the Middle and Far East. Construction in the United Arab Emirates and China is advancing at a pace never before witnessed. There are rules to abide by but in this boom there seems to be little restriction on what does and doesn't get built apart from a prohibitive cost. The resulting architecture is dramatic and at times alarming both in terms of aesthetic considerations and a lack of consideration for issues such as sustainability.

It seems that there is no definitive answer as to why a building does or does not get built: some just do and others do not. The architect is the punch bag in the midst of financial, political and regulatory sparring. With every project designed and for every building completed there are many more that don't see the light of day. This is no bad thing because it makes designers strive to reach greater metaphorical heights on their next competition or commission. And, contrary to what some might believe, no one, not even the star architects get every design built.

Even now, nearing thirty years after the formation of her practice, Hadid is still designing things that don't get realized. Her first permanent building in the UK, a new headquarters for the Architecture Foundation, has foundered due to a lack of ambition on the part of the developer and a downturn in the economy. Hadid's design for the 2012 Olympic swimming venue is also causing a furore, as the very people who commissioned this radical architect now fear that they have bitten off more than they can chew. The architect, public and International Olympic Committee wait with baited breath.

However, whether a competition, lack of funding, new dictatorship or fear of public opinion, put paid to the projects in this book, it makes them no less extraordinary and exciting and *Unbuilt Masterworks of the 21st Century* will bring you some of the best from a very ambitious start to this century.

1.
ARTS AND ENTERTAINMENT

Considering that it is something that has no physical presence at all, sound is potentially one of the most important design considerations for many architectural projects in the arts and entertainment sectors. This can mean the transmission of sound, its reception, the eradication of noise or the amplification of certain aspects for optimum performance and entertainment.

The implications for architectural projects are astounding. Material choices are important; the volume and shape of auditoria have to be considered; potential ingress of unwanted sound has to be minimized; and base elements such as vibration have to be guarded against. For example, the International Convention Centre in Birmingham, UK, houses a world class concert hall, but the venue is built directly over a main railway line. The design of the building includes soundproof lobbies to all conference halls, while the concert hall is actually built as an entirely independent structure within the overall building. Every wall and floor of the concert hall that connects with the rest of the centre is cushioned by a rubber vibration joint. Moreover, the entire concert hall rests on immense pad foundations that sit on rubber dampers which cut out any vibration from the trains passing underneath.

The reason for these drastic and often unseen design decisions, be the venue an opera house, theatre, art gallery, leisure centre or cinema, is to enhance visitor or viewer satisfaction. As with all good architecture, the user comes first. But while in offices or railway stations calculated corners can be cut, if a theatre does not perform well, visitors will not come back, and it will be classed as a complete failure.

To this end, the architect must next consider how the venue will operate as a whole with regard to those who will use it. Many arts and entertainment buildings will experience periods of semi-dormancy followed by short periods when thousands of visitors will expect to enter and wander freely without getting caught up in queues or bottle-necks. The venue has to be able to cope with large numbers, but it must also be easily navigable. And, in the case of visitors' centres and art galleries, they must also enhance the visitor experience by assisting in the understanding of the attraction therein.

The Centre Pompidou in Paris is a venue that does this very visibly. Architects Richard Rogers and Renzo Piano designed the building to keep exhibition spaces as clear as possible. They eradicated internal columns and moved all services and some circulation outside, tacking them onto the exterior of the building. Completed in 1977, the Pompidou now attracts 26,000 visitors each day, five times as many as it was designed for: it still performs well.

These ground rules for almost all entertainment venues have been in existence for a long while now. The difference in today's entertainment sector buildings from those of, say, one hundred years ago is that they are becoming accessible to all, not just the rich and privileged. This influx of visitors is not always used to the etiquette of an opera house or the nuances of a theatre, and as such the architect's role must be to guide them and offer prompts as to what, where, when.

In addition to all of these rules, procurers of arts and entertainment venues also want the architect to create a venue that is a visitor attraction in its own right. This has long been the goal for the designer. In 72 CE the Romans were treated to the opening of the Colosseum, an entertainment venue like no other. And, we have recently witnessed the completion of perhaps the modern world's nearest comparable creation, the Bird's Nest Stadium for the 2008 Olympics in Beijing. Both have triumphed in the dual feats of working as a venue and becoming an iconic building in their own right. Both are unique.

Another undoubtedly unique entertainment venue, and one that was only erected temporarily, was Le Corbusier's design for the Philips Pavilion at the 1958 World Fair. The architect described the concept for the design of the building as that of a 'stomach', in which to contain the 'Poème Electronique', a futuristic multimedia display featuring images, coloured lighting, and music and sounds. He wanted a pavilion with a twisted path for entrance and exit and warped, curving walls on which to project the colours and images. Internally, there was to be an auditorium, where five hundred visitors could see the images projected on all the walls around them.

Critics of the time slammed the architecture as 'not a fulfilled architecture... not a clear composition... only the indication of new architectonic dimensions'. However, the impact of the music in Le Corbusier's amalgamation of architecture, film and sound was great. The composer Varèse's score, while not enthusiastically received by the public, influenced an entire generation of avant-garde composers: justification for a bizarre venue in no uncertain terms.

When considered in this way, the success of an entertainment venue is easy to judge. If those who visit come away having been influenced, moved or simply having enjoyed the spectacle, then the venue can be said to have worked. If, in addition to this, the building is lauded as a masterpiece too, then the architect and owner have achieved great things. The skill in designing a successful arts or entertainment building is juggling these two aspects perfectly, while always giving priority to the former.

ARABIAN PERFORMANCE VENUE, UAE
AEDAS

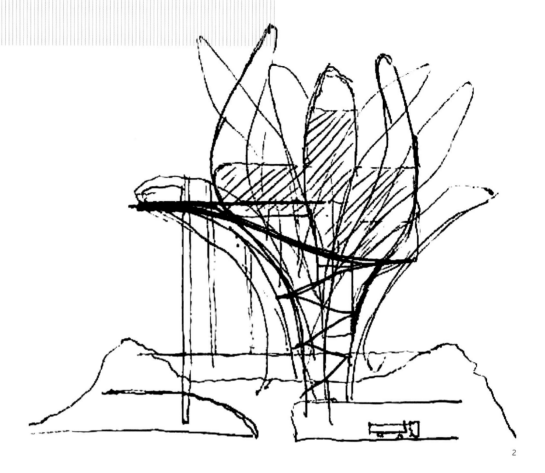

Surrounded by the desert sands and occupying its
own island in the middle of a nature reserve, the opera house for Dubai
is, according to its architects Aedas, organically tied to both its context
and use: 'The venue is experienced through an entry sequence of surprise
and discovery.'

The island is connected to the mainland via long-span bridges for
both vehicles and trains, but approach by boat offers the best spectacle.
Entrances are cut into the mounded landscape of the island. They open
into a water-filled cavity with walls which contain water leading to the
main entry foyer and a museum/exhibition centre.

Dropping down from the main foyer, a lower concourse travels
underneath the water into a darkened space dappled with reflections
from the water above. Here, restaurants surround a 'black box' performance theatre in the centre of the space. Inside this underwater
world there are splashes of light from above, emitted from glass tubes
that house forty-four elevators. Entering the elevator, visitors rise out
of the water and the walls open up to allow for 360-degree views of the
surrounding landscape.

1 'Petals', as
   inspiration
2 Concept sketch
3 Aerial view

The elevators arrive at a traditional forecourt for the 2,500-seat performance venue situated some 100 m (328 ft) off the ground. It is surrounded by seven giant structures that the architects dub 'dancing figures', which rise up to 284 m (932 ft) into the sky above. This entry platform also serves as a public observation area, allowing views beyond to the migrating birds which flock to the surrounding lake.

In the centre of four of the dancing figures is another performance venue. The main lobby of the hotel sits on top of it, enclosed in an outer glass shell. The lobby is reached via its own express lifts, while the four dancing figures that flank it are accessed via sky bridges. These figures house three hundred hotel and service apartment rooms.

Two of the three other figures house places for the public to eat and drink, and provide shade to the forecourt. The last, at the rear of the building, contains supporting facilities for the performance venue itself.

4   The approach
    by road
5   The entire island
6   Pedestrian
    circulation

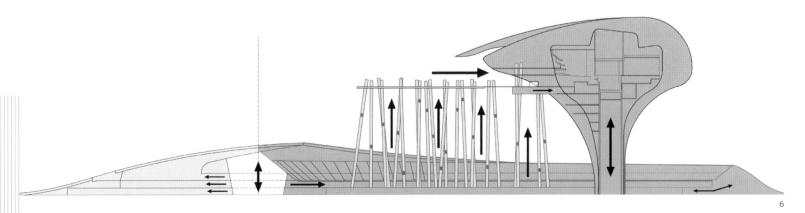

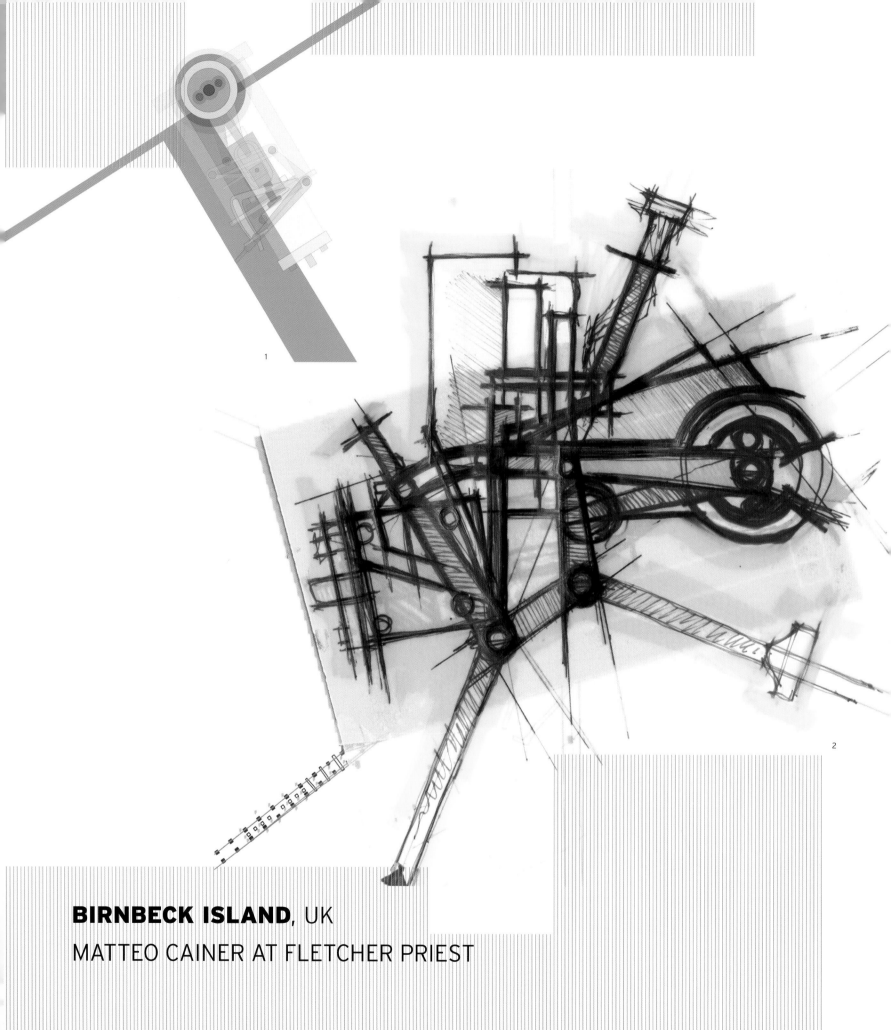

1

2

BIRNBECK ISLAND, UK

MATTEO CAINER AT FLETCHER PRIEST

Bustling seaside towns and busy ports full of small
fishing and pleasure boats encapsulate the romance and character of the
English coastal resort. For over two hundred years they provided an escape
from the grime of industrial centres such as Manchester and London.

Weston-Super-Mare was one such traditional holiday resort, located
on the west coast of the UK, and Birnbeck Island is a small, rocky island
just off the coast of the town. It is joined to the mainland by a long pier
which was built in 1866. The island has in the past been used as a steamer
pier and a weapon testing area. It also featured recreational facilities and a
pier-head ride for many years, but as holidaying in the UK lost its appeal,
the pier and island have fallen into disrepair.

1   Steam engine
    as inspiration
2   Concept sketch
3   Aerial model view

Developer Urban Splash acquired the island and pier in 2006 and launched an architectural competition to redevelop it. The 21st-century vision of Matteo Cainer at Fletcher Priest Architects is for the historic seaside attraction to take advantage of the isolated location in order to create the perfect setting for a hedonistic lifestyle, based on health and well-being. It includes, among other things, a tower hotel and restaurant, multi-therapeutical baths with thalassotherapy (therapies using seaweed and saltwater, etc.), training and fitness facilities, and beauty and health spas.

The architect's proposal reinforces the access to the island and enhances it through an extraordinary mechanistic structure that incorporates and interlocks with the remnants of the Victorian infrastructure of buildings and piers. Its elements are expressed as a steam engine whose qualities are further articulated in the detail of the design.

The design takes the static geometrical structure and combines a machine aesthetic with dynamic components, and by flooding basins and driving turbines it achieves the attributes of a working engine. The project not only appears to 'work', it also harnesses and generates power from the high tidal surges in the area, as well as wind and solar power.

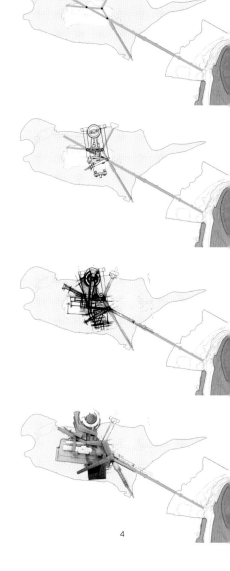

4

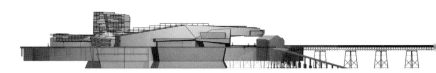

5

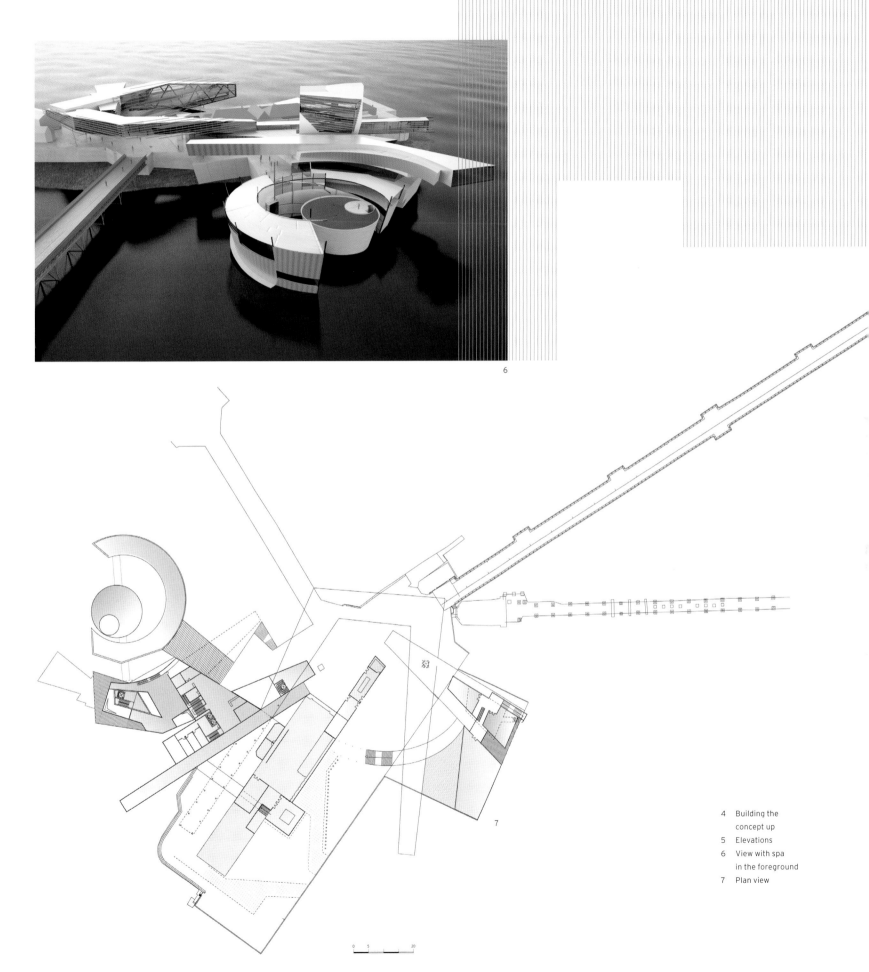

4 Building the
concept up
5 Elevations
6 View with spa
in the foreground
7 Plan view

1

2

CIUDAD DEL MOTOR, SPAIN

UN STUDIO

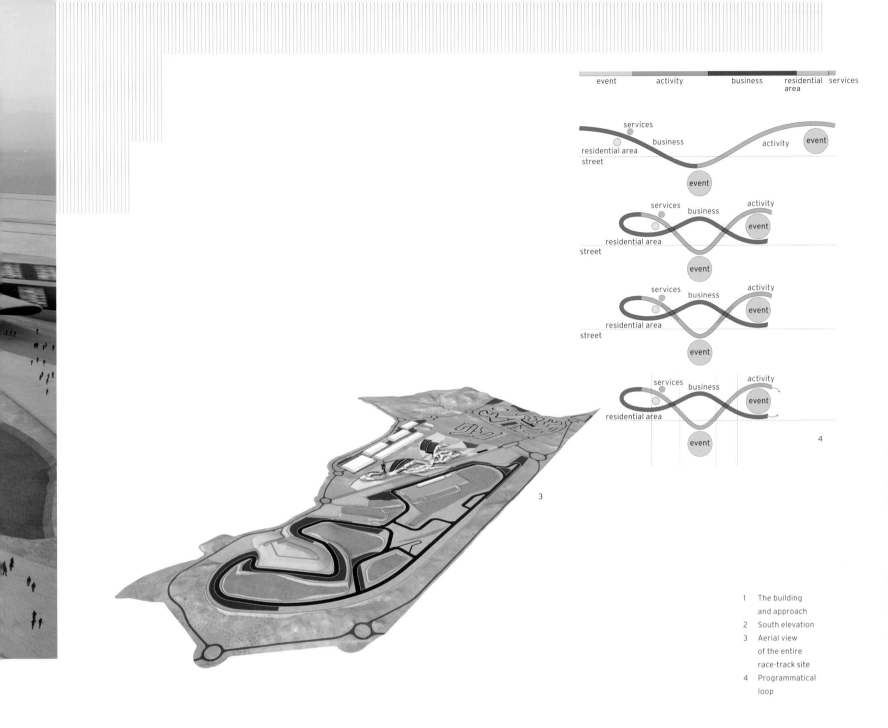

event   activity   business   residential area   services

1   The building
     and approach
2   South elevation
3   Aerial view
     of the entire
     race-track site
4   Programmatical
     loop

UN Studio's Ciudad del Motor was designed to be the centrepiece of a world-class location for racing development in Alcaniz, Spain: its concept is to link diverse racing tracks and connect different groups of users, while generating a coherent, iconic image. The design provides a built structure that blends landscape racing excitement into a uniquely configured sculptural object.

Architecturally, the design is indicative of the radical expressionism that the architect is known for. The loops and knots merge to form a three-dimensional 'race-track' of a building, which swoops and speeds from one element to the next. However, aesthetics were not the main driver for the design. UN Studio carried out analysis of the location and the potential user groups as well as research related to similar developments worldwide. This resulted in a proposal that put emphasis on the experience centre, a new type of interactive environment offering multiple visitor experiences all related to the topic of speed and movement.

This careful integration of diverse programmes and activities into one coherent building creates an attractive and sustainable environment that is well connected with the most important element of Ciudad del Motor, the tracks. However, while the main focus of activity on race days will be the tracks, the building is designed to be wholly sustainable on an economic as well as environmental level, and as such the retail and cultural 'sideshows' are of paramount importance.

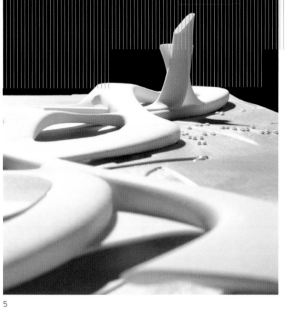

5

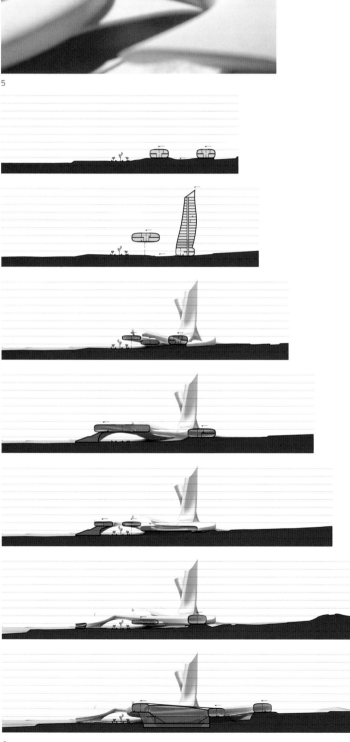

The building is organized like a continuous loop with two crossing points. The loop contains what the architect describes as programmatic topics – different areas specializing in technology, sports, leisure and culture. The grandstand is accessed via a bridge, while the shopping mall, experience centre, museum of movement, a multifunctional hall and the hotel and housing towers are connected to each other via 'knots' in the building structure. These knots, or routes, serve as a binding element, bring the independent building elements, and diverse experiences such as shopping, special events and motor sport, together, as you would find on a grander scale in a city.

The building structure strengthens the diagonal axis of the site and combines the locations of the attractions with the planned area of the grandstand. Parking facilities are positioned to become nodes offering quick access to the tracks, the grandstand and the extra-income activity areas. As such, UN Studio's design is based on generating maximum interaction with the building and the surroundings, especially the tracks, and providing multiple experiences to the visitor. Thankfully, it also creates a fabulous, slick design that is suited to the glamour of the sports that it serves.

5   Model detail
6   Various sections
7   Floor plan
8   View from the
    boulevard

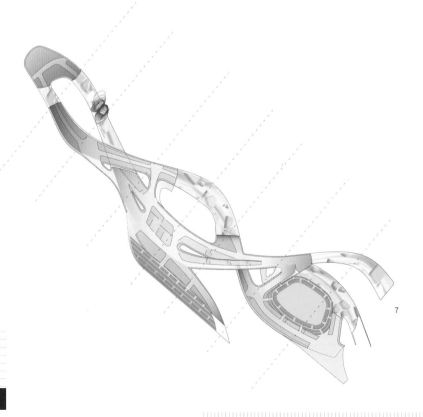

7

6

8

CRYSTAL PALACE, UK
WILKINSON EYRE ARCHITECTS

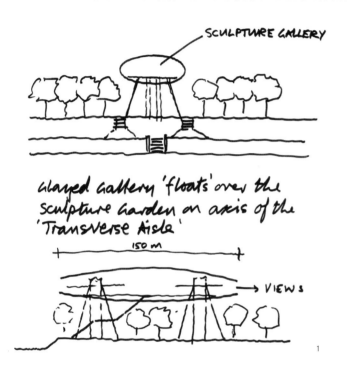

Plans for a 150-m (492-ft) long glass palace in the sky the first new building on the site of the old Crystal Palace since it burnt down in 1936, were revealed by Wilkinson Eyre in 2003. The scheme, set in what was to be the only dedicated sculpture park in London, aimed to restore Crystal Palace to its position as an internationally renowned cultural focal point for the UK capital.

Elevated 54 m (177 ft) above Crystal Palace Park in south London, the £45 million (US$65.4 million) glass structure respects the heritage of Joseph Paxton's visionary Victorian palace of glass. Wilkinson Eyre's arts venue floats above the space of the transept of the original palace: it is the same height, and follows the same line of its transverse aisle and yet retains the open space of the Grade II listed parkland in its entirety. The 150-m (492-ft) long two-storey building is designed to be constructed entirely of glass. Glass sculptural ribs support a laminated glass grid shell of minimal structure, with only the decks in the enclosed space supported by steelwork. An intelligent skin of photovoltaic cells encapsulated in the glass provides solar shading while also collecting solar energy to power the building. Vent-like louvres or 'gills' on the underside will control natural ventilation.

1   Concept sketches
2   The gallery in context
3   The gallery with the Crystal Palace TV transmitter in the background

Crystal Palace Wilkinson Eyre Architects 27

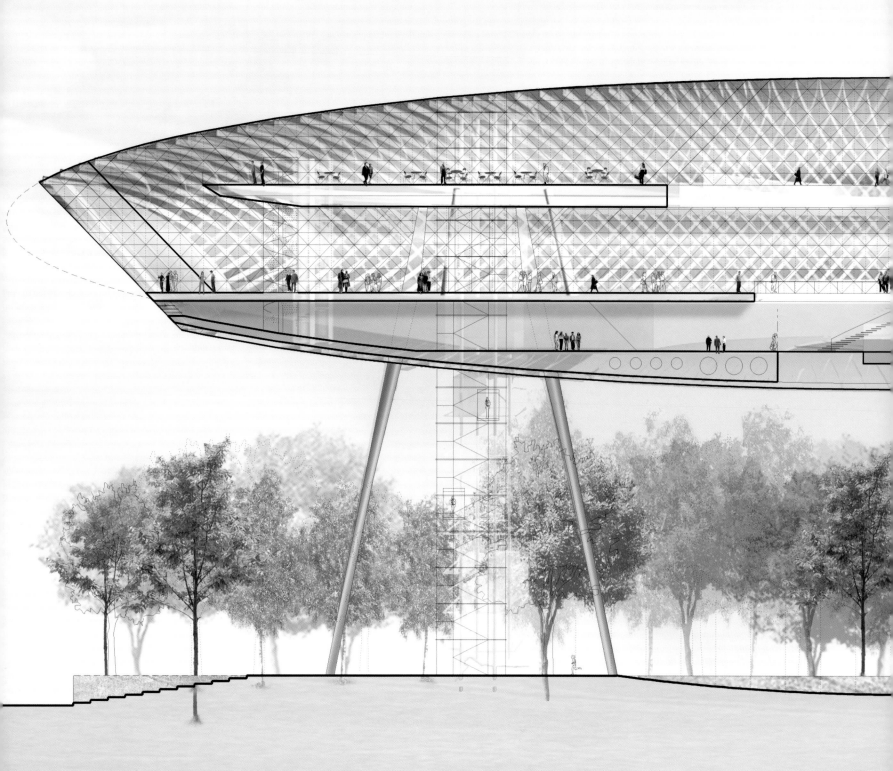

5

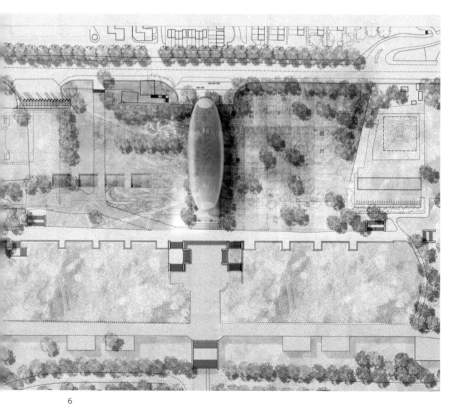

6

7

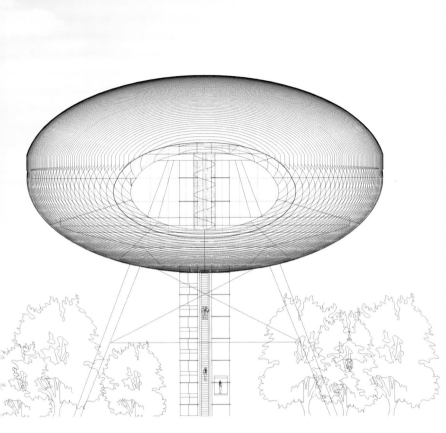

A moving stairway, the longest in the world, lifts visitors high above the park and the tree line into a 4,500 m² (48,438 ft²) exhibition space for changing displays. A mezzanine level will sit above with restaurants and bars.

With the focus on height not mass, Wilkinson Eyre has responded with a solution that is equal in its architectural vision and yet avoids the temptation to dwarf its surroundings, the area taken up being just ten per cent of the original Crystal Palace.

Wilkinson Eyre's vision for a sculpture park draws upon the unrivalled collections of statues that stood in the parklands surrounding the Crystal Palace, and it will provide an opportunity for new art installations and exhibitions. Sculpture courts spread out along the site underneath the elevated building. New tree planting and landscaping reinforce the original palace's central axis through the park, and the remaining original terracing and stairs will be extensively restored.

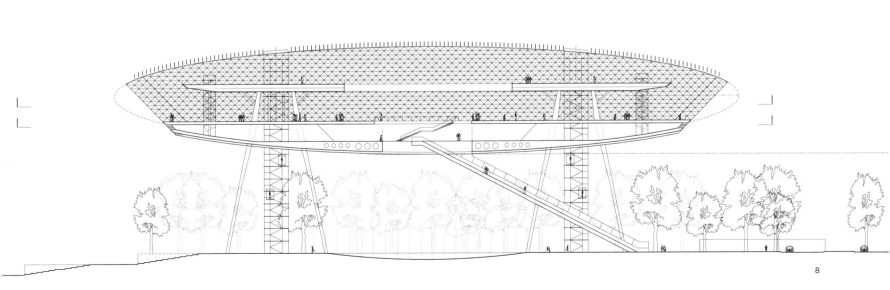

8

MUSIK THEATER, AUSTRIA
ODILE DECQ BENOÎT CORNETTE ARCHITECTES URBANISTES

1

2

This extraordinary design for a new 30,000 m² (322,917 ft²) opera house for the city of Linz in Austria was conceived by Odile Decq Benoît Cornette Architectes Urbanistes (ODBC) as a building that extolls the founding principles of the 'Musik Theater' – being a symbolic creative centre for the town – taking into consideration the complexity of functional constraints in this urban setting.

In terms of urban planning, the project is committed to providing a wide variety of contacts with the local environment, while creating a symbolic impact as a large-scale public building in the town. Accordingly, this architect's design is an object that shows three different faces on three different sides.

The lateral façades of the Musik Theater are adapted to their surroundings. The workshops and rehearsal rooms are arranged on the town side in a succession of divided and longitudinally staggered units, which match the fragmented pattern of façades on the other side of the road.

Along the railway tracks, in a completely linear elevation, dressing rooms and offices are stacked one above the other behind the shelter of a double-glazed façade that provides acoustic and thermal insulation. Punctuated solely by roof gardens and vertical access shafts, its horizontal lines seem to vibrate constantly in response to the random movement of coloured interior blinds. On the town square, approach and park side, the foyer reaches out to encompass the space of the concert hall and presents an expansive face to the town, with a seeming myriad pathways housed under a glass vault.

Externally, a similar pathway spans the crossroads, providing pedestrain access above the busy streets from various directions, including the station, the town centre and the edges of town. This raised walkway is taken up in the foyer by a further series of ramps, walkways and stairways, leading to the various rooms and performing spaces within.

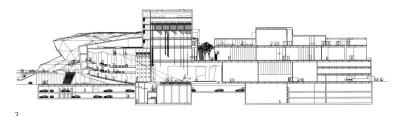

3

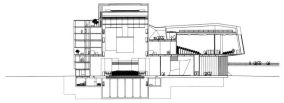

4

1 East elevation
2 South elevation
3 Long section
4 Short section
5 Night view from the street
6 Aerial master plan

5

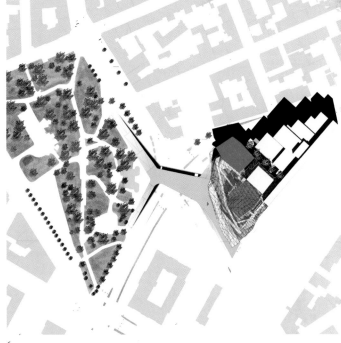

6

NATIONAL PORTRAIT GALLERY, AUSTRALIA
SEAN GODSELL ARCHITECTS

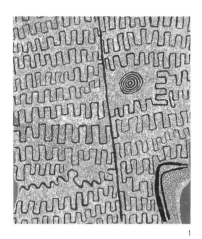

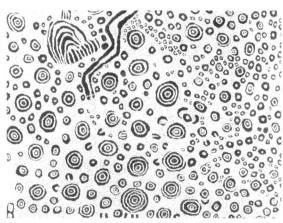

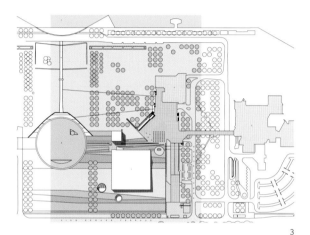

1

2

3

Through a series of built and unbuilt projects over the last decade Sean Godsell Architects has investigated the potential of the outer skin of a building. The aim of the practice's research is to emulate the physical properties of human skin: protection from injury; regulation of body temperature; excretion of waste; sensitivity to touch, temperature and pain; conversion of external stimuli into energy; and social communication. The question was how to inject these qualities in the 'lightweight enclosing membrane' of buildings.

The 'cells' which form the building skin of the National Portrait Gallery (NPG) proposed in Canberra, Australia, comprise 2-m (6.6-ft) diameter by 1.5 m (4.9 ft) deep oxidized steel tubes. Each tube has the capacity to house air filters, photovoltaic collectors, moisture sensors, sprinkler heads and so on. When combined over a large surface area, this façade has the potential to emulate human skin – to 'sweat' to help keep the building cool, to absorb energy and to protect the internal environment from impurities. In tandem with a comprehensive building management system, the gallery becomes more self-sufficient in terms of energy consumption as well as relying less on CFC-based cooling.

4

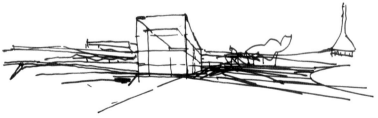

5

Burying the building so that only one floor is above the ground also assists in its environmental performance; however, this was not the main reason for this decision. Godsell says: 'Canberra is a wasteland of mediocre public architecture, sitting politely on greenfield sites. All is the same scale and most disappointingly predictable. Given its proximity to the High Court – a brutalist building on an artificially raised site – I was concerned that the same old Canberra response [incidentally what the government ultimately selected] would destroy the presence of the High Court in its urban context. Lowering the gallery was a deferential gesture.'

The earth removed as a result of this idea was to be retained on site and sculpted into a series of corrugations, within which the building is placed. Natural light is omitted from gallery spaces; Godsell chose to internalize them within the building's heart, pushing all of the other public activities to the perimeter of the building. This naturally lit 'veranda' space engages directly with the folding landscape beyond, and ebbs and flows around the building depending on function and location.

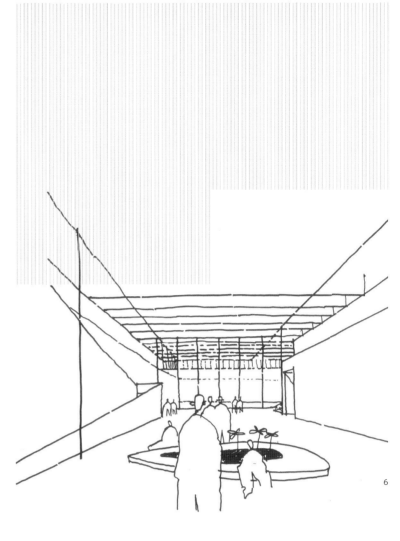

1, 2   Artistic inspiration
3   Site plan
4   Site sketch showing underground elements
5   Sketch from a distance
6   Interior sketch
7   Sections and skin conditions

6

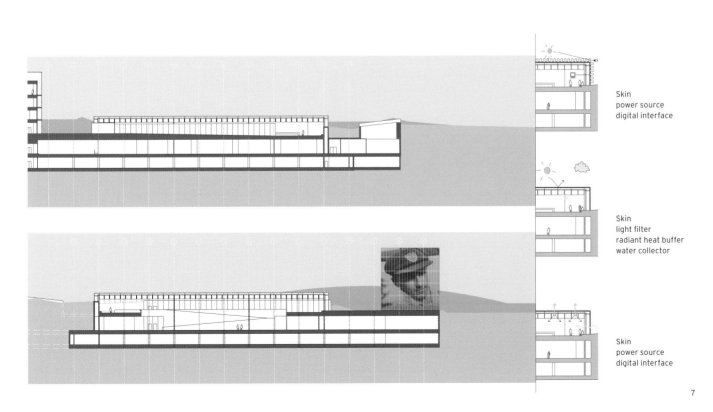

Skin
power source
digital interface

Skin
light filter
radiant heat buffer
water collector

Skin
power source
digital interface

7

1

The client, Strategic Hotels & Resorts, commissioned Morphosis to design an 8.1 ha. (20 acre) master plan for New Orleans in the USA, including a new National Jazz Center with outdoor auditorium, new city government buildings, a civil courts building and redevelopment of the Hyatt Regency site in 2005.

With a budget of £68.8 million (US$100 million), the architect's master plan for the performance arts park includes relocating some buildings to create a great lawn that stretches six city blocks. This was an important part of a core concept plan to integrate, improve and utilize existing architecture and infrastructure in a design that creates for the first time a world-class National Jazz Center and Park.

The creation of the National Jazz Center itself transforms the Hyatt area into a year-round destination for tourists and local people. Its facilities include a performing arts centre with 900-seat performance hall, 350-seat studio theatre, rehearsal and classrooms, museum, restaurant and event lobby.

The park starts at the foot of the National Jazz Center and extends north across green space for six blocks to a new, public outdoor amphitheatre. Throughout the park interactive art, gardens and fountains reflecting the culture of New Orleans and the American South create an oasis for visitors and their families. A dynamic bridge links the Superdome to the great park, unifying major elements of the area into one grand destination.

Prior to Hurricane Katrina, the largest office complex in Louisiana surrounded the Hyatt-Superdome District site. Many of its business inhabitants have been exploring ways to downsize or leave the city entirely. By creating a world-class destination at their doorway, the architect believes that firms would be enticed to stay, and other businesses will be drawn to the area.

Archaic city government facilities and civil courts are moved into a new state-of-the-art court building. By refurbishing and occupying other buildings that were under-utilized before Katrina, the city and parish would be able to modernize operations at a low cost, while other buildings are razed to make room for the park and National Jazz Center building.

NEW ORLEANS NATIONAL JAZZ CENTER AND PARK, USA

MORPHOSIS

1 Exterior from
  the approach
2 Main entrance
  and plaza
3 Section through
  model
4 Long elevation
5 Site plan in
  context with
  the city

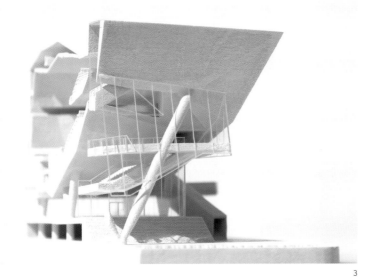

3

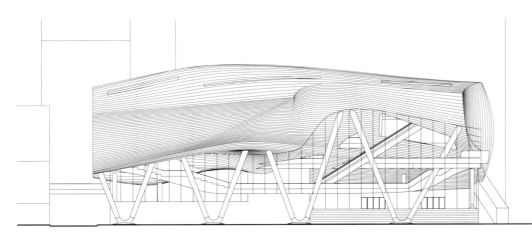

4

PERFORMING ARTS CENTRE, SOUTH KOREA
ATELIERS JEAN NOUVEL

Seoul in South Korea is a western-influenced city in a country divided in two by political unrest. The city itself is also split by the Han River, and in the middle of this large waterway is Nodul Island, a barren piece of land for which Jean Nouvel has designed a new performing arts centre with two auditoria. In fact, he went one step further than the Seoul Municipality required, and set out plans to design an entire 'mythical island'.

When any large city commissions a new opera house it aims to create an iconic building. Nouvel is doing this here, not by making an overt architectural statement but by designing a sense of excitement and wonder on a unique site within Seoul. His design creates a natural environment in the centre of this metropolis. 'A meeting of nature and music', he calls it, seeking to hark back to a time before Korea was split by political turmoil, when it was, in his words 'linked to the rock,

1   Aerial view
2   View from the
     river bank

2

1

3

to the trees, to the horizon... and also to the water'. Then into this natural habitat are placed two golden gems in the form of an opera house and a concert hall.

Nouvel describes the opera and concert venue interventions as like putting two musical instruments into the landscape: the opera house, a musical instrument of the human voice; the concert hall, an instrument of all the music of the world. And, to differentiate these two 'instruments' from afar, the gold hue given off by each building would differ – reddish for the opera house, more yellow for the concert hall.

With a gross floor area of 53,000 m² (570,000 sq. ft) and a budget of €250 million (US\$315 million), the project is no small undertaking. It includes road access to the island via a double bridge crossing and a tunnel straight through the island. Even this element gets radical treatment:

3   Section through   5   South façade
    the island   6   Opera interior
4   East façade   7   Theatre interior
                         8   View from the
                             main highway

4

according to Nouvel, 'When cars go through, the island has to become a kind of new world, you are inside the island. I propose to have rocks, I propose to have falling water because the noise of falling water hides the noise of the cars, but also when you are inside you could have perspective through the falling water in the landscape and you could see trees. It's not only a bridge through an island, it's really an urban architectural sequence linked to the new spirit and the new vocation of the island.'

1

QINTAI ART AND CULTURAL CENTRE, CHINA
ARUP ASSOCIATES

This entry for a 2003 competition to design the new Qintai Art and Cultural Centre in Wuhan, China, is a dramatic proposal that splits the complex into two large volumes resembling giant pebbles, shaped and smoothed by the sea. Arup Associates describes the massing of the buildings as reflecting 'a legendary relationship between two local personalities' – just who, we are left to guess.

The two buildings, although different, form a distinct pair; their characters separate and yet complementary in bulk and form. Their position in the landscape is also important to the scheme. The taller volume 'wears the earth like a cloak', sweeping upwards from the highest point of newly landscaped terrain to emphasize its verticality. Its more squat counterpart occupies a lower position that instead focuses its relationship with the water, as it juts forward to meet the gigantic artificial lake.

Arup Associates' design has the larger of the two buildings accommodating a 1,800-seat grand theatre, in a structure that rises 50 m (164 ft) above the surrounding ground levels. Its roof void is given over as a viewing platform, from which visitors can see across the lake to other new developments and pick out the key monuments of the city. The flatter volume is a concert hall, some 35 m (115 ft) high and seating 1,600 people; it is a quieter, more enclosed object that feels grounded, and as a consequence, more intimate.

Both buildings are conceived as layered spaces, with public access to a majority of areas. Transparent external envelopes swathe the solid performance halls within each volume, providing views out for theatre/concert goers as they make their way to the performances. The character of these inner performance halls is distinct and this is reflected in the treatment of materials. The grand theatre has staging capabilities that can easily be adapted to the demands of both Chinese and Western productions. It is the more static of the two spaces, and is clad in a sculptured stone surface. The concert hall, with acoustic properties that require a more dynamic volume, is characterized by a warm timber surface.

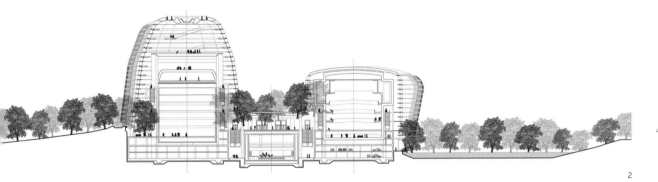

2

3

1 Qintai at dusk
2 Section (theatre, left; concert hall, right)
3 Sketch plan
4 Illuminated model

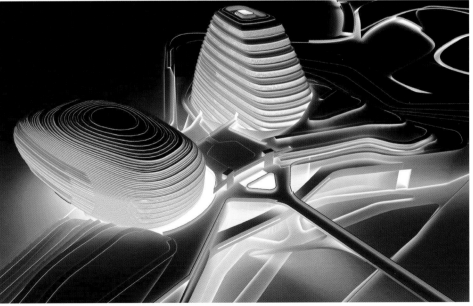

4

SARAJEVO NATIONAL CONCERT HALL, BOSNIA & HERZEGOVINA
URBAN FUTURE ORGANIZATION

This design for the Sarajevo National Concert Hall, in Bosnia–Herzegovina, emerged from Urban Future Organization's winning entry to an international architecture competition held by the Municipality of Rome and the Sarajevo Canton in Bosnia–Herzegovina.

The project extends the public surface of the city of Sarajevo into and under the ground. It forms a continuous space that wraps the foyers, the auditoria and the service areas, as well as creating an outdoor landscape above, which bleeds almost seamlessly into the surrounding open plaza and parks.

Conversely, the surrounding surface of the parkscape dissolves into and swirls underground in a whirlpool movement that allows access from several critical viewpoints. The bifurcated landscaping branches and forks to create openings for entrances and to allow natural lighting down into the building. The surface also expands and contracts on its way down, accommodating different events through the building.

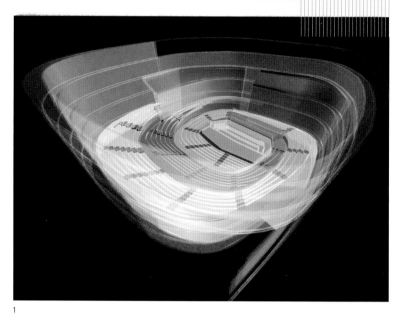

1

2

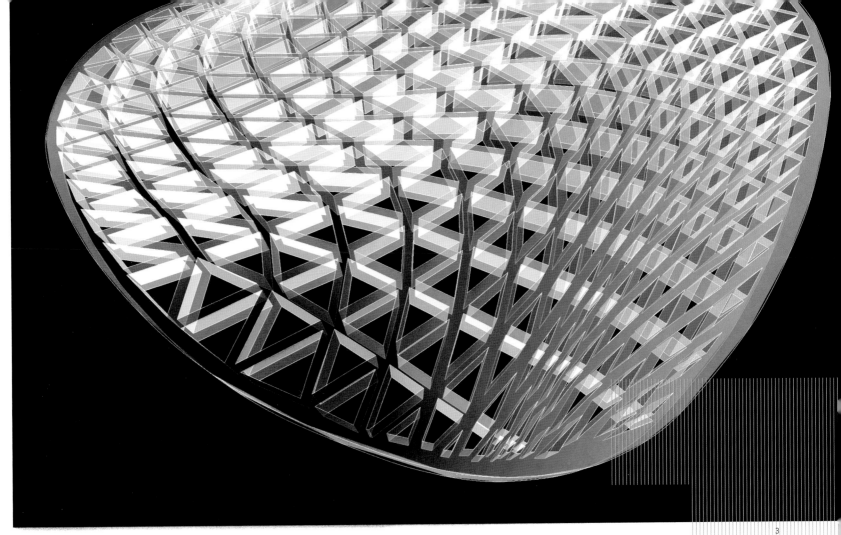

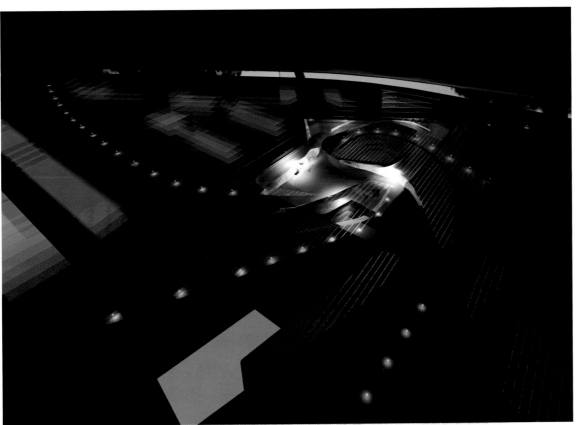

1   Abstract concept
2   Auditorium
    interior
3   Auditorium roof
    structure
4   Aerial night view

Sarajevo National Concert Hall Urban Future Organization   45

The landscape above is populated by public facilities. This relationship between exterior and interior events and activities changes according to the time of the day, weather conditions and seasons, meaning that the city's new addition would be far more than a concert hall. The open landscape allows an unobstructed flow of people across and within the site, creating a new public square for the city and again bringing all types of person into contact with the concert hall.

Most cleverly, however, is the planning of the building underground, which eliminates the potential conflict between the concert hall and adjacent buildings. The ground also acts as thermal mass which increases the energy efficiency of the concert hall. Solar gain is minimized, and overall the building's internal environment is stable and controlled. Also, acoustically an underground concert hall has no requirement for a sound-reductive external envelope.

This underground design is challenging to the norm, yet it fulfils all cultural requirements and presents a good argument for passive, environmentally friendly architecture.

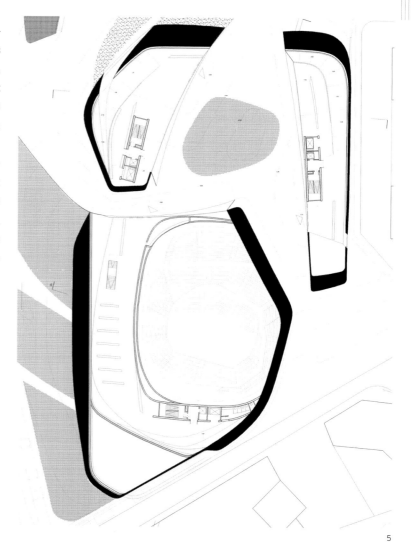

5

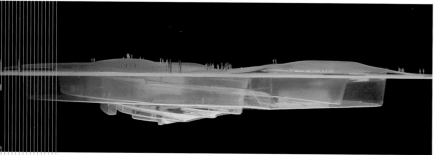

6

7

5 Ground floor plan
6 Model elevation
7 Artificial
  landscape
8 Urban positioning
  diagram
9 Sections

8

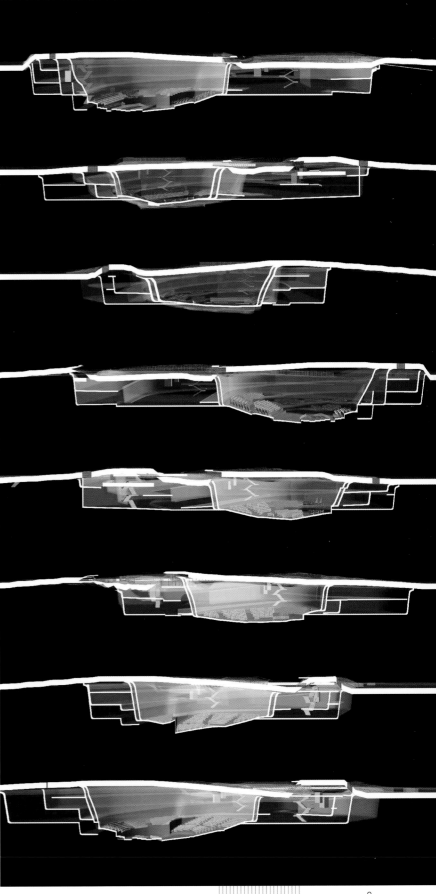

9

The Senscity concept was first developed for a site near Las Vegas, in the USA, then modified to suit the demands of another location in the United Arab Emirates. Behnisch Architekten's scheme combines elements of a typical theme park – a gaming arcade, theatre, auditoria, restaurants, public gardens, exhibition spaces and a series of playgrounds. Together, they create a super leisure experience over 86 ha. (212 acres) of artificial landscape outside Las Vegas.

The leisure park consists of two primary layers, each functioning independently of the other. At below ground level, exhibition halls, administrative and operational facilities are set firmly into the landscape. Above, the lush planted leisure park undulates across the rooftops before sloping down into a central valley and lake formed between the exhibition halls.

However, the creation of an outdoor green-landscaped leisure park in the desert in Nevada is not without its challenges. Behnisch's answer was to develop, in collaboration with structural and building services engineers, a series of giant multi-purpose tree-like structures. At up to 36.5 m (120 ft) high and spanning 90 m (295 ft), these 'trees' shade large parts of the park. Dramatic in size and appearance, the 'trees' are the crux of the entire Senscity scheme.

1

2

SENSCITY PARADISE UNIVERSE, USA
BEHNISCH ARCHITEKTEN

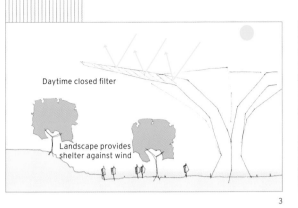

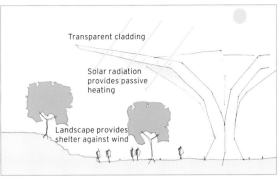

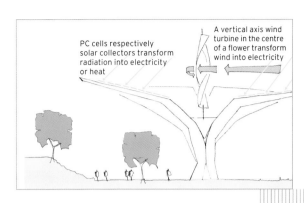

Daytime closed filter

Landscape provides
shelter against wind

Transparent cladding

Solar radiation
provides passive
heating

Landscape provides
shelter against wind

PC cells respectively
solar collectors transform
radiation into electricity
or heat

A vertical axis wind
turbine in the centre
of a flower transform
wind into electricity

3

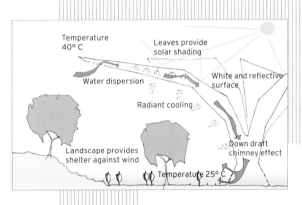

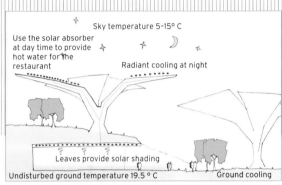

Temperature
40° C

Leaves provide
solar shading

Water dispersion

White and reflective
surface

Radiant cooling

Landscape provides
shelter against wind

Down draft
chimney effect

Temperature 25° C

Sky temperature 5-15° C

Use the solar absorber
at day time to provide
hot water for the
restaurant

Radiant cooling at night

Leaves provide solar shading

Undisturbed ground temperature 19.5 ° C

Ground cooling

1 Aerial
perspective
2 Plan detail
3 Environmental
design aspects
4 Daytime view
5 Night view

4

5

The design team calculated that the Las Vegas desert climate affords an ideal opportunity to take advantage of the phenomenon of evaporative cooling. Water pumped through hollows in the outspread leaves of the trees cools the surrounding air; this cooled air is displaced by rising warm air and falls to ground level, generating beneficial down-draft airflows. The cold air streams into the valley, dramatically improving outdoor temperature and humidity levels. The park's distinct topography will also shelter against prevailing winds and hold a stratum of cool air within the valley.

The trees also function as exhaust shafts for the natural ventilation of the exhibition halls below ground, as well as energy providers. Photovoltaic cells or solar collectors on their upturned leaves are capable of transforming radiation into electricity or heat, which can be used to operate an absorption chiller for use in the exhibition halls. Cooling loads for the halls are further reduced by the park's insulative properties, which take advantage of the relatively stable temperatures below the earth's surface. Finally, at the centre of each flower is a highly efficient, stamen-like, vertical-axis wind turbine that will transform wind energy into electricity.

Behnisch sees its design as a large-scale inhabitable educational tool capable of demonstrating how the inhospitable local climate – sun, wind and extreme temperature ranges – can, through a progressive, sustainable design approach, be tempered to benefit the immediate microclimate, creating an oasis in the midst of the desert.

SHERWOOD FOREST VISITORS' CENTRE, UK
MAKE

1

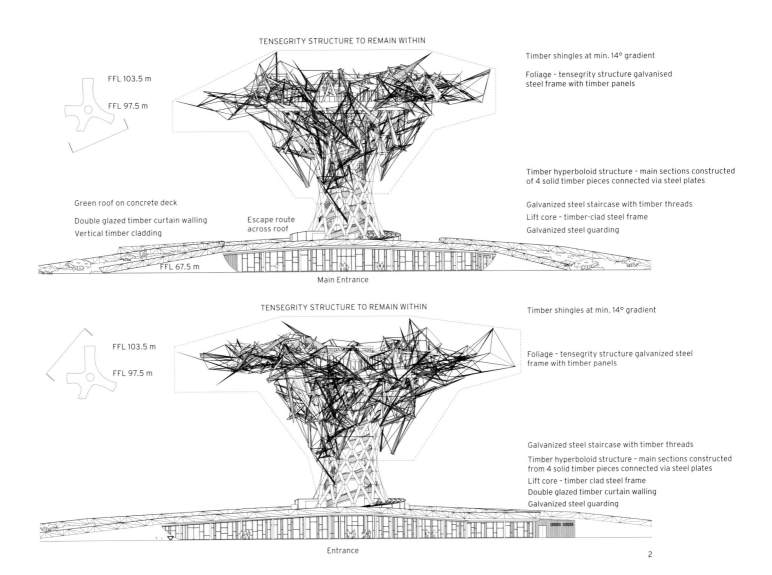

TENSEGRITY STRUCTURE TO REMAIN WITHIN

FFL 103.5 m

FFL 97.5 m

Timber shingles at min. 14° gradient

Foliage - tensegrity structure galvanised
steel frame with timber panels

Timber hyperboloid structure – main sections constructed
of 4 solid timber pieces connected via steel plates

Green roof on concrete deck

Double glazed timber curtain walling
Vertical timber cladding

Escape route
across roof

Galvanized steel staircase with timber threads
Lift core - timber-clad steel frame
Galvanized steel guarding

FFL 67.5 m

Main Entrance

TENSEGRITY STRUCTURE TO REMAIN WITHIN

FFL 103.5 m

FFL 97.5 m

Timber shingles at min. 14° gradient

Foliage - tensegrity structure galvanized steel
frame with timber panels

Galvanized steel staircase with timber threads
Timber hyperboloid structure – main sections constructed
from 4 solid timber pieces connected via steel plates
Lift core - timber clad steel frame
Double glazed timber curtain walling
Galvanized steel guarding

Entrance

2

3

1   Aerial
    perspective
    with forest
2   Structural
    detail views
3   Concept sketch

This competition-winning scheme to design a new
visitors' centre for Sherwood Forest near Nottingham proposes an utterly
unique landmark structure that enhances access to and appreciation
of the ancient woodland's historical, regional and ecological importance.

Inspired by tree-houses past and present, the scheme consists
of a dramatic timber trunk that emerges from a podium structure resembling a network of roots and rises 30 m (98 ft) before branching out into
a 'tree' canopy at the apex. Core visitor facilities are housed at ground
level, while a staircase and lifts within the trunk lead up to a viewing
platform set within the building's canopy.

This structure is integrated into the site by the root-like base, which
extends outwards in a radial system of accommodation, paths and places.
Timber walkways lead visitors between the hub of the visitor centre and
the forest beyond. The built elements of the root structure, meanwhile,
house functions including an education centre and conference facilities.
The spaces between are occupied by playgrounds and picnic areas. At the
boundaries of the site, new habitats such as meadow, grass, heath and
coppice are created.

4 Looking towards
  the main entrance
5 View from the
  main entrance
6 Interior view
7 Site plan

The structure has been designed to use timber in its organic state, with the tree trunk formed using hyperboloid geometry that allows member dimensions to be limited to a range of naturally occurring solid timber sizes. The scheme also incorporates a range of strategies to achieve a carbon-neutral status. An array of wind turbines located within a nearby coppice grove generates electricity for the complex, while the coppice itself contributes fuel for a biomass heating system. Other sustainable measures include rainwater collection and reed bed waste recycling systems.

huge billets of pewter-toned burnished metal. According to the architect they 'establish an image of solidity, strength and timelessness without recourse to stone, masonry or concrete, or direct association with Stonehenge'.

There is no sense of the usual building imagery on the site; no apparent windows or architectural embellishment. It is testament to the architect's design that the building's volume is unreadable from outside, so little is given away externally. Viewed from a distance, the centre appears as a long, sweeping wall, marked only by the entrance, a single break in its surface. Internally, the centre opens out to provide space for historic exhibits and multimedia displays telling the story of the history of the monument.

Associated works within the World Heritage Site included the removal of site roads and execution of related archaeological works. A nearby trunk road was proposed to be placed in a tunnel for the section next to Stonehenge, while part of another road was to be removed completely to reinstate a landscape similar to that which existed when the monument was initially built.

6   Approach to   8   Aerial showing
    the entrance   arrangement
7   Internal   of billets
    exhibition space

6

7

8

TAICHUNG METROPOLITAN OPERA HOUSE, TAIWAN

ZAHA HADID ARCHITECTS

1　2

3

1　Aerial view
2　Integrated
　　external
　　courtyard
3　View from
　　pedestrian
　　approach
4　Promenade
　　design

The Taichung Metropolitan Opera House was designed to give the city of Taichung, Taiwan, an exciting cultural venue in its new civic district. Housing a 2,000-seat grand auditorium, an 800-seat drama theatre and a 200-seat black box theatre, the design is of immense proportion and complexity.

The proposal envisions an opera house that is defined by an internal elevated urban plaza, which serves as the main foyer. The three auditoria are clustered around this area, with the grand auditorium on the south of the building, the playhouse on the north, and the black box theatre elevated on the west side. This allows the main foyer to slip underneath and provides for a secondary west entrance.

The exterior black granite skin of the building wraps around the auditoria into the main foyer, heightening the sense that this space is an extension of the public realm. The ceiling of the main foyer and the internal bridge are also clad in the same black granite. The windows, skylights over the main foyer and curtain walls at the entrances have mirror finished dark-tinted double glazing, with a low-emissive coating.

4

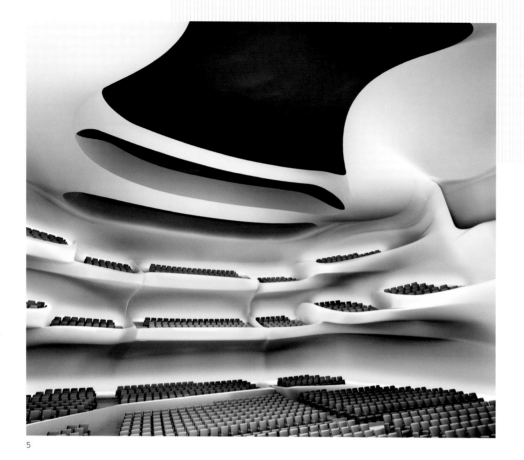

5

5   Grand auditorium
    interior
6   Above the
    courtyard
7   Main foyer
8   Night view

The landscaping is designed to merge with the building. This build-up, manifested as earth mounds, fades as it moves away, radiating like waves. Indeed, part of the building itself merges into the landscape, further blurring the boundary between building and ground.

Inside, the grand auditorium and drama theatre both have grand staircases within secondary foyers that connect the various levels of seating, while an escalator leads directly from the main foyer up into the black box theatre foyer. An internal bridge connects balcony foyer levels from the opera house to the playhouse and stretches through the main space. Against this, the roof with its elongated skylights, appears as a kind of membrane tearing apart as it is stretched between the two large auditoria.

6

7

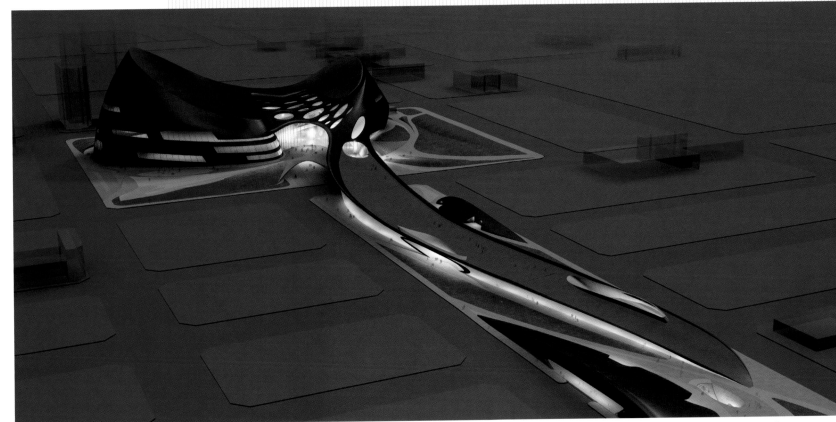

8

2.
ACCOMMODATION

At a time when a credit crisis is gripping vast parts of the western world, it is not difficult to understand why many architectural projects do not make it past the drawing board. Residential property prices are falling, while construction material costs rise: the combination is one that frightens all but the most committed or foolhardy of clients.

Conversely, a global recession could be seen as the perfect time to invest in property, while prices are weak and sellers are looking to off-load quickly. However, this type of gamble is only for the bravest, and as financial pressures heighten most public and private residential developments are put on hold.

This is dangerous from a design perspective because the longer a client has to deliberate over financial outlay the more likely they are to want to slash budgets and reduce costs, cheapening not only the value but also the architectural merit of the proposed project. This accountant-led number crunching almost always brings about compromises in the design, and what was conceived as high-quality accommodation soon slips into the realms of mediocrity, similar to much of our modern housing stock.

Financial constraints are the bane of every architect's creative ego. While some say that they are good, in that they act to bring about a more rigorously thought-out design, every architect will at some point want to break free from them. It is in the housing and hotel sector that the results of these monetary constraints tend to be noticed most sharply. And, because we live in the outcome of these financial battles, any construction failings are magnified. It seems idiotic then that our homes are so often designed and built to the minimum standards with little or no imagination, flair or daring. Why is this?

The vast majority of the population is consigned to mediocre accommodation because large housing providers in both the public and private sectors look to make a quick profit at the expense of quality design and construction. The trouble is, we seem to have become used to it and to expect little more. Even when an individual has a large budget to spend on 'the home of their dreams', so often it is a pastiche of a past vernacular – half-timbered, pillars, porticos, etc.; devoid of any architectural merit and completely lacking in good design philosophy. Think of the countless images of tacky architecture in glossy magazines devoted to the lives of the rich and famous.

All is not lost, however. Two potential saving graces for our residential housing stock are global warming and oil prices. With pressure mounting on everyone to use less fuel, save energy and become more efficient in every aspect of their lives, environmentally conscious housing is an important area for architects and developers to tackle. Suddenly houses are not simple boxes offering shelter; they need to be intelligently designed, the materials must be properly and locally sourced, and construction needs to be professionally completed to ensure that we reduce our energy use to an absolute minimum.

Until now, sustainable designs have been the ones often dreamed of and designed but then put aside because the costs did not add up. Everyone would like to live in an environmentally friendly home, or stay in an eco-resort, but until oil prices escalated beyond all comprehension, fossil fuels were almost always cheaper than renewable energies such as wind, solar or hydro power. Now, all that has changed: traditional fuel prices are so high that these green energy sources become viable, while home design must be improved to reduce energy consumption and conserve heat.

Housing is currently at a crucial point in its evolution. Capitalist instinct is to stick to the same course and build cheaply. However, governments and private sector developers are being put under increased pressure to build sustainably, and with that comes the prospect of well designed housing.

This does not necessarily mean our homes and other places of accommodation will automatically sprout wind turbines, solar panels and bio-fuel boilers. It will hopefully encourage architects and their paymasters to consider valuable design lessons from our past: the way in which traditional homes in Pakistan use chimneys to naturally ventilate and cool their interiors; ground source temperature stabilization, as used by the Romans; or the use of thermal mass for insulation.

These relatively simple steps make a big difference. They should be adopted where suitable. However, they also take us out of our literal and metaphorical comfort zone – away from the norm of air conditioners and gas-fired central heating – and so we tend to be reticent about using them. Architects have to drive this green revolution and play a leading role in convincing the private and public sector that environmentally conscious designs work and that the public is ready for them.

Financial constraints and environmental aspirations are not the most likely of bedfellows, but if the energy crisis is to be ridden out and global warming slowed we have to take bold steps. There is some evidence of this being done, with entire new town quarters being built sustainably in Scandinavia and Germany. However, large parts of the world such as the USA and Russia are yet to be convinced, and the race from Third to First World for global powers as mighty as China and India means that the message of intelligent environmental design is one yet to be fully taken in.

1

2

BATTERSEA WEST HOTEL, UK

ARUP ASSOCIATES

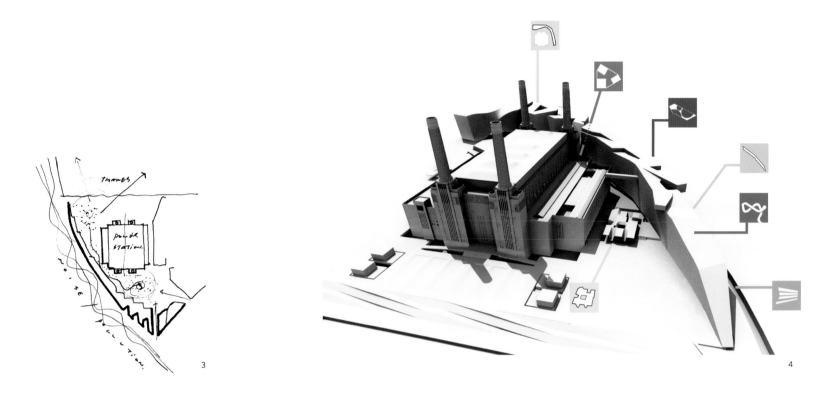

Designed in 2005 as part of the larger but now defunct Battersea Power Station master plan in London, UK, the West Hotel by Arup Associates is a re-appraisal of hotel design. It is upside down. The public levels, which include a spa, restaurants and lobby facilities, are all arranged across the top of the building and expressed as a series of sharply cantilevered volumes that project towards views of the river Thames and London beyond: the bedrooms, meanwhile, are below.

This articulation is in response to the master plan and the hotel's position within. Both in its shape and massing, the West Hotel forms part of a larger wall of buildings that collectively define the western perimeter of the Battersea Power Station site, shielding it from a major rail link across the river. But, rather than designing the hotel as an obvious obstruction, Arup Associates has graduated its height, sloping the building downwards towards the river to create exciting outdoor spaces and provide interesting, and gradually revealing, views of the historic power station.

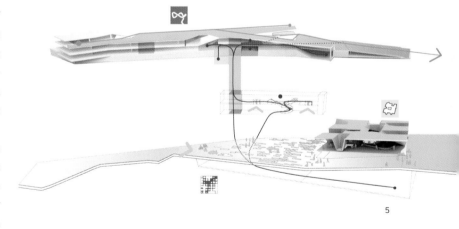

1	West elevation with power station	3	Sketch plan
2	Concepts for rooftop garden	4	View from north of river
		5	Circulation routes

6

At riverside, the roof of the 461-room hotel actually meets ground level. Then, as it graduates backwards, rising to form the shield, this warped ground plane continues up and over the hotel itself. The architect calls it the 'Great Wall Walk', a series of levels that form an inclusive, publicly accessible route across the landscaped roof of the building. The walk 'weaves' directly into the public areas of the hotel at upper levels and provides extraordinary views over London.

Additionally, in its form as a shield, the West Hotel is used to create special wind-sheltered places for people. Pedestrians are free to use the interconnected sequence of walkways that lace across the surface, from the public gardens to the river walk.

6   Internal views
7   External views
8   Hotel roof garden
9   Ground level
    covered spaces

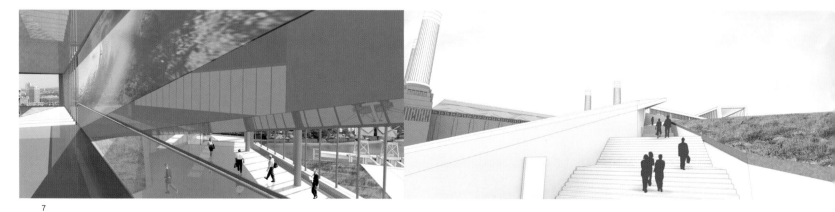

7

9

8

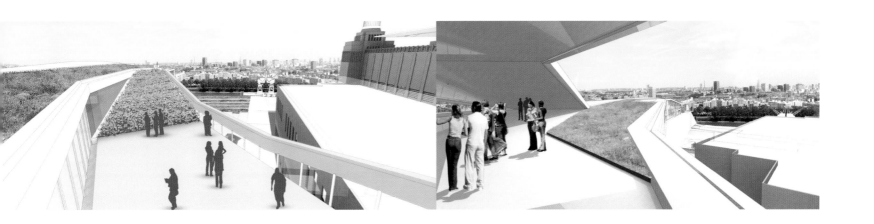

BLUEWATER, CANADA
TAYLOR SMYTH ARCHITECTS

1

2

Bluewater is a prime example of high-end Canadian residential architecture. The country has some of the best scenery in the world and as a consequence luxury homes are designed to make the most of it. Located along a natural ridge, the house follows the curve of the top of a bank as it bends into an adjacent ravine. It is sited as close to the top of the slope as possible to maximize the views of the beach and the lake below.

Bluewater has two distinct aspects, which are discovered gradually. The back or east face of the house consists primarily of a multi-storey zinc-clad wall that deforms to follow the ridge. Larger openings cut into the wall provide views out to the lawn. Small random windows break the formality of this large wall. The lawn slopes up to an outdoor terrace and the obligatory screened-in porch off of the great room. In all, there are four porches to offer shelter from direct sunlight and insects.

The front, west side of the house faces the lake. It is distinguished by two multi-level volumes that cantilever out over the ground floor to take full advantage of lake views. The relationship between the interior and the natural environment outside is blurred by continuous planes of floor-to-ceiling glass at key spaces.

Internally, the great room is a glass-clad volume that contains the double-height living room. It is oriented towards the steepest part of the ridge, with views southwest down the beach and west towards the setting sun over the horizon. At the upper level of the great room is a library and reading room, partially enclosed by bookcases. Both rooms focus on the symbolic centre of the house, the stone-clad fireplace that rises up through the overhanging roof of the great room. At the end of the library, a screened-in porch protrudes out of the exterior glass wall like a tree-house, providing a sheltered outdoor place to read.

The kitchen and dining room are located under the library. A sliding panel separates the two spaces, allowing the kitchen to benefit from the natural views. The dining table is located along the outer glass wall, capitalizing on views of the lake through the trees.

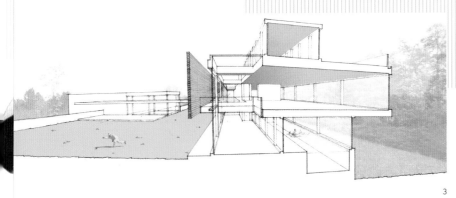

3

4

1 West elevation
2 East elevation
3 End section
4 Main living space
5 Night view of
   main façade
6 Site model

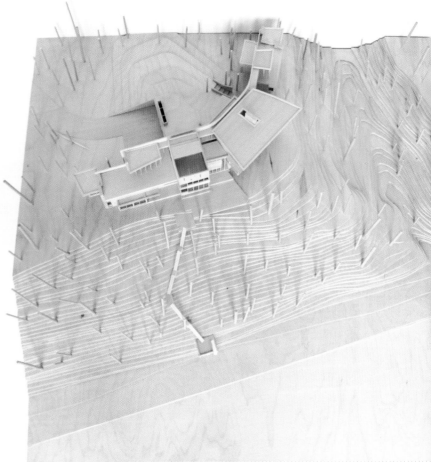

5

6

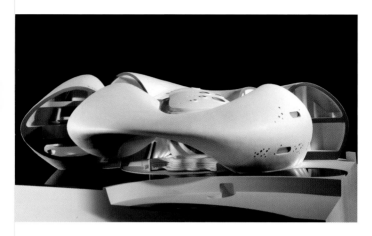

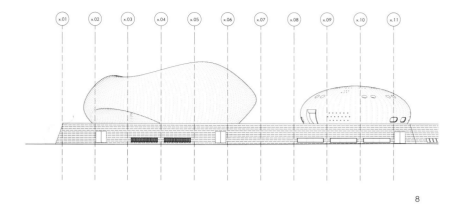

8

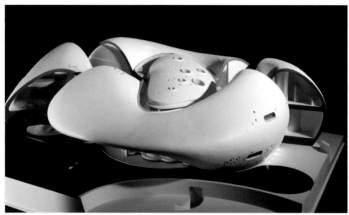

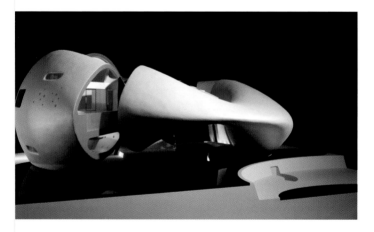

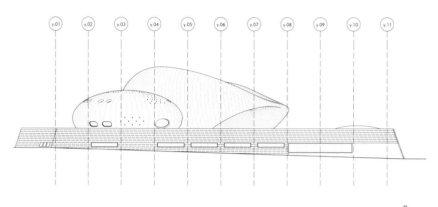

9

Reflecting the unique place and responding to the intense environmental conditions, the design moderates the transition between outside and inside, public and private. It is informed by the cultural typology of a courtyard house. The entrance passes under the floating form to an interior courtyard, from which the sequence of spaces vary and become finer as one moves through into the most intimate areas of the house. Each layer of spaces becomes more closed and more private from the first order of rooms off the main space through to the private suites on the upper levels.

The architects designed the property to be constructed from concrete cast in digitally cut formwork. The external temperature in Doha required a sensitive approach to control heat, and the villa is organized to take advantage of the mass of the form enclosing the courtyard, while allowing light and ventilation through the canopy. The concrete mass of the building also moderates temperature changes.

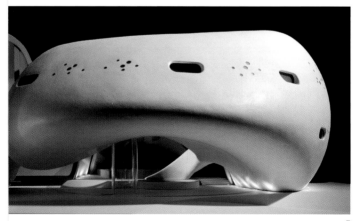

7

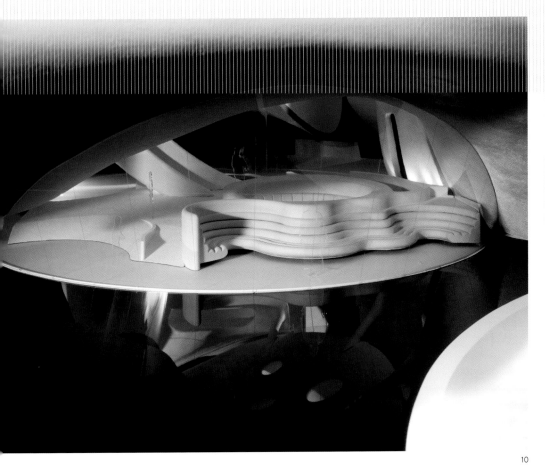

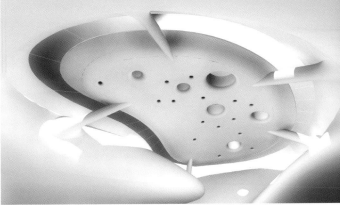

7 Model views
8 West elevation
9 South elevation
10 Interior model
11 Ceiling / roof
detail from below
12 Sections

10

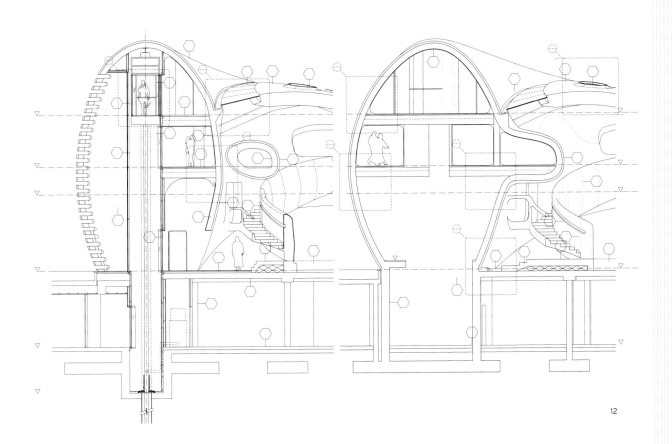

12

Doha Villa **Ushida Findlay** 75

FACTORY 798, CHINA
BERNARD TSCHUMI ARCHITECTS

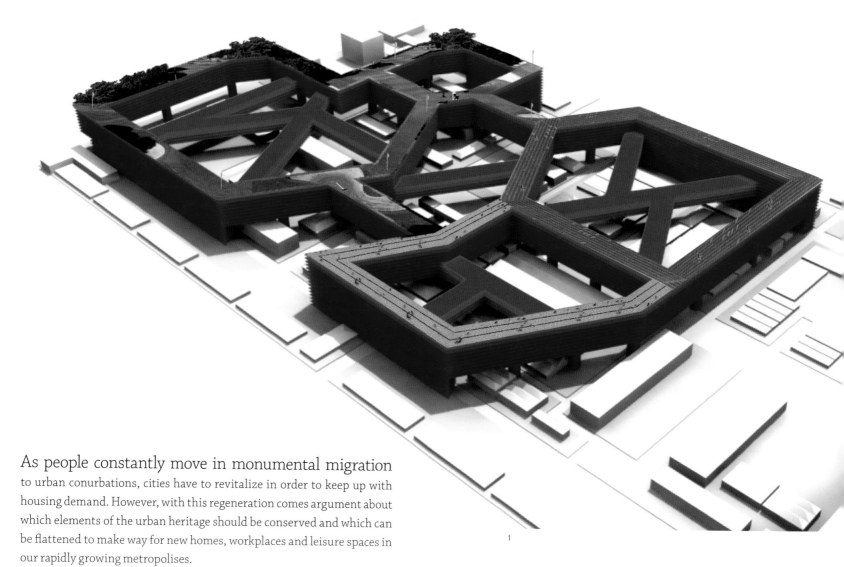

1

As people constantly move in monumental migration to urban conurbations, cities have to revitalize in order to keep up with housing demand. However, with this regeneration comes argument about which elements of the urban heritage should be conserved and which can be flattened to make way for new homes, workplaces and leisure spaces in our rapidly growing metropolises.

Bernard Tschumi Architects has addressed the potential problem of conflict between developers wishing to demolish and build anew, to supply housing for a community of artists who have occupied an unused manufacturing facility in the northeast of Beijing.

In recent years, this vibrant art community has grown and flourished in an industrial neighbourhood dominated by Factory 798. Artists' studios, lofts, galleries and bookstores have taken over the spaces of the old manufacturing plant, which was built in the 1950s. However, developers have proposed that Factory 798 and its surrounding fabric be demolished and the site developed into one million m² of residential towers. The proposal would wipe out the livelihoods of almost all of the existing community.

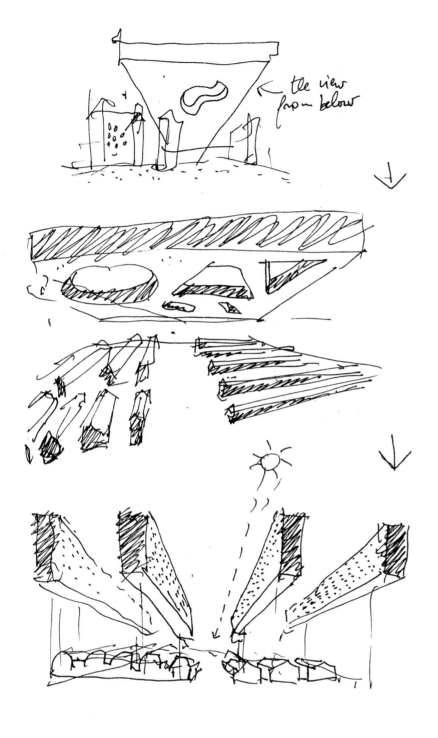

the view
from below

22 NOV. 03
The In-between
Beijing 798

2

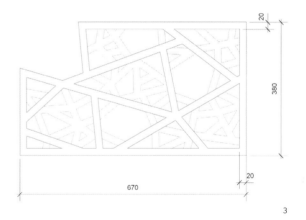

3

1   Aerial view
2   Concept sketches
3   Lattice form
    progression

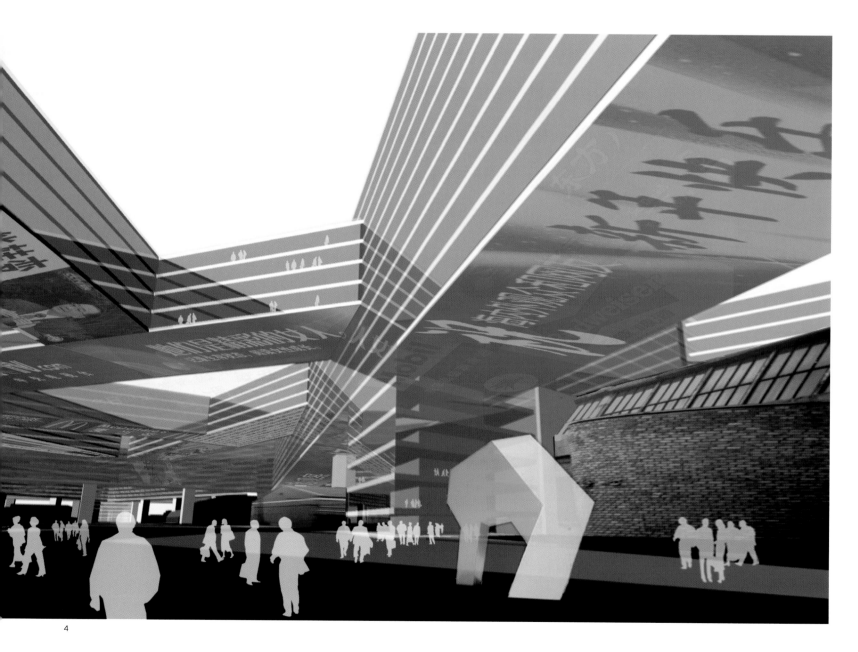

4

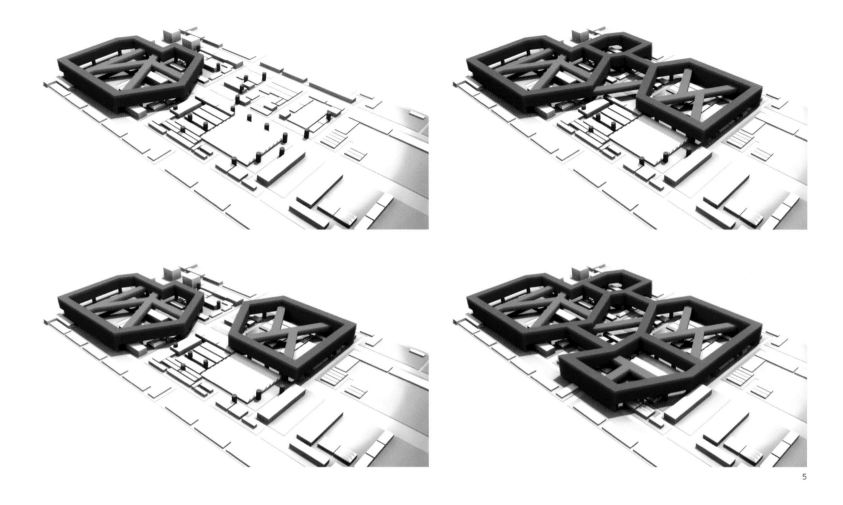

5

Tschumi's answer is audacious but it would create the required number of new homes, preserve the artists' community and present a new architectural landmark for Beijing. The architect's plan sees the existing Factory 798 buildings retained at ground level. Over these is superimposed a new high-density residential quarter, a horizontal city hovering 25 m (82 ft) above the ground.

This new residential building takes the form of a maze of inter-connecting streets with wide gaps between to allow light down into the existing spaces below. The new housing development will create over one million m² of living space at an estimate of £406 million (US$600 million). Occupants would be able to use garden areas on top of their development. They would also bring new trade to the artistic community below.

The design acknowledges the inevitable confrontation of old and new and is an innovative alternative to the wholesale demolition of the existing urban fabric. It is a strategy of in-betweens, which creates new while preserving the old, and Beijing is richer for it.

4   View from ground
    level
5   Potential growth /
    phases of the
    scheme

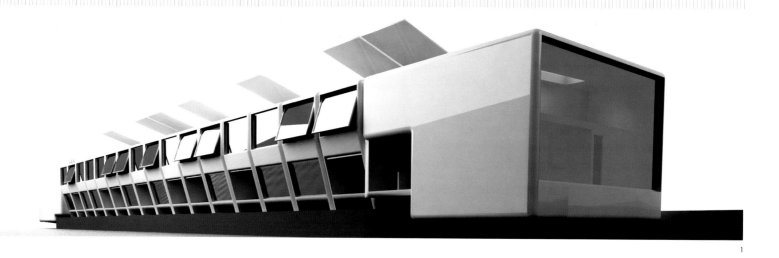

FREIGHT SHIP CONVERSION, CZECH REPUBLIC

IVAN KROUPA ARCHITECTS

Constructed in a decommissioned freight ship, sixteen luxury apartments are created in an exclusive dock for downtown Prague by Ivan Kroupa Architects. The location, on the riverbank beneath Vyšehrad, provides direct links to the historical core of the city and clear views of Little Town and Prague Castle. Each of the four living levels on the ship offers habitable space in a functional yet spatially reconfigurable way with different characteristics and qualities – space, light, views and communication with the surroundings.

The main habitable level has one closed-off façade oriented towards the riverbank. This offers the possibility of individual entrances for each apartment. The more open part of this level looks out over the water through a sloping glazed curtain wall.

Below, small private courtyards offer views of the sky, intimacy and a quiet atmosphere for working, as well as access to the connecting corridor. While above, the rooftop terrace is accessible upon opening the roof itself. The operable part of the roof projects, shielding the terrace area and improving intimacy.

Common areas are divided into two parts. The publicly accessible entranceway is at the ship's stern. It includes the security office, reception, a small catering area, and a double-height multifunctional space with a view upstream, a café, dining room and dance hall. The forepart of the ship is solely for the use of residents. A bar in an extended-height space has a spectacular view of the river, the city and the castle. A sky-lit swimming pool, changing rooms, a sauna and a massage studio feature, as does a fitness club below deck, which is lit in part via the glazed swimming pool floor.

From a constructability perspective, the modular steel structure of the new additions ties into the original transverse bulkheads of the freight ship and is supported on a load transfer grid at the below-deck floor level. The exterior surfaces of the apartments are finished in laminate. The interiors are similarly styled, in combination with solid wood.

1   Main façade
    of apartments
2   Rear entrances
3   Roof level
    external space
    provision
4   Cabin plan details
5   Section through
    the ship
6   Plan view of
    cabins

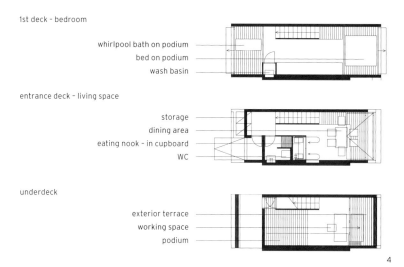

1st deck - bedroom

whirlpool bath on podium
bed on podium
wash basin

entrance deck - living space

storage
dining area
eating nook - in cupboard
WC

underdeck

exterior terrace
working space
podium

4

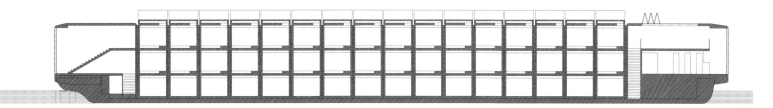

5

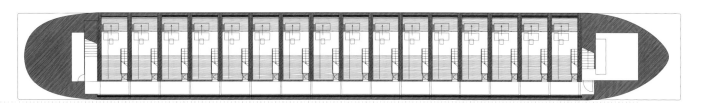

6

HOTEL PUSHKIN, RUSSIA
JAN STÖRMER PARTNERS

1

On a prime site in the centre of Moscow a new boutique hotel is to be built. The Hotel Pushkin will become one of the luxury tourist destinations of the city, being situated in the heartland of Moscow's nightlife, in close proximity to numerous restaurants, theatres, bars and shops.

The client, Basic Element LLC, held a design competition in 2006 to discover an architectural aesthetic to achieve these ambitions. Jan Störmer Partners answered this competition call with a design for the €26 million (US$32.8 million) development that brings together these varied functions in a way which it believes 'generates an identity of space, using form, colour and different materials to define each separate zone within the building'.

The exterior of the hotel contrasts sharply with its neighbours: a rippling glazed façade standing out between the more conventional stone frontages. To the rear, the façade is less glitzy but equally striking, as storeys are denoted by solid strips that undulate horizontally.

2

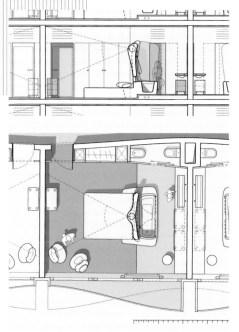

3

4

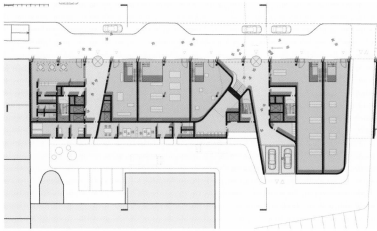

5

6

This glamorous external covering is a precursor to an interior where the architects have let their imaginations run riot, to create an aesthetic design indicative of a new age. While the price of a room will be high, the internal design does not take on the traditional 'upmarket' or classic approach. Instead, Jan Störmer Partners has generated a space that 'integrates' with the guest, an internal environment that adapts and changes, in short, a concept that is flexible and changeable, not stuck in time.

The ground and first floors will be populated by retail outlets. Entrance to the actual hotel is gained via a sweeping staircase rising through 'lively' surroundings that indicate what is to come. Internal walls are adorned with almost garish patterning, while furniture in restaurants and bars is contemporary in style and bespoke. A typical room includes a king-size bed at its centre, an overhead projector, and more very modern styling.

1	Hotel in context	3	Structural
2	Façade detail		support at
			ground level
		4	Bedroom section
			and plan
		5	Ground floor
			layout
		6	Bedroom concept

HOUSE IN THE ANDES, CHILE
CHETWOODS ARCHITECTS

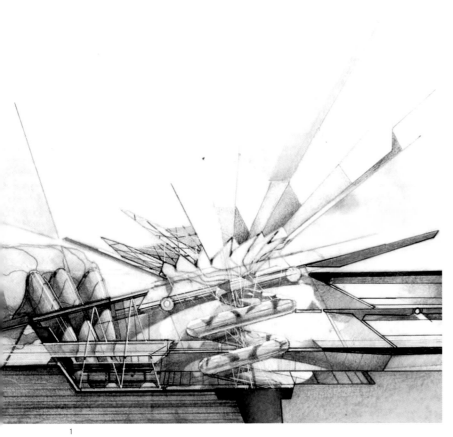

1

2

A hilltop site in the foothills of the Chilean Andes is the setting for this dramatic residential project, designed by the British practice Chetwoods Architects. The house is the first element of a family enclave nestling within a 5 ha. (12.4 acre) area in the dense rainforest.

While the location of the site sounds idyllic, the surrounding environment can be harsh, with temperatures reaching desert highs in the day before dropping below freezing at night. In addition, due to its remote location, the house has to be entirely self-sufficient to counter the lack of utilities.

Chetwoods' solution is to create a property that will physically react to the environment around it. The design takes as a metaphor a flower, which opens each day to soak up the sun's warmth and energy and closes as dusk falls to protect its fragile innards from the cold of night.

3

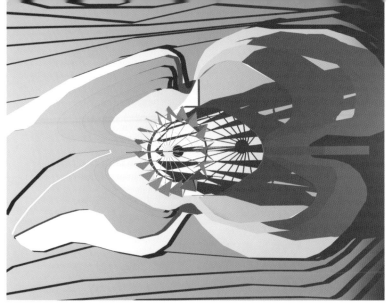

4

The house in the Andes mimics the flower's abilities: in the daytime the roof, formed as an array of huge petals, opens upward and out to provide stunning views out over the rainforest, while shading the entire property and allowing cooling breezes to filter through. At night, the petals close, enveloping the glazed façade, insulating the house.

The roof petals are also adorned with photovoltaic panels, while their overall shape forms a shallow funnel which operates as a large rainwater collector. This water source is supplemented by a solar-powered pump, which pulls water up from a natural spring deep within the hillside.

At night the house is warmed by the natural heat sink formed by the bare rocks on which it is built. During the day these rocks heat up in the warmth of the sun, then, at night, they release that warmth back into the atmosphere, passively heating the house.

Building in this pristine environment puts pressure on the designer to excel in the field of sustainable design. This building fully utilizes the available natural resources to create a beautiful and workable home that sits lightly within its surroundings.

5

1   Concept sketch
    section with open
    canopy
2   Concept with
    closed canopy
3   Aerial view of
    model
4   Plan with closed
    canopy
5   Plan with half
    open canopy
6   Plan with fully
    open canopy

6

1

On a site opposite the new Tretyakov Museum in Moscow, Russia, Erick van Egeraat Architects (EEA) designed five residential blocks. But these are not the usual concrete slabs that are indicative of much of the city's housing: each is themed on a painting by a famous artist from Russia's Avant Garde period in the 1920s. The paintings are housed in the museum.

The designs, proposed in 2001 for the developer Capital Group Moscow, include the Rodchenko Tower, which is based on Aleksandr Rodchenko's *Linear Construction* (1920). A layering of continuous glass skins hints at the artist's intended fluidity of space in his paintings, as well as an ability to find accidental and non-orthogonal manifestations in a chaotic world.

Moving to Kazimir Malevich's *White on White* (1918), EEA has used detailing and subtle variations as well as graduations between solid and transparent, heavy and light materials in the Malevich Tower to convey the artist's desire to discover beauty in the smallest of things as a viable architectural design.

The Popova Tower – referring to Lyubov Popova, *Painterly Architectonic with Three Stripes* (1916) – uses a variety of tools to convey the ambiguity between space and depth, creating a three-dimensional form from two-dimensional objects. This method is similarly used on the Kandinsky Tower, based on Wassily Kandinsky's *Yellow–Red–Blue* (1925). The spatial depth of the painting leads to an architectural design using several layers.

MOSCOW AVANT GARDE, RUSSIA
ERICK VAN EGERAAT ARCHITECTS

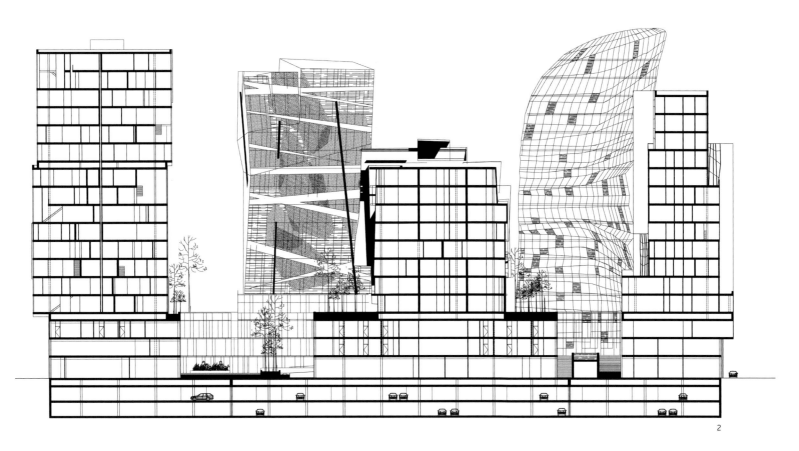

2

3

4

7

10

13

5

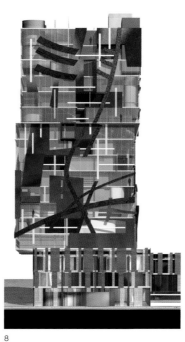

8

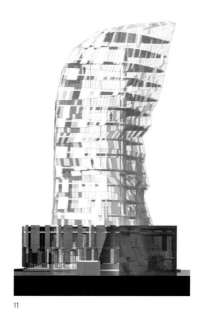

11

14

6

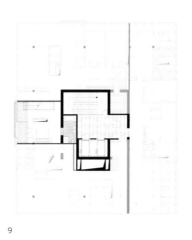

9

12

15

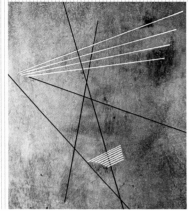

16

17

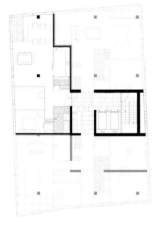

18

Finally, Alexandra Exter's *Sketch for Costume for 'Salome'* (1921) informs a folding concept for the building. This is the most direct interpretation of art into architecture on the Yakimanka complex.

EEA conducted extensive studies to understand the intrinsic compositional structure of each painting and to discover an appropriate interpretation for each of them. The towers house between twenty-one and thirty-one apartments each, with individual property sizes ranging from 145 m^2 (1,561 ft^2) in the Popova Tower to 270 m^2 (2,906 ft^2) in the Kandinsky Tower. Overall there is a gross floor area of 55,570 m^2 (598,150 ft^2).

EEA's approach to the project is at odds with the historic architecture of Moscow. However, in 2001, as Russia was really beginning to feel the influence of the outside world, the designs were a brave attempt to bring artistic flair to the city on a grand scale.

(previous pages)
1   Towers and the cityscape
2   Section through the riverside towers
3   View from the river
4   Exter painting
5   Exter Tower
6   Typical floor plan, Exter
7   Kandinsky painting
8   Kandinsky Tower
9   Typical floor plan, Kandinsky
10 Malevich painting
11 Malevich Tower
12 Typical floor plan, Malevich
13 Popova painting
14 Popova Tower
15 Typical floor plan, Popova
16 Rodchenko painting
17 Rodchenko Tower
18 Typical floor plan, Rodchenko
19 Ground level site plan

19

PIZOTA HOTEL, MEXICO
ESTUDIO CARME PINÓS

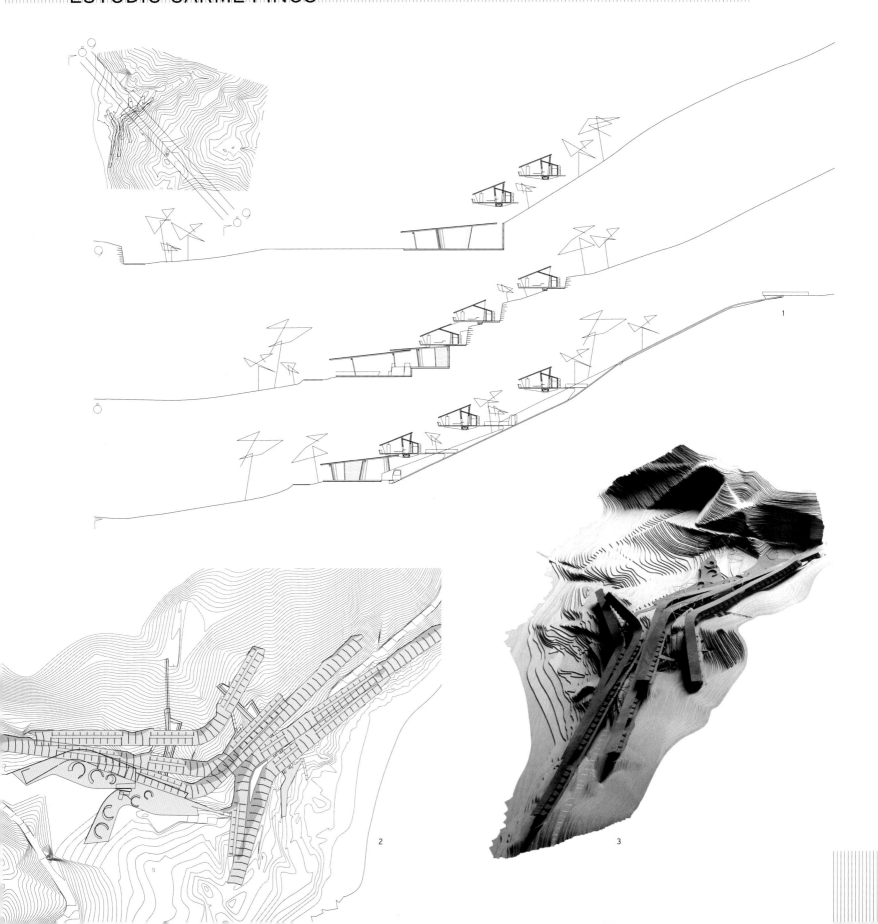

1   Site section
2   Site plan
3   Model showing
    gradients
4   Detail of stepped
    façade
5   View towards the
    bedroom suites

The Pizota is a 150-room hotel design for Puerto Vallarta in Mexico. It is situated in the dense jungle and is only accessible by boat, given that the closest roads are some 60 km (37 miles) away and the only route passes through jungle and over ground hardly touched by human feet.

The site for the hotel is set over a steep gradient, and as such the design flows over different levels in sinuous strands. Surrounding the hotel are dense vegetation and massive ancient trees. Estudio Carme Pinós has dealt with the site and hotel requirements in a way that is ambitious and yet aims to tread lightly without destroying the characteristics of this paradise-like place.

From the beginning, the architect's intention was to create a project that is enlaced with the surrounding nature; a building that cannot be read as a single volume with different floors but which instead captures the essence of the vines that entwine the trees.

Pinós started with the idea of drawing lines into the mountains, demarcation of the gradients on which the hotel was to stand. These lines became belts of thatched roofs that sheltered the rooms. However, the problem of communication and transportation between these linear arms of rooms became apparent. The team did not want to create a simplified design, as this would entail moving massive amounts of earth on the site and destroying the natural flow of the landscape.

Instead, the final solution was to create ribbons of accommodation that follow the topography of the site but also jump it when it gets too complicated. This creates terraces of rooms, each with fabulous views across the sloping terrain. The result is a building design that creates a stunning hotel without making a dramatic aesthetic impact on the environment. The buildings are in tune with their site to the extent that they follow contours and hug the hillside. If it had been built, you can imagine this hotel in years to come shrouded in the vines that its design aimed to mimic.

SENTOSA ISLAND, SINGAPORE
TANGE ASSOCIATES

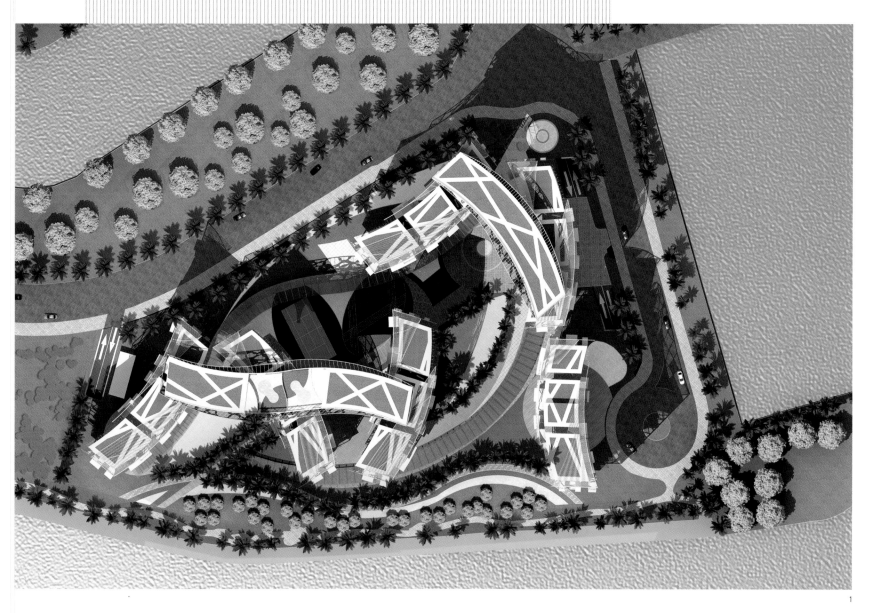

1

Tange Associates submitted two schemes for a competition held in Singapore in 2007 to determine the development rights of a property on Sentosa Island, close to the centre of Singapore.

The area is rapidly changing into a premier resort quarter, used by the high fliers of the city. A new casino resort is soon to open and the site for this new project is near the southern bay. It creates a gateway to the marina and presents a strong first impression as the landmark of Sentosa Island.

Tange Associates' two schemes each create approximately 350 residential units and leisure facilities within multiple twenty storey towers. In the first proposal, named the 'Breeze of Sentosa', the layout of the towers is a primary feature. They are sited as if breezes are passing

2

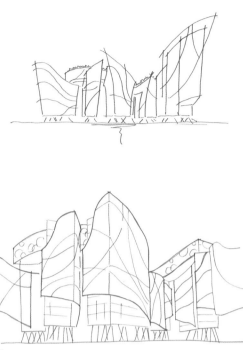

3

4

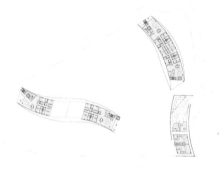

Breeze of Sentosa:
1   Aerial view
2   Multi-tower design
3   Concept sketches
4   Typical floor
    plans

through them. The free and varied shape of the louvres on the external façades expresses the breeze and is designed to present a light and refreshing image.

The second proposal, the 'Forest at the Cove', makes roof gardens a major part of the design. They connect nine towers and are populated by sports facilities and a park where people can relax and gather. Openings located in the roof garden allow sunlight to filter down to the lower floors.

Tange Associates says: 'Architecture is man made, often existing in contrast to nature. However, we tried to express the "Breeze" and "Forest" as parts of nature and to include our approaches toward ecology. We believe there is a simple and fundamental way to be ecological without

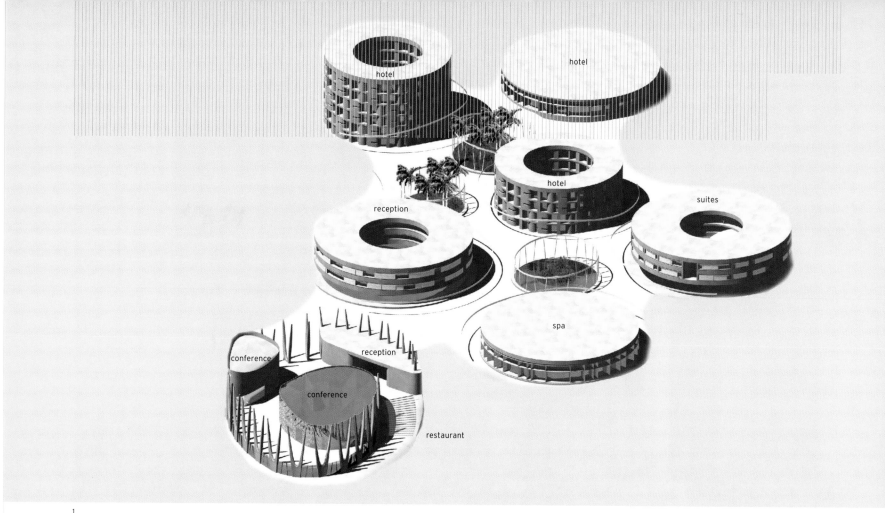

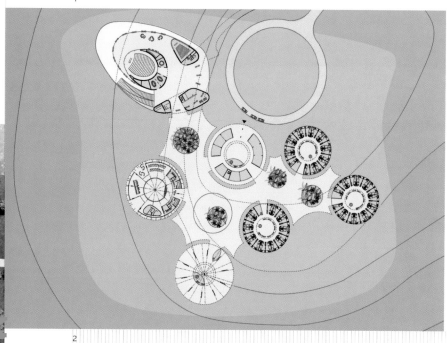

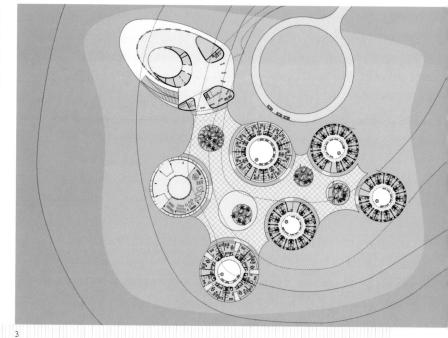

SOUTHERN SUDAN PALACE, SUDAN

JAN STÖRMER PARTNERS

4

1   Exploded
    axonometric
2   Ground floor plan
3   First floor plan
4   View of gardens
5   Conference area
    foyer
6   Internal / external
    meeting and
    circulation area

Sudan is a very troubled country, in which civil unrest dominates everyday life and simple survival is the most important aspect of many people's lives. However, Juba, the main city in the south of the country, has been slated as a good place to develop as the new capital of Southern Sudan.

This kind of step is a long way off while fighting still persists and many people are displaced in refugee camps. But with such a proposal comes the need for new architectural interventions, and Jan Störmer Partners was commissioned to design a hotel for Juba by Becken Investitionen & Vermögensverwaltung in 2005.

The architect came up with a circular building form, characteristic of traditional housing in south Sudan. This premise forms the basic urban planning component, from which the core of a congress centre and hotel complex is developed. The appeal of the 35,000 m² (377,000 ft²) Southern Sudan Palace complex arises from the spaces between the 'houses', which are surrounded by natural light and air. Roofed shaded aisles connect the entrance building with the restaurant, the hotel rooms, a spa and fitness area and, if necessary, office buildings.

Instead of one structure housing all elements, this group of circular buildings of differing heights and sizes collects together the different aspects of the hotel in a gathering similar to that of a traditional Sudanese village. This both creates less immediate visual impact and provides ample outdoor space for visitors to enjoy.

Building such a major project in a region which does not have anything comparable presents a great opportunity for local people. The architect's concept is therefore not to bring in an expensive workforce and materials from far away, but to use local skills and labour in the construction of the hotel. Small accommmodation units have also been developed for workers to live in on-site. These would, at a later date, be used as a staff village on the hotel premises.

5

6

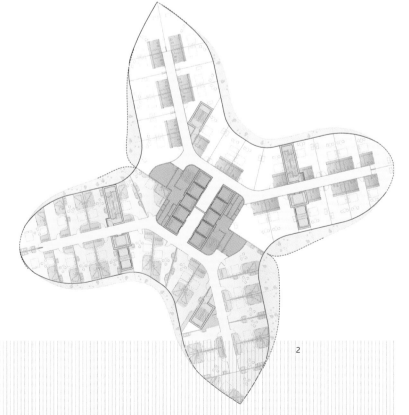

URBAN OASIS, SINGAPORE

UN STUDIO

The Urban Oasis development is located on Beach
Road, a strategic point within Singapore's city centre that connects three
districts and forms a confluence point and hub for business. UN Studio's
design for a mixed-use development comprising office, hotel, retail, and
residential components within a garden setting is influenced both by the
location and the implementation of low-tech sustainable design.

The 3.5 ha. (8.6 acre) island site commands panoramic views while
also enjoying a high degree of visibility from within the city. The public
plaza at ground level is designed to create a lively urban park, activating
and vitalizing the area. The development comprises minimum forty per
cent office use and minimum thirty per cent hotel related use, with the
remaining property reserved for residential and retail components.

The two high rise structures – an office tower and a mixed-use residential and hotel tower – are designed as slender volumes, anchored
between the massive existing neighbouring structures. The architect describes their design as having 'virtual movement', which can be
perceived depending on the viewpoint, due to the formal variation
of the façade.

Sustainable design considerations start with the external envelope. Variations of spatial solutions react to the tropical conditions: sky gardens, sun and rain shelters, balconies, terraces and bay windows are not added to the design by mere multiplication and repetition but by specific allocation in order to transform it into a climatic skin that interfaces with the surrounding environment both aesthetically and organically. The façade and its variants breathe for the building.

The office tower offers large floor plates and features sky terraces on almost every level. The lower section of the second tower allows for two luxurious business hotels with accommodation for more than six hundred guests.

The residential component is situated on the twenty-two levels above the hotels, offering spectacular views of the sea and the city. The units are high-end, luxury apartments with refined interiors and spacious balconies.

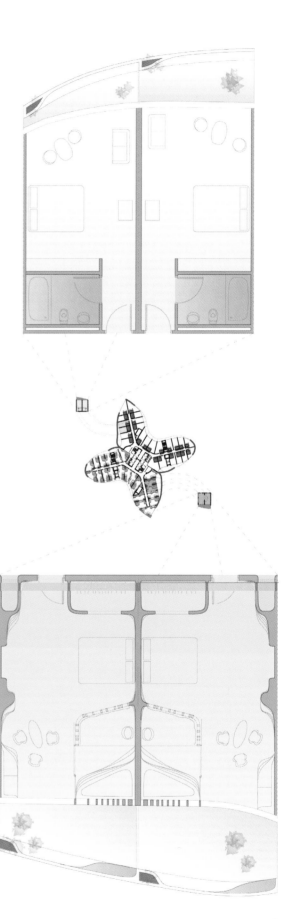

6

7

6 Evening view from Knight Plaza
7 Hotel room plan
8 View downwards from tower summit
9 Pool deck

8

9

W HOTEL, UAE
ATELIERS JEAN NOUVEL

1

This design for a dramatic harbour-front hotel in Dubai, UAE, was taken little further than concept stage by client W Hotels Worldwide. In pulling the plug on the project, the hotel chain missed out on a well-considered architectural proposition by Jean Nouvel that moves away from the brash, overstated construction that blights much of the area, in favour of something far more integrated.

The 2006 proposal for this international hotel with 350 rooms, serviced apartments, a pool, spa, nightclub, retail outlets and restaurants covers a gross floor area of 52,000 m^2 (560,000 ft^2) and would have cost around £72.2 million (US$105 million).

Nouvel conceived the hotel as an extension of the harbour promenade. 'Like a dock, it is set into, and becomes a part of, Dubai creek according to a principle of horizontal platforms in relationship with the water,' he says. The building appears as a series of wooden platforms that stack vertically from the promenade level up through the hotel floors to the roof.

2

3

1   Hotel on arrival   3   Public space,
    by boat   internal / external
2   Aerial view   4   Bedroom
                          5   Private living
                              space
                          6   Public internal
                              area

4

5

The building can be read as a great sailing ship with its bridges and decks, wrapped on the outside in layers of vegetation which extend the surrounding park up onto the building. The architectural vocabulary is linked to boats, sails and water, and carries an idea of luxury that pervades the building inside and out, blurring the line between interior and exterior.

The floors of the hotel are stepped back from the harbour as they rise, creating private balconies at each level. Internally, timber is used extensively, layered and slatted to provide semi- and fully shaded spaces. This technique also allows Nouvel to 'play' with light effects to change the mood between spaces and create different ambiences depending upon the time of day.

The principal hotel wing reaches out over the water, creating a protected space sheltered from the hot desert wind and sun. Here, the architect envisages outdoor activities of all kinds – a public promenade, pontoons, restaurants, bars – all organized around water and boats.

The other wings of the hotel form borders around a sheltered harbour, where residents can moor their luxury yachts. The scene is similar to that pictured at conventional U-shaped hotels, which border a swimming pool. Here, though, as with everything in the UAE, it is on a grander scale.

6

3.
MASTER PLANS

AKTAU CITY EXPANSION, KAZAKHSTAN

KOETTER KIM & ASSOCIATES

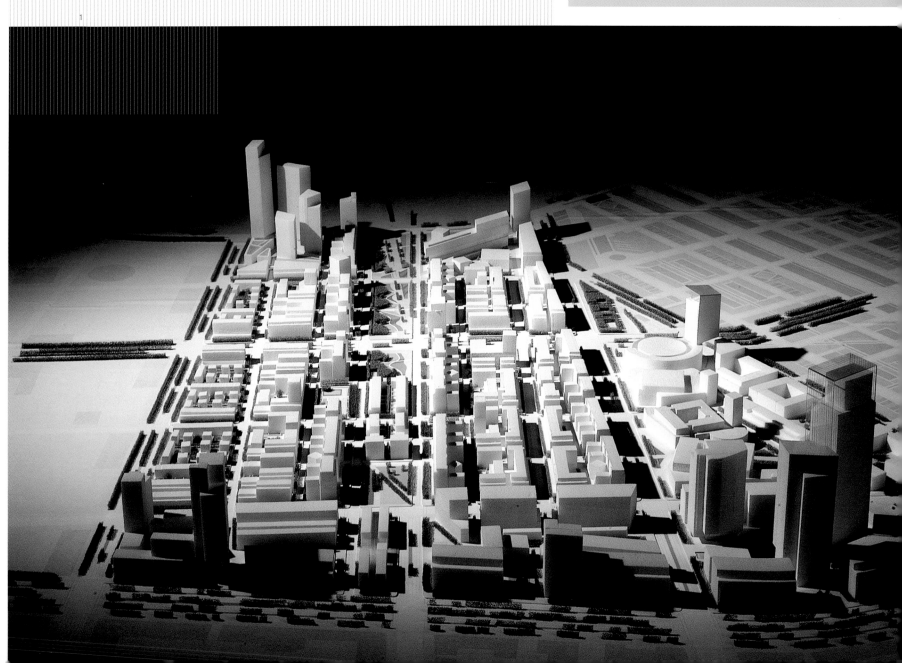

Koetter Kim & Associates was commissioned to design this 4,450 ha. (11,000 acre) expansion to the city of Aktau in Kazakhstan. Atkau is the nation's primary city on the Caspian Sea, and the project seeks to enable the small city to capitalize on its strategic location. It establishes a mixed-use urban pattern and framework for growth that will promote positive development, business investment, tourism and fostering a sense of community by creating a 'green city in the desert'.

The site extends north from the existing Soviet-era port city of 125,000 inhabitants. The region has faced decades of environmental degradation and desertification, and Koetter Kim's proposal therefore incorporates numerous strategies to reintroduce vegetation and promote sound ecological practices that will work hand-in-hand with development.

The master plan design is conceived as a constellation of mixed-use districts of unique identities, 'little cities within the city', which maintain a connection to neighbouring districts and the existing port city to the south. An open space network and multi-modal transportation and pedestrian routes knit the various districts together, while what the architect describes as a 'mosaic' of activities and destinations – including municipal, educational, and residential components – define the different districts.

2

1 Master plan
   model
2 Plan view
3 Aerial night view

3

4

4　Tree-lined avenue
5　Municipal centre
　　at night

6　Residential
　　promontory
7　Concept sketch
8　Plan with parks
　　highlighted
9　Residential
　　square

5

6

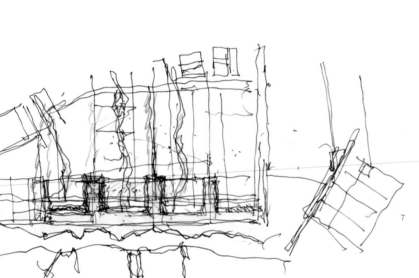

7

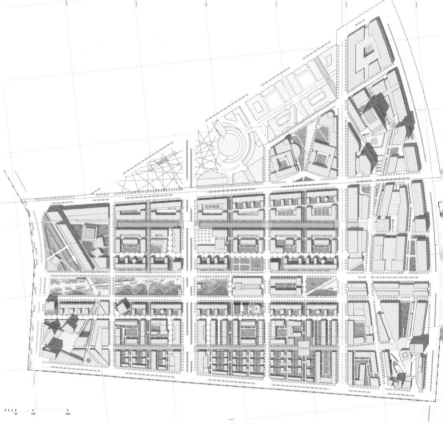

8

9

10

Water Basin
Pump House

Corporate Campus

Festival City

Water Park

Southern
Residential Court

11

10 Canal Park
11 Sea water cooling
12 Aquarium
13 Sea water cooling
    detail

One of the major environmental measures considered was seawater cooling. Investigations indicate that Caspian Sea water may be feasible as an effective and economical cooling agent for the seasonal cooling of the city centre district of Aktau.

Stated simply, cool water from deep in the sea can be pumped up to an energy transfer station in or near the city that transfers the cool low temperature of the sea water to a closed-loop chilled water system; this distributes the water to the buildings of the district. Following the energy transfer, the warmer sea water is returned to the sea.

Koetter Kim animates the sea water return via a system of basins, water gardens and seaside wetland/salt marshes. The basins and water gardens form an important part of a unique city centre public open-space waterway and landscape system. This is in addition to the Aktau Parks District, which serves as a model for subsequent district and neighbourhood development.

12

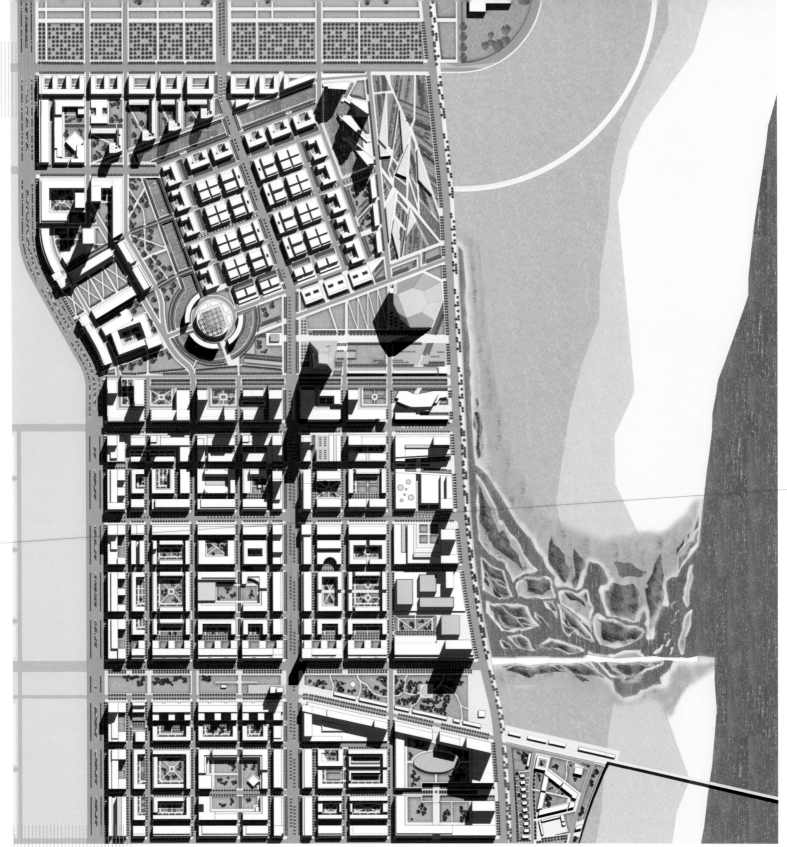

Aktau City Expansion Koetter Kim & Associates 121

Arup's Advanced Geometry Unit (AGU) created a master plan for the 405,000 m² (4.36 million ft²) site on the banks of the river Thames in London, which includes the Grade II listed Battersea Power Station. The design creates a brand new entertainment, cultural and commercial destination for London.

The AGU's involvement started with an invitation to put forward a concept for the South Park, the area to the rear of the power station. The practice designed a combined underground car park and cinema incorporating a double helix, with pedestrians and cars traversing separate inclined ramps. AGU's design brief was subsequently extended to encompass the entire site because of the unit's exciting use of inclined planes and unusual sight lines.

The inclined planes emerging from the car park now spread across the landscape, creating multiple levels, piazzas and secluded courtyards. These subtle changes in gradient alter the way the buildings are viewed and create alternative appreciation of space. They extend into the multiple architectural elements on the site, literally tying the buildings into the overall master plan too, a process that AGU calls 'deep planning'.

This desire to achieve a real integration or connection of all elements of the site forms the master plan. The landscape does not stop when it reaches a building but moves into it, creating a continuation of space that links the external plane with the interior of the building, achieving a greater level of engagement and a more integrated plan.

1

BATTERSEA POWER STATION, UK

ARUP AGU

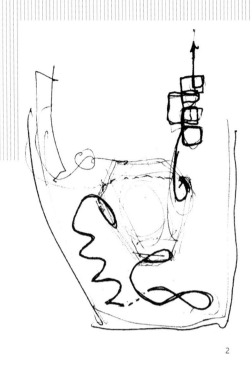

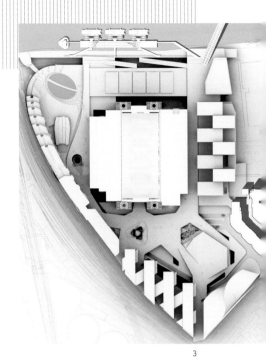

1 Master plan night
   view
2 Concept sketch
3 Building form
   concepts
4 Section
5 Circulation ideas

2

3

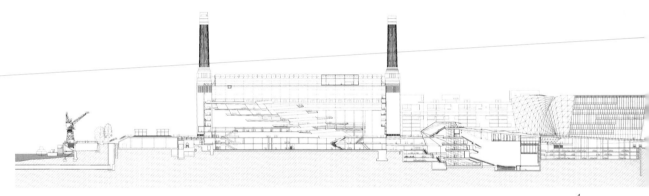

4

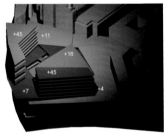

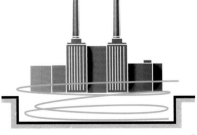

5

The design is seen as a new spatial concept, created to achieve fluid movement throughout the site. The master plan includes eight major architectural interventions such as hotels and residential and office blocks, as well as the power station itself, melded together by this innovative landscaping strategy. Designers involved in the project include Grimshaw Architects (power station refurbishment), Scéno Plus (theatre and cinema), Benson & Forsyth (residential), UN Studio (the Weave office), Arup Associates (West Hotel), West 8 and Gustafson Porter (landscape architecture), Ron Arad (power station rooftop hotel) and the AGU (hotel, car park and cinema).

The complexities involved in a project of this nature demand that all parties work cohesively towards a common goal. The AGU's 'deep planning' strategy ensured that this would happen.

Moxon Architects designed a master plan and major architectural interventions for Daejeon, South Korea's fifth largest city, which was highly commended in this 2007 international competition.

The Daejeon Urban Renaissance competition called for a plan to revitalize the old central urban district of the city, and Moxon's aim is to treat the city as a response, both to the specifics of the location and the way cities will be used in the future. The master plan injects life into the district with a number of differing design ideals, spelt out as 'seasonal architecture'.

Towers symbolize spring, reaching skyward and looking remarkably like new growth from tulip bulbs. Summer comes in the form of medium-rise development, dense growth, and 'ground cover' in the form of private and public buildings overlaid by green pedestrian ways. Smaller buildings and bridges represent autumn and the breaking up of a rigid city fabric. Finally, winter comes as open space, ready to begin over – for future development or temporary events and activities.

DAEJEON URBAN RENAISSANCE, SOUTH KOREA
MOXON ARCHITECTS

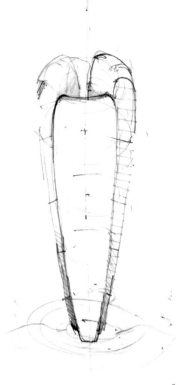

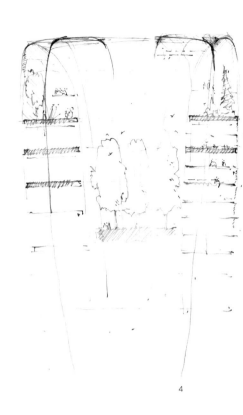

2

3

4

1 View of tower
  tops
2 Site perspective
3 Tower concept
  sketch
4 Tower summit
  detail
5 Activity massing
  diagrams

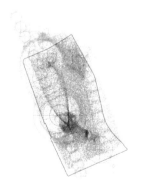
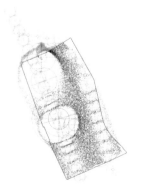
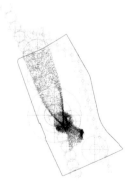

5

Daejeon Urban Renaissance Moxon Architects 125

The poetic nature of this competition submission is cleverly tailored to the Korean mentality.

At a more prosaic level, Moxon envisages the linking of two cultural exchanges, to the north and south of the master plan, via a figure of eight piazza with wide public spaces and fewer vehicles than inhabitants are used to. The exchanges will feature an art gallery, concert hall, cinemas, nightclubs, exhibition space and public squares.

Three distinctive towers provide high-density office accommodation and spectacular leisure and residential areas at the heart of the city. Their form is designed to maximize the daylight reaching the internal floor plates, minimizing the need for artificial lighting and creating stunning internal views.

To maintain a human feel to this vast new intervention into the city, smaller pockets of shared public space beyond the central area will include neighbourhood cinemas and shopping centres to encourage the creation of lively local communities. Housing is situated by the creek to provide the best all-round environment for families and creative people.

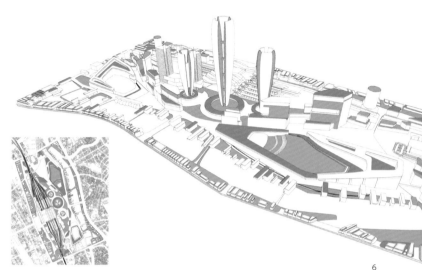

6

7

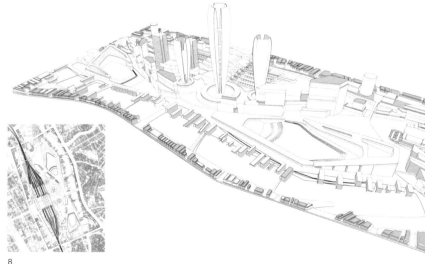

8

6   Green areas
7   View from across
     the city
8   Residential
     massing
9   Aerial view

9

Henning Larsen Architects' design for this collection of five colossal towers, which come together to create a new city in the desert, is not unique in concept, but it is in design. At 1,022 m (3,353 ft), the tallest tower would be the highest in the world.

The project suggests a gathering of towers rising up from a public oasis, like palms from a waterhole. It envisages a vertical city in which people live, work, shop and relax within the five vertiginous giants. The two tallest towers (1,022 and 640 m/3,353 and 2,100 ft) house office space and public services; tower 3, at 530 m (1,740 ft), is a hotel; and towers 4 and 5, diminutive in comparison, at 420 and 250 m (1,378 and 820 ft) respectively, are extensively residential. Ironically, a shopping centre is deemed by the architect as the 21st century equivalent of an oasis; it nestles at the base of the vertical city.

Everything about this design is big. The shopping centre would be the largest in the world, spreading some 2.29 million m^2 (0.88 mi.^{2}) over five storeys and including two public gardens. If this sounds hellish, Larsen has subdivided the retail areas into smaller clusters with secondary pathways leading to internal local courtyards. Throughout the mall the bases of the towers reveal themselves, and skylights allow the visitor glimpses upwards to their summits.

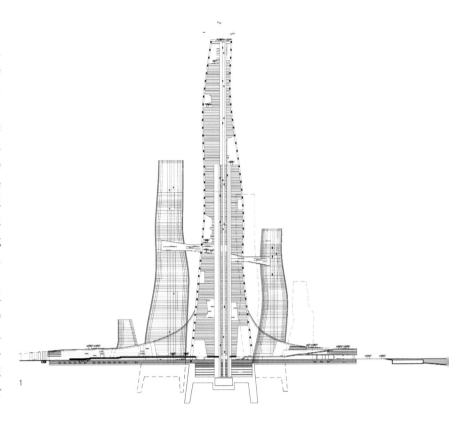

1

1   Cross section
2   View up towers
3   Plinth and sky
      bridge

2

MURJAN CITY, SAUDI ARABIA
HENNING LARSEN ARCHITECTS

3

The façade of the massive towers is directly related both to the geometry of Islamic patterns and to coral, an historic building material in the area. An integral part of this patterning is the primary megastructure of the towers, which is designed as a shell on their exterior. The different layers of the façade go on to interpret traditional patterns operating in different scales, from the macro of the main load-bearing structure, and a secondary structural bracing at openings; to the micro of solar shading panels that filter the harsh light coming into the building. The architect describes the resulting design as a 'structural pattern interwoven and emerging from the landscape, evolving and becoming the façades of the towers'.

With towers that range from 40 to 200 storeys high, the world's largest shopping centre and some 38.5 ha. (95 acres) of garden, Murjan City is a project possibly too extravagant even for the powers behind the new colonization of the Middle East's deserts. While the world's tallest, largest, greenest, glitziest are all being built in and around Saudi Arabia, this scheme never quite made it past the drawing board – a pity given that its collective design is more readily readable than the plethora of individual projects currently rising out of the sands.

4

5

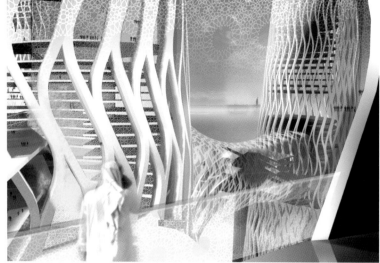

6

7

8

4   Model morning
    view
5   Evening
    panorama

6   Small sky lobby
7   Sky lobby detail
8   Ground level
9   Section through;
    façade details

Perforated solar shading

Glazed openings

Secondary grid
structure

Primary grid
structure

Glazed openings

perforated solar shading

Secondary grid structure

Primary grid structure

9

1 2

1 View from a tower
2 Aerial view
3 Site elevation
4 Site plan
5 Looking outwards

Zaha Hadid's designs for the New York 2012 Olympic Games were brought to an abrupt end when the bid was lost to the UK. However, this 19.4-ha. (48 acre) Olympic Village master plan would have created a new high-rise residential district, set amidst green space in Queens, New York, following the games.

The proposed collection of fourteen residential towers presents a dramatic Olympic icon to Queens. The tower footprints are minimized to offer an open, undulating space around them, which extends between the East River and Newtown Creek. The ground is lifted to absorb parking below, and then shaped to define varied settings to encourage different leisure pursuits above.

Together, this textured ground and the towers establish a strong formal presence. The architect says: 'Although the sheer beauty of the towers may stand as their most immediately noticeable advantage, the integrated landscape achieves important planning aims. It offers a land-scape that opens itself to a rich pattern of activity and highlights the role of recreation in contemporary lifestyles, and this plan also draws future residents close to the area's increasing employment opportunities, while lending critical mass to the small shops and services already in the neighbourhood.'

Along the East River the ground lifts to sweep over the main Olympic dining hall: a double-height space facing out towards the skyline of Midtown. This is the more muscular waterside, matching the scale of the river and its ferry infrastructure. Along Newtown Creek, however, a closer engagement with local life takes shape with mid-rise housing that takes inspiration from the warehouses and industrial structures along the creek. Ground-level shops and workspaces, as well as small-scale boating facilities, encourage a sense of connection between this new development and the existing urban fabric of Queens. These two very different waterfronts are linked by a continuous promenade extending around Hunters Point.

SEWOON DISTRICT URBAN REDEVELOPMENT, SOUTH KOREA

KOETTER KIM & ASSOCIATES

1 Aerial view
2 North elevation
3 South elevation
4 East elevation
5 West elevation

Koetter Kim & Associates has conceived this four-block sustainable urban district in the heart of Seoul, Korea. The planning of close-knit mixed-use buildings, largely built upon existing street patterns, aims to maintain and intensify the active, street-oriented life that characterizes this historic district. The programme includes retail, commercial and entertainment uses as well as public and cultural activities.

The master plan incorporates an intense web of street-related building and activity that is on a juxtaposition of two major public spaces: the west to east path of the newly reclaimed historic Cheonggyecheon Canal (dating from the 15th century), and a proposed new north to south linear park system, called Central Park, running through the city from north of the canal to the southern hills.

The canal and park bring nature back into the heart of the city and help re-establish Seoul's traditional 'closeness to the earth'. The master plan achieves a new integration between the historic city and its magnificent green setting; redeveloping natural and managed watershed conditions; and providing an ecologically balanced meshing of the natural and built environments.

SHENZHEN CULTURAL CENTRE, CHINA
LAB ARCHITECTURE STUDIO

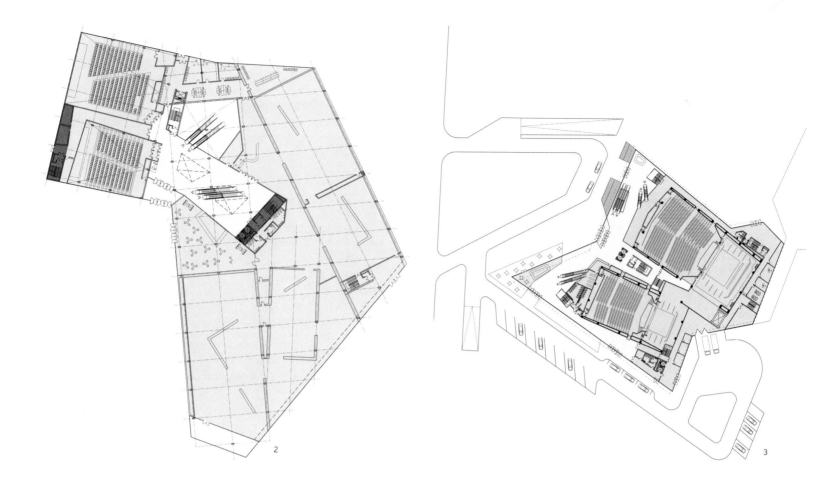

With a gross area of 75,406 m² (812,000 ft²) LAB Architecture Studio's proposal for the Shenzhen Cultural Centre is located in Bao'an, on the southern coast of China. LAB has conceived the four potential sites as one master plan that consists of cultural and performing arts structures placed side by side to form an urban edge along the city's central park. The design considers the urban and natural landscape as interconnected with and inseparable from the buildings, which seem to grow out of the ground like crystalline formations that define the boundary between built and landscaped environments.

LAB proposes three buildings: a library, a combined arts and youth palace, and an opera house. All are designed similarly, their façades based upon a dynamic Voronoi pattern, generated from the geometry of the buildings. Three different types of façade materials are used: dark metallic cladding, textured stone panels and two different shades of glass. This use of contrasting materials creates surface changes in the appearance of the façades, ranging from matt black to light grey and reflective, according to the light at different times of the day.

1 Aerial view
2 Library plan
3 Opera house plan
4 Library elevation
5 Opera house
   elevation

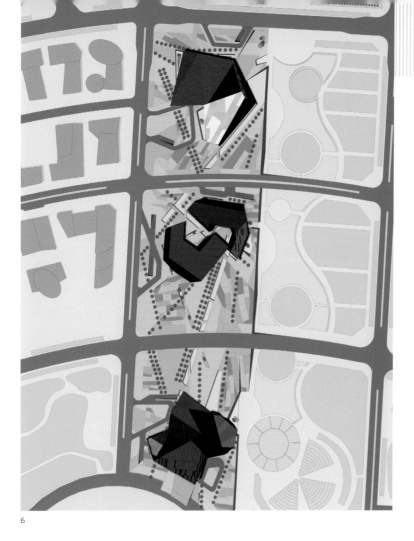

6

The library is located at the northern-most site in the precinct that the cultural centre creates. Entry to it is drawn into focus by a spectacular south-facing overhang which soars over 20 m (66 ft), providing year-round shade.

The arts and cultural centre and the youth palace are integrated as a single site, in a figure of eight. Both buildings have clearly identified ground-level street frontages with defined entries, but they are also connected by sunken gardens with stairs providing access from a below-ground level to the public plazas.

Landscaping to the master plan has been designed so that the 'architecture' of the landscape becomes the building and vice versa. Moving between the buildings and the landscape, pedestrians circulate through courtyards, plazas and parks, which encourage people to meander rather than simply take the fastest linear route connecting public spaces and the building entries.

7

The West Kowloon Cultural District is a 40 ha. (99 acre) site set in a prime location in Hong Kong harbour. It was offered by the city to developers with the brief to bring maximum revenue while creating a new urban leisure experience for Hong Kong.

Requirements for the site include 200,000 m² (21.5 million ft²) of cultural facilities and a 220,000 m² (2.37 million ft²) canopy, the concept of which was taken from an earlier competition won by Foster & Partners for the site. All other aspects of the site could be developed as the bid teams saw fit.

Aedas's master plan, in conjunction with Richard Rogers Partnership as joint master planners and architects, shuns what it describes as the 'architectural iconism' of Foster's original design and instead concentrates on providing for civic need. Aedas commissioned star architects including Herzog de Meuron and Jean Nouvel to provide architectural glamour to a 10,000-seat performance venue, museum of modern art and three theatres.

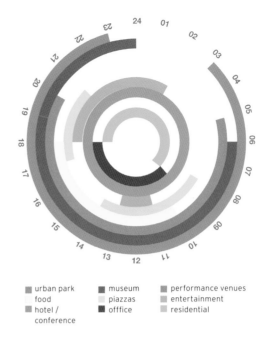

urban park   museum   performance venues
food   piazzas   entertainment
hotel /   offfice   residential
conference

1

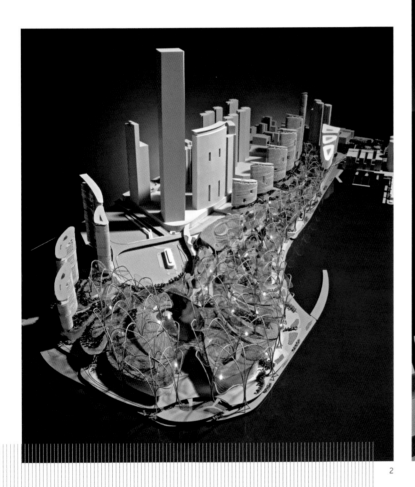

2

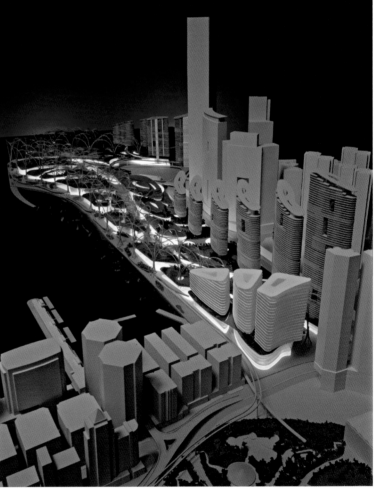

3

WEST KOWLOON CULTURAL DISTRICT, HONG KONG
AEDAS AND RICHARD ROGERS PARTNERSHIP

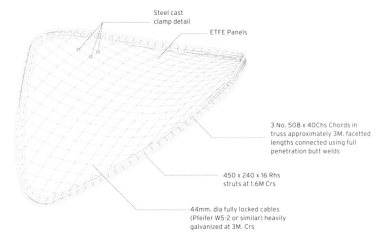

Steel cast
clamp detail

ETFE Panels

3 No. 508 x 40Chs Chords in
truss approximately 3M. facetted
lengths connected using full
penetration butt welds

450 x 240 x 16 Rhs
struts at 1.6M Crs

44mm. dia fully locked cables
(Pfeifer W5-2 or similar) heavily
galvanized at 3M. Crs

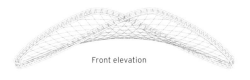

Front elevation

Side elevation

4

5

6

1	Land use diagram	4	Cable net canopy	6	Theatre interior
2	Aerial view		design	7	Site plan
3	Aerial view from	5	Under the		
	inland		canopies		

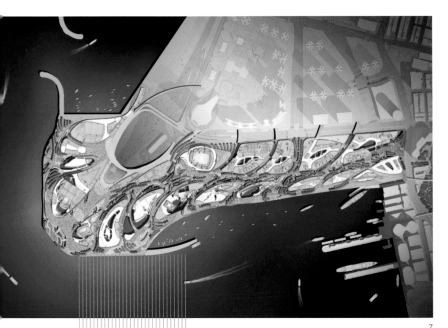

7

However, most precious to the inhabitants of Hong Kong is outdoor leisure space, and this master plan features a continuous 25 ha. (62 acre) park, which stretches over the roof of the entire low-rise cultural and commercial facility. It provides a much needed central park for Hong Kong, equivalent in size to all the existing parks put together.

The park is covered by a continuous translucent canopy that allows in maximum amounts of natural light, while shielding against the elements, including some of the sun's harmful rays. Undulating below, as the canopy arches above, is the green parkland that features myriad walks and scenic points to look out over Hong Kong harbour. Beneath this new park is a similar series of routes that meander between cultural venues, restaurants, cafes and retail outlets.

The scheme, with its all-shrouding canopy, is a futuristic vision similar in its aesthetics to those dreamed of in sci-fi literature. It did not win the competition; but with the climate changing so rapidly, be prepared to see similar elsewhere in the near future.

WEST KOWLOON CULTURE PARK, HONG KONG
MOSHE SADFIE & ASSOCIATES

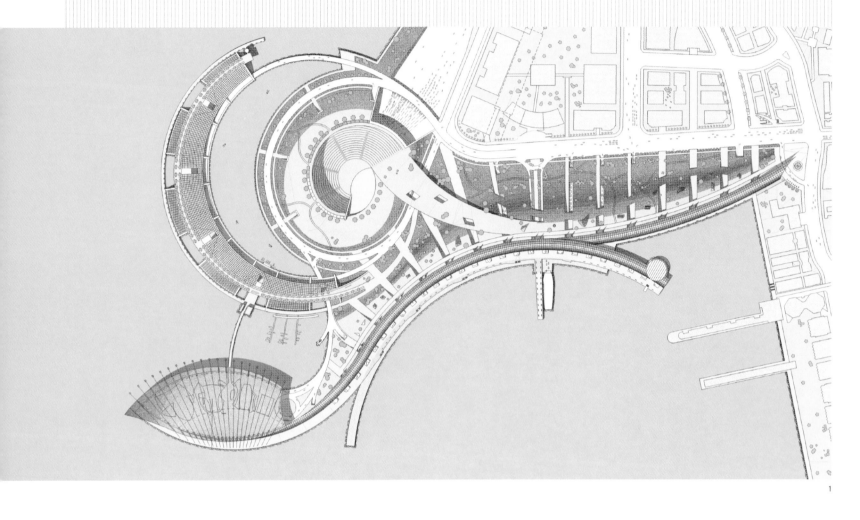

1

The creation of a vast 60.5 ha. (150 acre) culture park on the shore front of West Kowloon was the subject of a competition held by the Planning and Land Bureau of the Hong Kong Special Administrative Region in 2001.

Moshe Safdie & Associates' sweeping design, which arcs out into the bay between the mainland and Hong Kong Island, is a striking scheme that contrasts with the high-rise towers surrounding it and yet lives with them for its breathtaking audacity.

The architect designed a concept that would combine green landscaped areas and open promenades with an 'intensely animated cultural boulevard', along which a huge variety of entertainment can be found. The low-rise design doesn't block the views from towers behind it and presents a dramatic sculptural addition.

The scheme includes 26 ha. (64 acres) of publicly accessible parks and open spaces, 318,000 m² (3.42 million ft²) of cultural and entertainment venues and 220,000 m² (2.37 million ft²) of hotel and retail space. This creates 538,000 m² (5.79 million ft²) of new institutional and commercial development, plus new roads and 3,500 parking spaces to service it.

The design features flamboyant architecture such as the pier-end concert venue which is shrouded in a transparent skin of glass. Numerous venues feature water views from two aspects, and retail spaces are housed in sloping units which have roofs that double as public space. A long series of masts and a covered walkway flows from the mainland to the tip of the scheme, while towards its centre pedestrian bridges lead to a main external public space, which winds in on itself like the pattern of a snail shell.

The entire development is a direct contrast to the crowded, cluttered streets that lead into the midst of Kowloon. If built, the culture park would have been a major draw for residents of the city; not necessarily for its cultural content but purely as a space to relax and enjoy the outdoors, similar to squares such as that under the HSBC Building on Hong Kong Island.

2

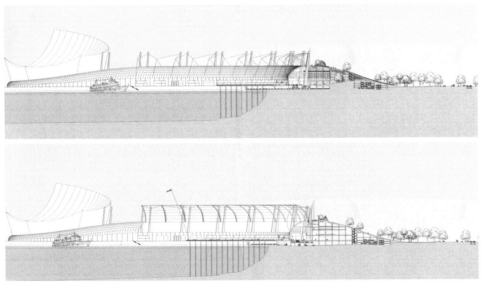

3

4

West Kowloon Culture Park **Moshe Safdie & Associates** 153

4.
MUSEUMS

CANADIAN MUSEUM FOR HUMAN RIGHTS, CANADA

ANTOINE PREDOCK

1

2

Both carved into the earth and dissolving into the sky on the horizon of Winnipeg, Canada, the Canadian Museum for Human Rights by Antoine Predock is a 23,500 m² (253,000 ft²) colossus of symbolic meaning. Designed to be built in the relative flatlands of Manitoba, this towering building cuts a dramatic presence, unlike anything previously seen anywhere in world, let alone a central Canadian province.

The architect describes his design as 'the abstract ephemeral wings of a white dove, which embrace a mythic stone mountain of 450 million-year-old Tyndall limestone, in the creation of a unifying and timeless landmark for all nations and cultures of the world – a symbolic apparition of ice, clouds and stone set in a field of sweet grass.'

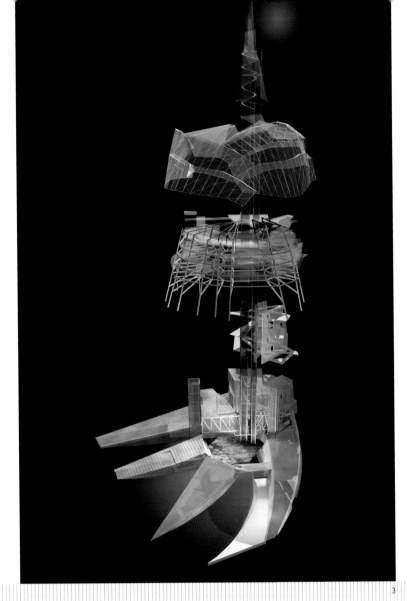

The visitor's journey begins with a descent into the earth, a symbolic recognition of the earth as the spiritual centre for many indigenous cultures. People enter the museum at its base, past giant roots: protective stone arms that suggest an ancient geological event. These roots are positioned to block northern and northwestern winds and celebrate the sun, with apertures marking paths of equinox and solstice: they also contain the essential public interface functions of the museum and create a framework for ceremonial outdoor events, with roof terraces and amphitheatre seating.

Arriving at the heart of the building, the Great Hall evokes the memory of ancient gatherings of people of the Forks of First Nations, and later, settlers and immigrants. The Garden of Contemplation is Winnipeg's winter garden. Here, water and medicinal plants define space and act as a purifying 'lung', reinforcing the fundamental environmental ethic of the building.

The journey through the museum galleries culminates in an ascent of the Tower of Hope with panoramic views of the city and natural realm. 'The tower symbolizes the life-affirming hope for positive changes in humanity,' says the architect.

Predock has not finished there, though. Even the back-of-house support facilities are swathed in meaning. These are ensconced within the Cloud, which is envisioned as light-filled and buoyant, in marked contrast to the geologic evocation of the roots and stone galleries. It is meant to provide a visible reminder of the power and necessity of hope and tolerance.

3

1   Scale model
2   Concept sketch
3   Exploded model
4   The garden
5   Great Hall

4

5

1

How to design a museum for cultural artefacts from an area as diverse as Europe and the Mediterranean? Tod Williams Billie Tsien Architects' (TWBTA) entry for a competition to do just that evolved into an exciting new structure in Marseille, France, shrouded in a filigreed net and connected to an ancient fort by a slim pedestrian bridge.

Located at the entrance of the old port in Marseille, the new museum and the old fort structures contain gallery space. The new museum is comprised of three separate volumes, held together visually by the net, to form a distinct silhouette, seemingly suspended above the ground. The form of the net is an inversion of the battered walls of the fort, sloping outwards to the sky. Its semi-transparent design could allude to Moroccan decoration, a heritage long associated with this southern French port. The new museum also makes direct reference to the fort in that it is a group of distinct forms or buildings surrounded by the net, as the fort is a series of built volumes surrounded by a wall.

1   Aerial view
2   Perspective
    showing bridge
    between new
    (left) and old sites

CIVILIZATION MUSEUM OF EUROPE
AND THE MEDITERRANEAN, FRANCE
TOD WILLIAMS BILLIE TSIEN ARCHITECTS

2

The three building volumes of the museum create an inner spatial maze, through which the public access stair weaves to a sky terrace and lobby. By encapsulating the volumes, this inner void becomes a dynamic space where public and museum visitors overlap.

TWBTA sees the zones that extend from the three buildings to meet the sloping form of the net as a buffer space. These zones form extensions to the formal space: ambulatory gallery spaces, the auditorium foyers, and exterior terraces, creating tightly interwoven areas that connect each of the built volumes.

On the fort site, the architect's approach has been to reinforce the existing nature of the site by creating modestly sized volumes that nestle within or above the historical structures. This strategy of infusing the old with the new enables the design to distribute the museum's programme throughout the site without dominating the existing ruins. It also allows for the preservation of the unique identity of the fort.

3

4

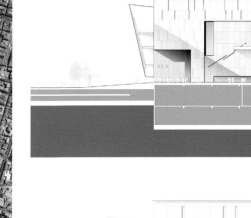

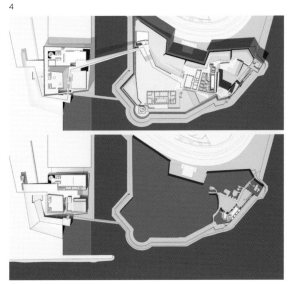

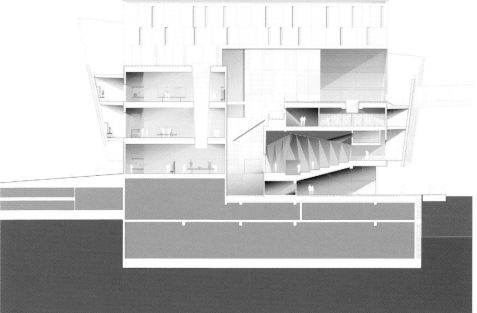

5

6

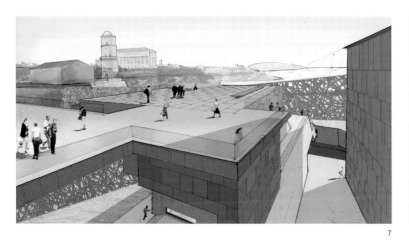

7

8

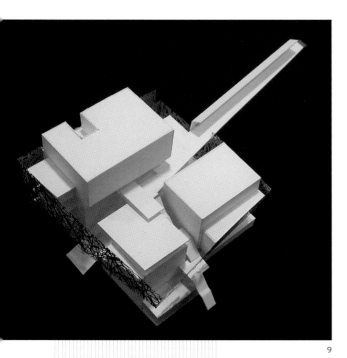

9

3 Aerial view with
existing fort to
the foreground
4 Site location
5 Site plan
6 Section and detail
7 View from
museum sky
terrace
8 Main courtyard
9 Concept model
10 Site elevation and
main section

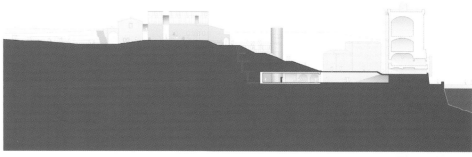

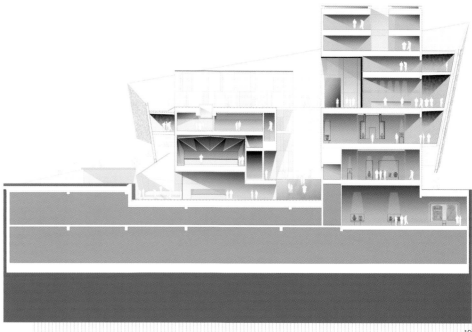

10

ESTONIAN NATIONAL MUSEUM, ESTONIA
GIANNI BOTSFORD ARCHITECTS

1

Philanthropists Jakob Hurt and Jan Jung began the journey to create the Estonian National Museum by asking the Estonian people to bring together artefacts from all parts of the country to form a collection that tells the story of this proud European nation. Gianni Botsford Architects' (GBA) competition proposal symbolically reflects the artefacts' journey from all corners of the country in its form as a solid mass with a series of incisions that relate to journeys depicted across a map of Estonia and locally to the site and city of Tartu.

The museum reveals itself in a series of layers, which are controlled by differing levels of light. The public spaces contain views and openings which connect the interior to the landscape setting of the museum, as well as controlling daylight and sunlight. A deep reveal in the façade draws you into the main entrance lobby – a dramatic space where a series of staircases wind their way up, connecting the main public elements of the museum, with light penetrating through deep projecting reveals, skylights and incisions. A restaurant opens out on to an outside terrace on the upper level.

The museum complex is organized on three floors, with the open non-exhibition zone located to the east of the building, the open exhibition zone centrally to the north on two floors, the closed collection zone to the south, and the closed non-collection zone to the west. The carefully controlled incisions in the building's façades form views and connections with the overall site; they allow in daylight where required; and they symbolically link the form to the emergence of the museum's origins.

Tallinn ●   Rakvere ●   Johvi ●

Kardla ●   Haapsalu ●   Rapla ●

Tartu

Parnu ●   Viljandi ●

Kuressaare ●

Polva ●

Valga ●   Voru ●

Narva road

vahi street

Boss street

2

1   Model view
2   Geographic
    regions and site
    layout similarities
3, 4 Illuminated
     perspectives

3

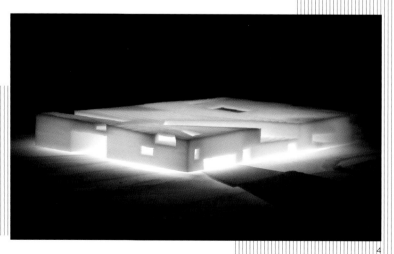

4

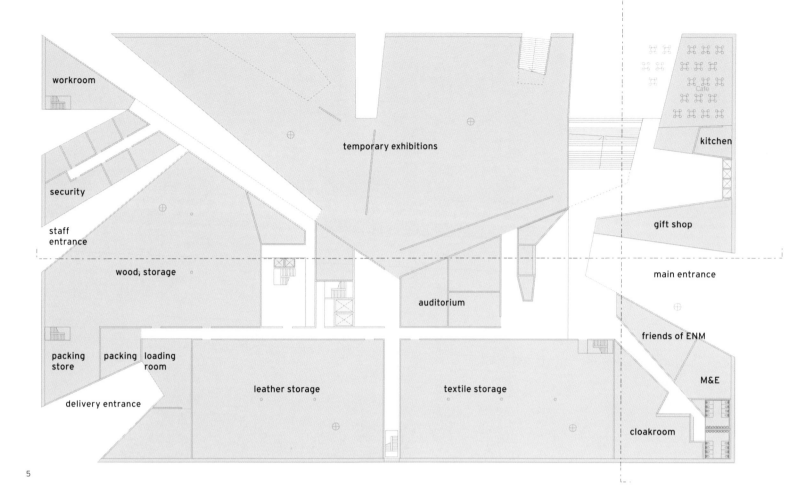

workroom

security

staff
entrance

wood, storage

packing
store

packing | loading
room

delivery entrance

temporary exhibitions

auditorium

leather storage

textile storage

Café

kitchen

gift shop

main entrance

friends of ENM

M&E

cloakroom

5

6

7

5   Ground floor plan
6, 7   Internal concepts
8   Circulation
    routes
9   Exploded zoning
    diagram
10   Site layout and
    sight lines

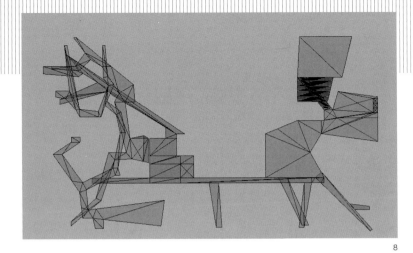

8

Internal materials are exposed concrete and timber lining, display cases are in materials ranging from stainless steel, glass and aluminium to wood. The darkest materials are used in the heart of the museum, the galleries, diminishing to the most open elements such as the lobbies, restaurants and cafés, which are lined in lighter materials throughout.

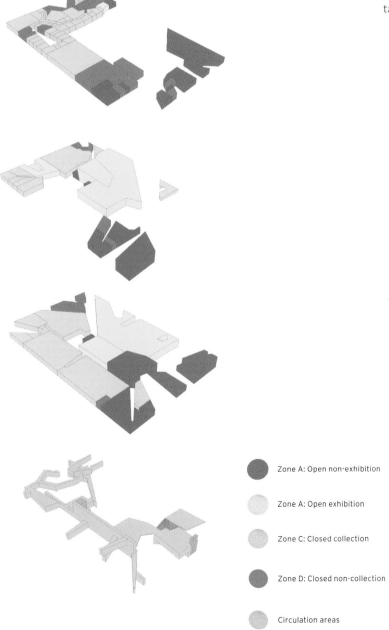

9

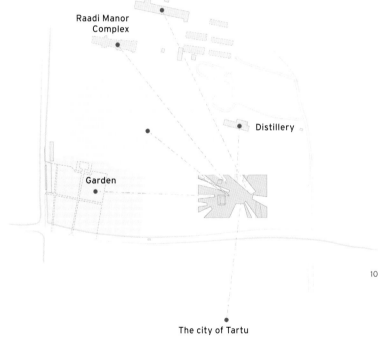

Raadi Manor Complex

Distillery

Garden

10

The city of Tartu

● Zone A: Open non-exhibition

○ Zone A: Open exhibition

○ Zone C: Closed collection

● Zone D: Closed non-collection

○ Circulation areas

1

Designed in 2001, the dramatic 21st century aesthetic for the museum is described by its architect Diller Scofidio + Renfro as having a 'hybrid nature that provokes an architecture of cross-programming and spatial interweaving'. The use of IT terminology has become commonplace now in architectural description, but just a few years ago it provoked excitement, as did the designs for Eyebeam.

The museum of art and technology was to be located in Chelsea, New York, amidst the conventional brick buildings of this warehouse district. Diller Scofidio + Renfro's design concept begins with a pliable ribbon, which partitions the spatial programming of the building in two: production spaces to one side (blue) and presentation spaces to the other (grey).

The ribbon undulates from side to side as it climbs from the street, floor folding into wall folding into floor, while the front elevation slips backwards gradually to fit the city planners' diminishing zoning envelope. With each change of direction the ribbon alternately enfolds a production or presentation space.

Museum staff use the east core and visitors use the west. However, each must pass through the spaces of the other when circulating between successive levels, ensuring that the diverse activities interconnect regularly – 'cross-programming and interweaving'. The ribbon is also sometimes sheared and slipped into alignment with a level above or below, conjoining a production and presentation space. These layers are both architectural manifestations and spatial demarcation, which provoke interaction.

EYEBEAM MUSEUM OF ART AND TECHNOLOGY, USA
DILLER SCOFIDIO + RENFRO

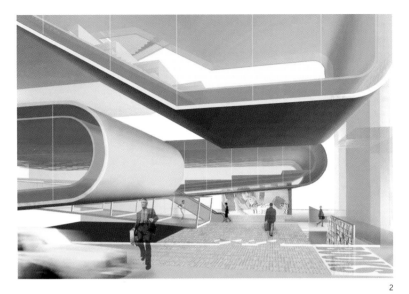

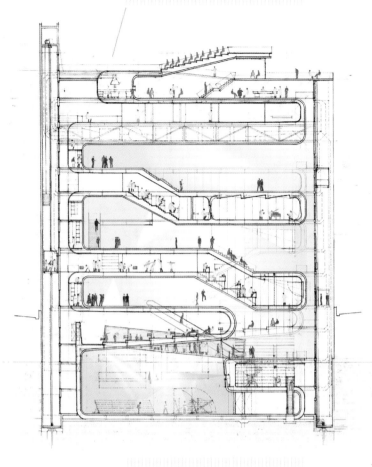

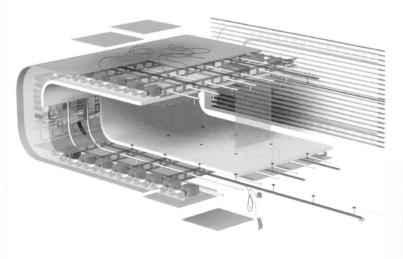

1	Main façade with spider	2	Internal circulation space	4	Internal exhibition space
		3	Section through layered design	5	Services layers

The ribbon is two-ply with a technical space sandwiched between layers, housing the building's 'nervous' system. The smooth concrete ply facing the exhibition space has a pattern of precast service points. The ply of modularized panels facing the workspaces permits easy access to the interstitial space for rewiring and servicing of exhibition spaces at specific locations below or above.

Diller Scofidio + Renfro believes that new institutions breed new spatial politics and codes of behaviour. The hybrid nature of the Museum of Art and Technology, both museum and production/education facility, is an example of a redirection in architecture that is at the forefront of a new age in museum design.

GUGGENHEIM MUSEUM, MEXICO
ASYMPTOTE

1

Asymptote's Guggenheim Guadalajara Museum scheme for Mexico sits perched on the edge of the city where it meets the vast Barranca landscape. The site itself presents an awe inspiring spatial experience for the visitor; and by lifting the museum off the ground, the architect literally heightens the excitement.

Designed for an international competition in 2005, the museum features outdoor 'gallery' space that projects towards the horizon as a spectacular urban balcony. Defined by the four sculptural building volumes and the sweeping undulating surfaces of the museum suspended above, this space is envisioned as a transition between the city and the extraordinary expanse of the canyon beyond.

While looking out over the canyon, visitors rise from the plaza level to arrive in a large-scale, twisting, cylindrical glass entry volume that extends the full height of the building interior. From there they move into the central atrium, which is the main interior public space of the museum. The atrium itself is oriented along the north–south axis. It terminates at large glazed openings in the building shell, affording dramatically framed views of the Barranca on one end and the city on the other.

The main exhibition spaces of the 25,000 m² (269,000 ft²) building are located on two upper levels connected by bridges and balconies that overlook the atrium space, while there is a multimedia gallery located on a lower level in the southwest corner. The upper galleries are reached via an over-scaled stair that rises from the atrium at the north end of the space. This stair functions both as a grand entry to the galleries and as a large theatre-like seating platform that provides a resting or gathering area for visitors.

2

3

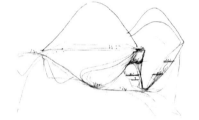

4

1   Main perspective
2   Viewing gallery
3   Exhibition space
4   Concept sketches
5   Bridge connection
6   Night view

The exhibition spaces are housed in generously scaled, flexible enclosures that are interconnected by horizontal bridges overlooking the atrium and vertical circulation that occupies the space between the gallery volumes and the building shell. A workshop and administrative offices are housed in a delicate tower structure that rises above the southeast corner. On the uppermost levels of the tower a restaurant offers views of both the undulating architectural form and the spectacular panorama of the Barranca.

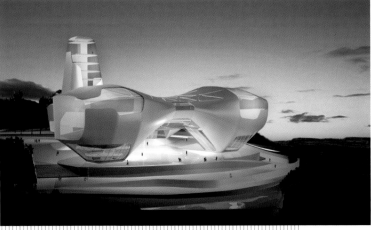

5

6

1

'The Basalt Mass': these are the first words from Jean Nouvel on his design for the competition to build the Guggenheim's outpost in Mexico. 'I see the museum as a basalt monolith balanced on the edge of the Barranca. It is a mass made of the matter of the ground of the site,' he says.

The design sees a series of viewing shafts cut through the mass of the building, through which the visitor recomposes the landscape from fragmented views. Via this spatial mechanism, framed views of specifics of the landscape, the elements of the site are heightened to arouse emotion.

Nouvel has expressed the areas within the museum as five 'worlds' – the World of Light, the Depth World, the Every Day World, the Abstract World and the Real World. Each world has its own character: the World of Light is a space dedicated to natural light. The Depth World is a dark space with imperceptible contours. The Every Day World is a space that is able to welcome large expositions or retrospectives but can also be partitioned for more modest events. The Abstract World is a sphere in which artists can 'intervene', with temporary exhibits. The Real World is a platform within the Barranca 130 m (427 ft) below the museum on a precipice.

These worlds define the internal atmosphere of the museum. The worlds of Light, Depth and Every Day take up 9,000 m^2 (97,000 ft^2), as requested in the brief, but Nouvel has gone further, suggesting the Abstract World and the Real World, where artists intervene within the strong spaces to produce unique works specifically for the Guadalajara Museum.

GUGGENHEIM MUSEUM, MEXICO
ATELIERS JEAN NOUVEL

2

3

4

5

Externally, the museum monolith is situated in a park leading from Plaza Independencia. Its grey basalt form, similar to the rock outcrops of the Barranca, sitting at a slight angle (three degrees), stands out when the sun reflects off it. The entrance is marked by a cascade of water showers from the corner of the southern façade, while LEDs encrusted into the rock illuminate to show diffuse images.

3 West elevation
   and valley
4 South elevation
5 Internal
   exhibition space
6 Daytime view
   of road approach
7 Night view

6

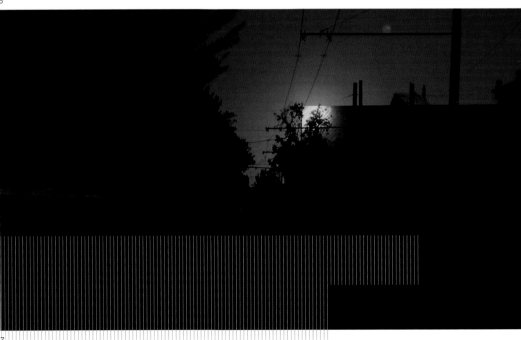

7

LIAUNIG COLLECTION MUSEUM, AUSTRIA
ODILE DECQ BENOÎT CORNETTE ARCHITECTES URBANISTES

1

The Liaunig Collection Museum in Neuhaus, Austria, is designed to house one of the most important private collections of Austrian art after 1945. However, the architect looks beyond cultural reference to explore and reinterpret the duality of what it describes as 'the contextual inscription and the immaterial escaping, of natural and artificial, heavy and light, shadow and light'.

Odile Decq Benoît Cornette Architectes Urbanistes (ODBC) talks of the museum's external form in a language more akin to dress-making – 'the envelope of the museum finds its origin in the slope of the site by its pleats and drapes in softly sinuous tension'. Lifted up, the curves of the slope are reinterpreted in volumes that compress and twist as they reach out towards the valley, the village and the castle in the distance.

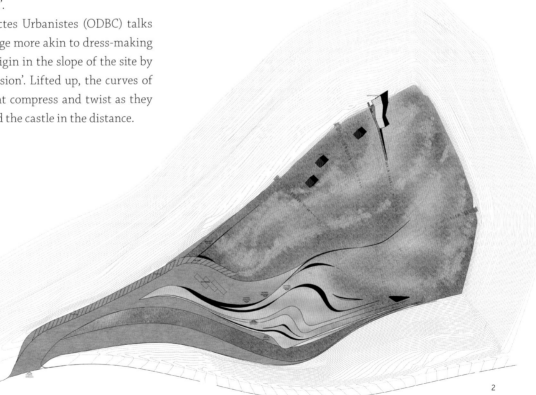

2

3

4

5

1 Site view
2 Site plan
3 Museum approach
4 Side perspective
5 Section
6 Roof view

On the building's façades lines, which mimic contours, become waves. Then in one movement the envelope swoops in on itself to form an internal wall or walkway: the outside becomes the inside, the enclosed becomes open, a building forms a landscape.

Internally, the walk through the building becomes a sequential discovery also. Every space is conceived to lead the visitor on, to suggest they move and travel through the building to experience the art exhibitions. Spaces are never centred and as such exhibits seem almost transitional. The essence of the design is to create a dynamism that gives visitors the illusion of constant discovery.

6

7

8

9

In addition to these internal spaces, TWBTA create a 'golden platform' on top of the hill. Here, the brooding concrete skylights are set on a platform of burnished bronze panels which shine in the sunlight. This external space provides views over the landscape to Aarhus Bay and to the manor house. It is also an integral part of an historic path running through the area.

TWBTA describes the design as an architectural and historical journey through space and time. The design is highly connected with the museum's subject matter, to the extent that it does not present an overt outward presence. This is sensitive architecture on a grand scale.

10

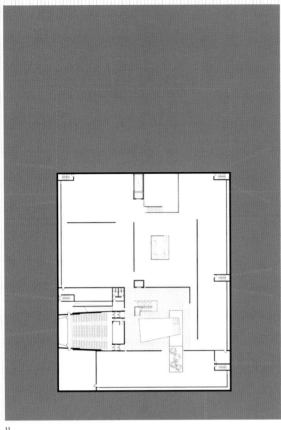

11

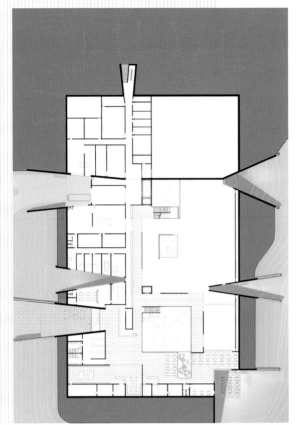

12

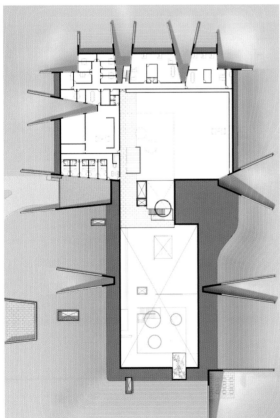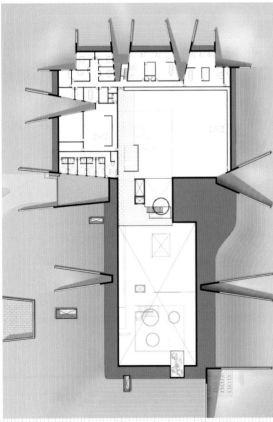

13

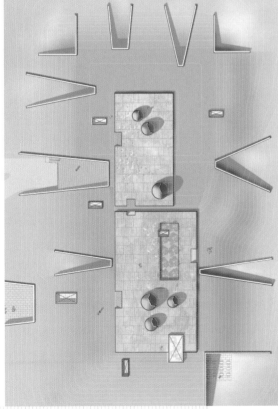

14

7 Internal view between floors	11 Basement
8 Interior with sales desk	12 Ground floor
	13 Upper floor
9 Interior with window slot	14 Roof
10 External approach	

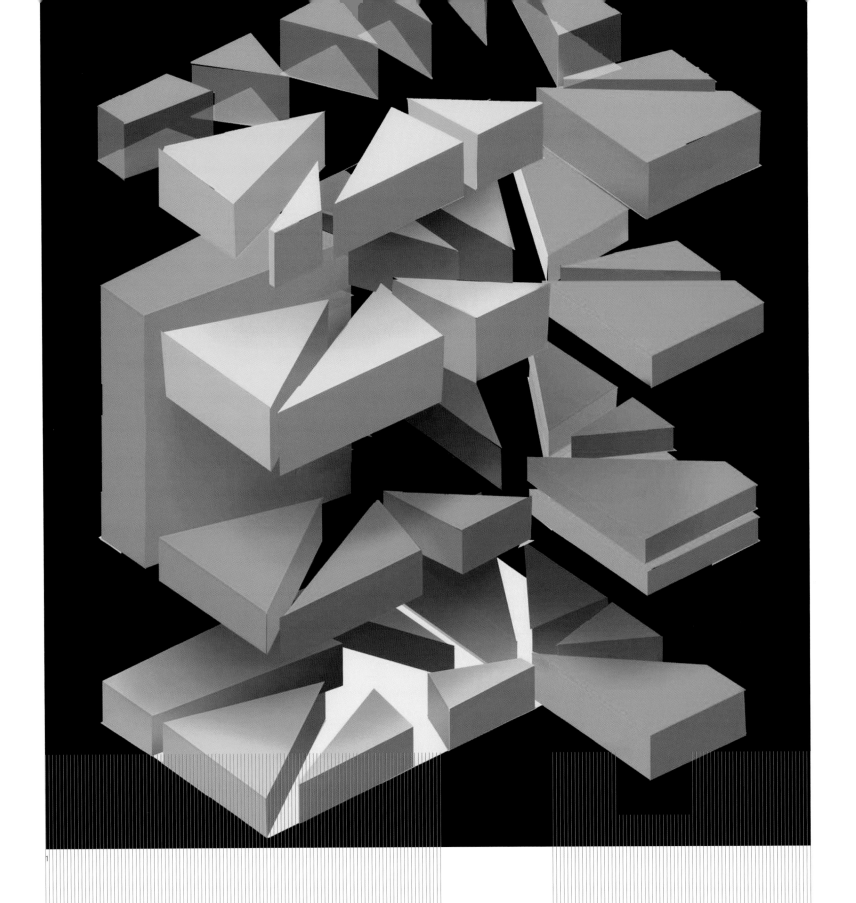

MUSEUM OF CONTEMPORARY ART WARSAW, POLAND

WHITE ARKITEKTER

1 Fractured
concept
2 Façade /
elevation
view
3 Museum in
context
4 Views from
the museum

Planned for a site next door to Warsaw's famous Palace of Culture, this design for the Museum of Contemporary Art Warsaw (MCAW), by White Arkitekter is a true departure from the museum as a monument. Instead, it seeks to create an aura of place in order to compete with other dramatic art museums around the globe.

'The architecture of the new museum must have the power to attract visitors from around the world, while fulfilling all the needs of an art museum for Warsaw itself,' says the designer. In this respect, the architect proposes the complete opposite of the Palace of Culture, an anti-monument that seeks to integrate completely into the city, instead of standing aloof from it.

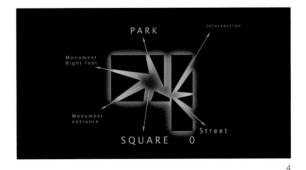

5

6

7

5　View from above
　　the square
6　Internal view
　　to the Palace
　　of Culture
7　Façade
　　perspective

The museum's overall plan is rectangular, in keeping with the city grid. However, its shape is radically altered from the centre outwards by a series of voids that burst from a central courtyard and create a museum complex fractured into a series of triangular elements. These voids or cracks are aligned with prominent landmarks around the city, making historic Warsaw always visible from within the new addition.

Exhibition halls are set within the triangular boxes; those on the third floor benefit from daylight, and others below are artificially illuminated to protect sensitive works. Connecting these halls is the full-height atrium at the museum's centre. This is more of an indoor district or mall than simple reception area. It includes a library, restaurant, shops, offices, café and apartments. However, to distinguish the museum from commercial premises, a large ramp connects the lobby to the first floor and exhibition areas.

The exhibition spaces themselves vary from small, intimate rooms to the largest space of all, the atrium itself, in which the designer intends large artworks to be displayed.

Materials play an important part of the design, and the limited palette presents a strong building. Limestone is the primary façade covering, its surface smooth at ground level but getting rougher the higher up the building it climbs. Glass elements join the cracks between the exhibition spaces. Vegetation also features extensively via a large roof garden that is also an external sculpture park.

8   Internal street
9   Imagined
landscape

SHEIKH ZAYED NATIONAL MUSEUM, UAE
MORIYAMA & TESHIMA

1

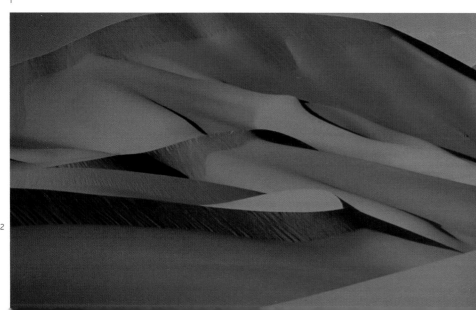

2

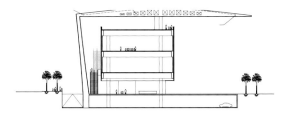

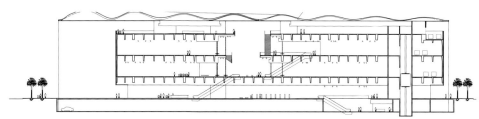

3

4

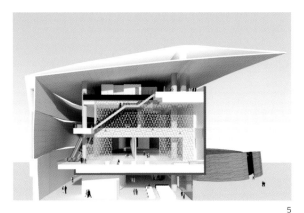

5

6

1	Southwest elevation	3	Short section north / south
2	Sands as inspiration	4	Long section east / west
		5	Illustrated short section
		6	Illustrated long section

Moriyama & Teshima wanted to evoke the rich traditions and cultural symbols of the UAE as inspiration for the Sheikh Zayed National Museum, Abu Dhabi, and it found this in the exquisite, uniquely shaped and crafted 'container' of a traditional writing case. The richly decorated vessel also emerged as a powerful metaphor intended to symbolize the centrality of 'knowledge and ideas' as well as the permanence of written history, to the life and rule of Sheikh Zayed, and to the unification, evolution and prosperity of the UAE.

The form that the architect gave to the principal museum is an apparently simple box: long and slender, proportioned similarly like a writing case and protected from the elements by a massive over-sailing canopy. The façades of the 'writing case' are adorned in artful Islamic geometries that can be found in Bedouin jewelry and the colours of the seven sands of the Emirates (white, RAK; light red, Abu Dhabi; red, Dubai; brown, Sharjah; blue, UAQ; cream, Ajman; black, Fujairah). This decoration is fashioned using ceramic tiles to form an exquisitely detailed façade.

The dramatic 'canopy' element that is folded over the museum protects against the harsh climate and glare of the sun. It is also symbolic, representing the scribe's parchment. Its inner face is partly 'etched' to record the past, and partly blank to invite untold possibilities for the future.

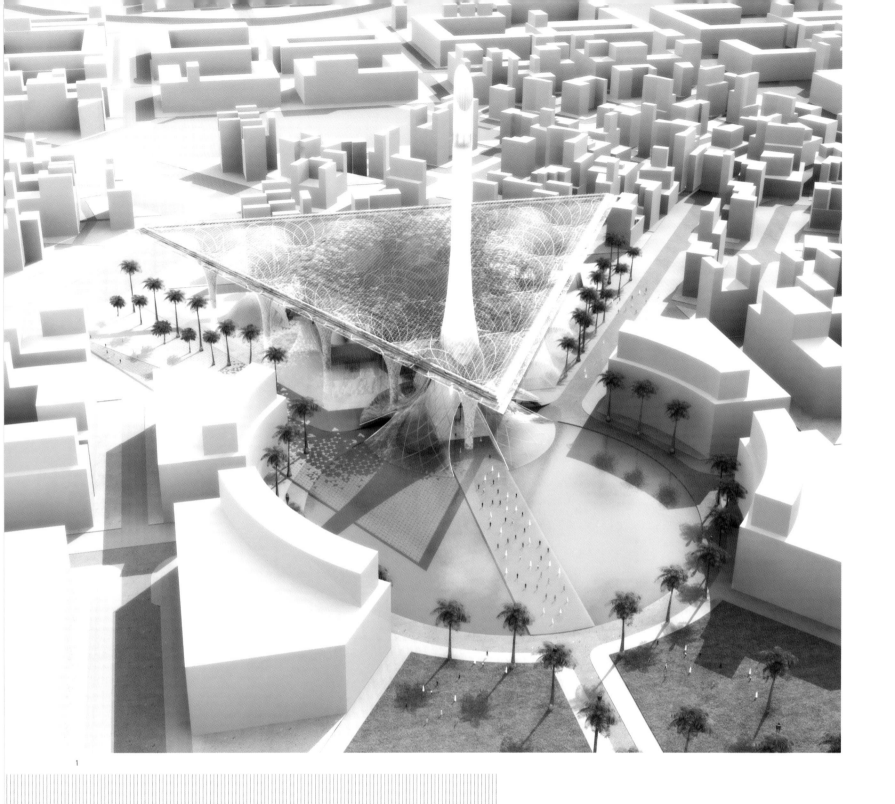

SHEIKH ZAYED NATIONAL MUSEUM, UAE

SHIGERU BAN ARCHITECTS

2

3

The defining feature of this museum design by
Shigeru Ban is its roof. A single decorative roof structure, it shrouds
seven individual buildings beneath – one for each of the seven emirates
of Abu Dhabi, Dubai, Ajman, Fujairah, Umm al Quwain, Sharjah and Ras
al Kaimah – which are connected by glass corridors.

Shigeru Ban describes each emirate building as echoing the historic and geographic characteristics of the state that it represents. Abu
Dhabi is a forum containing café, shop and ticket office. It is a large
space, similar to the dominating land mass of the emirate, on to which
the others are joined. Dubai is the administration building, clad in gold
tiles to represent its wealth and status. Clad in sand tiles and with a five-
peaked roof, the Fujairah building houses temporary galleries. The two
enclaves of Ajman are represented by two theme galleries, encased in
sand-like caves. The education centre is housed in the pearl-encrusted
tile building of Umm al Quwain: this follows a lesson learned by the UAE
in the early 20th century when Japan developed the mass production

1   Aerial view
2   Forum
3   Temporary
    exhibition
    galleries
4   Front elevation
5   Site plan

4

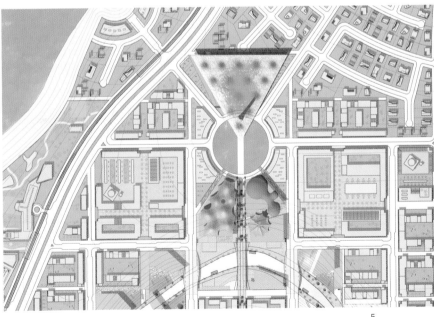

5

Sheikh Zayed National Museum **Shigeru Ban Architects** 195

VICTORIA & ALBERT MUSEUM EXTENSION, UK
STUDIO DANIEL LIBESKIND

1

The extension, called the 'Spiral', at the Victoria & Albert Museum was the predecessor to many radical museum designs including Herzog & de Meuron's ideas for London's Tate Modern. It is a celebration of public activities in a unique historical setting. The building represents a new awareness of the central role of contemporary museology, technology, arts and crafts in sustaining tradition and education in a spectacular cultural setting.

'The Spiral is not an architecture which imitates what already exists,' says Libeskind with considerable understatement. He qualifies this by saying: 'The V&A was not conceived as a repository for objects or a container for passivity and nostalgia. It was built as a set of exemplary spaces and inspiring experiences involving the public through participation in the ever-evolving drama of art.'

The Spiral only actually constitutes four per cent of the entire building mass of the V&A, a series of structures containing more than eleven km (seven miles) of galleries and diverse buildings built across a century by different architects. The extension is a unique structure but one which utilizes a simple, continuous, interlocking wall system, while offering a flexible structure requiring no supporting elements. The core of the building provides large uninterrupted spaces, while the

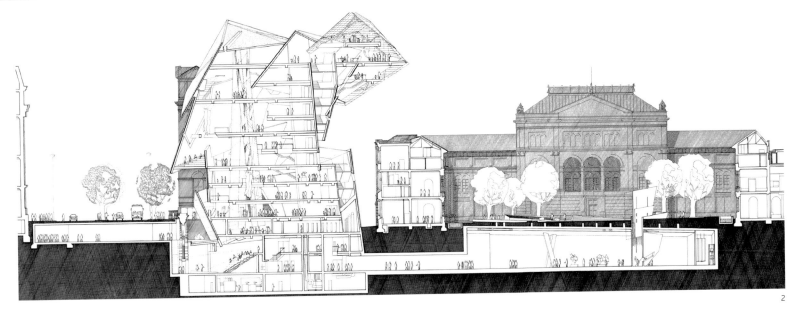

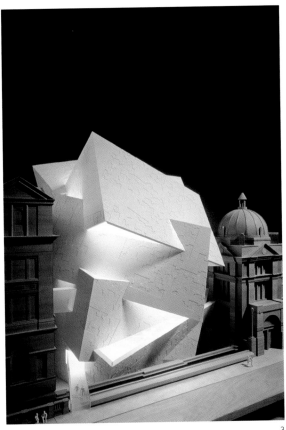

periphery creates smaller demonstration theatres which communicate with the galleries and are washed by natural light. The wall geometries extend the floor plates into a fully three-dimensional experience, an entirely new set of possibilities for contemporary media presentations.

The external façade is clad in a ceramic tile whose geometry forms a contemporary fractal pattern related to the Golden Ratio, a mathematical constant. The off-white tone of the tiles lies midway between the cold greys of portland stone (one of the materials the V&A is built of) and the warm ivories on the Natural History Museum across the road. The tiles are subtly graded and textured, giving the façade a shimmering life of its own and thematizing the light through the contexts of the composition.

In its spatial form and handcrafted quality, the Spiral embodies the tradition of the Victoria & Albert Museum. Libeskind also intends it to carry the message of inspiration and knowledge into the everyday experience of the visitor, creating an emblem for communicating and connecting arts, crafts and architecture into the 21st century.

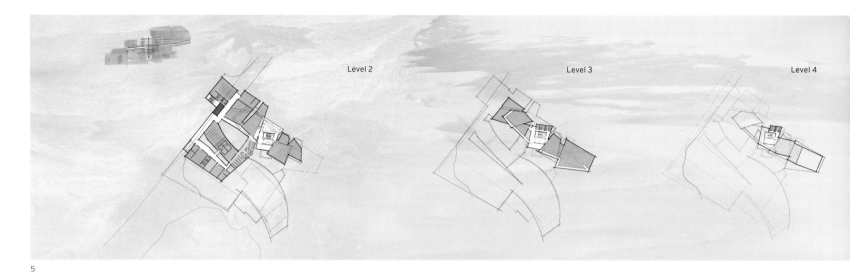

Level 2   Level 3   Level 4

5

6

From a functional perspective, the building is designed in response to the museum's pairing of research ambitions with exposition and education. Interface zones, such as the parallel use of the permafrost tunnels for both galleries and research, embed the relationship between ongoing investigations and exhibition. The bridging elements between the two halves of the building encourage intellectual cross-pollination between research, curatorial and public users.

Massive concrete and earth-sheltered enclosures insulate from the extreme conditions. In winter the titanium wrapping around the stacked gallery boxes traps air close to the 'body' of the building, allowing the sun's rays to warm the perimeter thermal mass. The building is oriented towards the southeast in anticipation of the rising winter sun, a Sakha object of worship. The central axis is aligned to the winter solstice sunrise, maximizing the morning sunlight penetration to the building entry. The stacked galleries inflect towards the sunrise angle corresponding to the Sakha Farewell to Winter celebration.

The building's circulation leads visitors to the Public Permafrost Galleries, which celebrate the preservation of prehistoric remains. On the building's northeast, the metallic wrapping of the Exposition Galleries admits natural light in a controlled fashion – light levels can be adjusted or the galleries fully darkened. A research zone is covered in tilted turf planes: its mass steps back down to the entry terrace with the central axis leading to public permafrost galleries deep within.

7

8

5.
BRIDGES
AND TOWERS

Towers and bridges are the most instantly recognizable and most lauded of architectural and engineering feats. They openly display the drama of structure and size in ways that cannot fail to impress. However, while the bridge is almost always a predominantly functional structure, a means of transportation from A to B, the role of the tower is rather less defined, its purely functional aspects being blurred by egotistical desire in a race to be the tallest.

The mid-size towers that pop up in almost every city on the planet – those of between ten and thirty storeys – are now very necessary parts of our high-density urban environment. Whether residential or commercial, they fulfil a basic requirement for space that cannot be met by low-rise buildings without massive expansion into green areas. Arguments are now being made that much higher-rise developments are doing the same. In exceptional circumstances this may be true.

Vertical cities are being planned, where every type of space – residential, office, retail, leisure, etc. – is combined within buildings of monumental height. These towering edifices cost inordinately more to build than medium- and low-rise buildings, but they are most frequently now conceived for the Middle East, where a lack of space is one of the least pressing concerns going, thanks to deserts that stretch to every horizon.

And it is here, in Dubai, where the Burj Dubai stands, scraping the underside of the heavens at over 800 m (2,625 ft) tall, that the distinction between high-density urban planning and egomaniacal architecture is at its greatest. The building is a brash statement of wealth and power. It does not need to be that high, and in fact it could probably have been built to half its size and still made quite an impact, while serving all of the needs of its owners. This is statement architecture at its best, or worst, depending upon your perspective.

When gazing in awe at Burj Dubai, Taipei 101, the Petronas Towers or even the now relatively diminutive Empire State Building, what we cannot get away from is that these towers are hugely impressive. And therein lies an innate desire within our human nature: we want to see who can build the tallest; we like competition; we strive to be bigger, better, stronger. All that tower architecture is doing is pushing this competitive spirit to the limits of architectural, engineering and construction know-how.

Bridges, on the other hand, exercise a different aspect of the human dynamic. Their design and construction is a challenge, not for competition's sake, but in order, quite literally, to overcome obstacles.

Here, some would argue, lies the difference between the architect and engineer. The former consider themselves, in some part at least, an artist, a creative; while the latter has traditionally been defined by numerical skills, precision and rigour. Now these descriptions are becoming ever more blurred as buildings and bridges get more complicated and extravagant – architects are realizing that without truly creative engineers they could not design the most exciting of buildings, and engineers are also taking guidance from architects to create spectacular bridges.

The results are exciting. Foster & Partners can currently claim the title of designer of the world's highest bridge, in conjunction with engineers EEG Simescol and Greisch, for the Millau Viaduct in France. This is a mammoth feat of engineering, which creates a new, far quicker route for traffic travelling on a motorway between France and Spain. The bridge is awe inspiring and yet at the same time it has been built to fulfil a functional role. The same can be said of the Hangzhou Bay Bridge in China or the Golden Gate Bridge in San Francisco. However, not all bridges are built with the adage 'form follows function' at the forefront of the designer's mind. Bridges can be egotistical follies too.

Santiago Calatrava – architect and engineer – is perhaps the most famous proponent of bridges that are recognized for their architectural or sculptural merit. And, while many span rivers as new road links, some, such as the Campo Volantin bridge in Bilbao, are little more than grand exercises in sculptural convenience for tourists, in this case wishing to visit the Guggenheim Museum. It saves no more than a few minutes walk, but it does create an extra spectacle for visitors. Similarly, Wilkinson Eyre's 'Winking Eye', the Gateshead Millennium Bridge, is a wonderful design that adds to the long history of bridges spanning the River Tyne in the north of England. However, unlike the road and rail crossings that came before it, this pedestrian bridge was designed as an iconic statement for the city, somewhat smaller but in the same vein as Bilbao's Guggenheim Museum.

Towers and bridges, these two dramatically different elements of our built environment, are the touchstones by which the vast majority of the general public judge architectural design as a whole. They are what inspire or annoy even those with little interest in the aesthetic of the built environment. Each, when executed well, can be a joy to see and use. They display design at its finest and elevate their creators to star status. The greatest challenge, however, is not who can build the highest or longest, but how to ensure that those which are built are the best that they can be. If one takes the designs shown in this book and compares them to some of the schemes that are currently being built, it is evident that we need to work much harder to make sure that good design always comes to the fore, and does not remain trapped in the pages of books such as this.

ALLEGRO ALTURA TOWER, INDONESIA
TANGE ASSOCIATES

Bandung City is located approximately 180 km (112 mi.) southeast of Jakarta in Indonesia. It is one of the largest cities in Indonesia with a population of over two million people. Surrounded by mountains, Bandung is a highland city, and Tange Associates' Allegro Altura facility was planned in 2006 for a 7 ha. (17 acre) site in the northern hills overlooking the city centre.

The government has designated this area as a tourism resort with the expectation that it will become a popular destination in the near future. The Allegro Altura project offers an architectural landmark in the 600-m (1,969-ft) tall TV tower, as well as office space for the TV broadcast company and a range of entertainment and convention facilities designed to attract international visitors.

A boutique hotel with 100 deluxe guestrooms is situated in the upper part of the tower, while a media centre is located half way up the structure. However, the main tourist attractions will be located under the massive roof at the base of the tower.

1

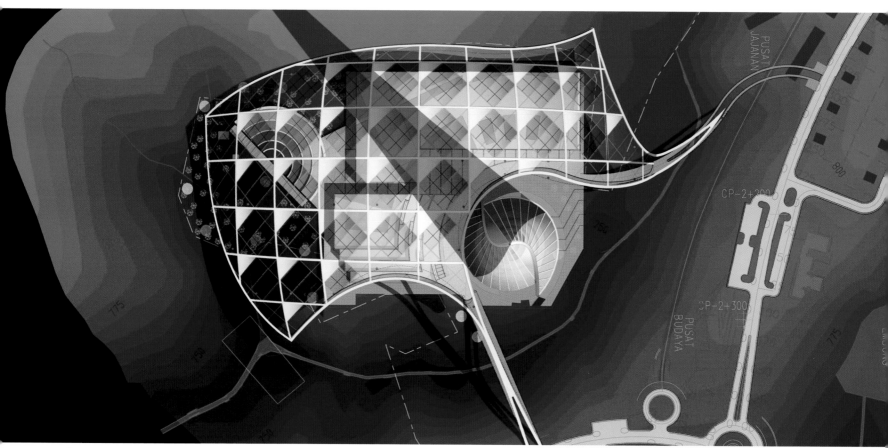

2

1　Concept sketch
2　Plan view
3　Night view

3

Located in Tulsa, Oklahoma, Crow Creek flows from the Arkansas river before winding through residential suburbs. The entire creek is due to undergo a dramatic reinvention to create a new feature among the residential and commercial areas, and provide links to nature for the local community.

Bing Thom's bridge spans 30.5 m (100 ft) across the creek. It is designed to serve as an anchor point at the gateway of the Crow Creek redevelopment, visible from the road, from the Arkansas river itself and along the footpath.

The design has obvious links to nature and natural form, its slender suspension system using a series of cables, from which hangs a thin wooden deck. Beyond the banks, a number of timber poles rise up into the air like clusters of trees to serve as the anchor points for the suspension cables.

Viewed together as a 'chaotic coppice', the seemingly random tree clusters and wires serve as a foil to the order of the bridge support cables: they ground the bridge in nature, rather than marking it out as a man-made structure. However, from a distance the clusters of timber poles and related support cables disappear into the tree tops, with the resulting effect that only the glistening triangular forms of the bridge support cables remain visible, creating an ephemeral 'outdoor room'.

1

CROW CREEK BRIDGE, USA
BING THOM ARCHITECTS

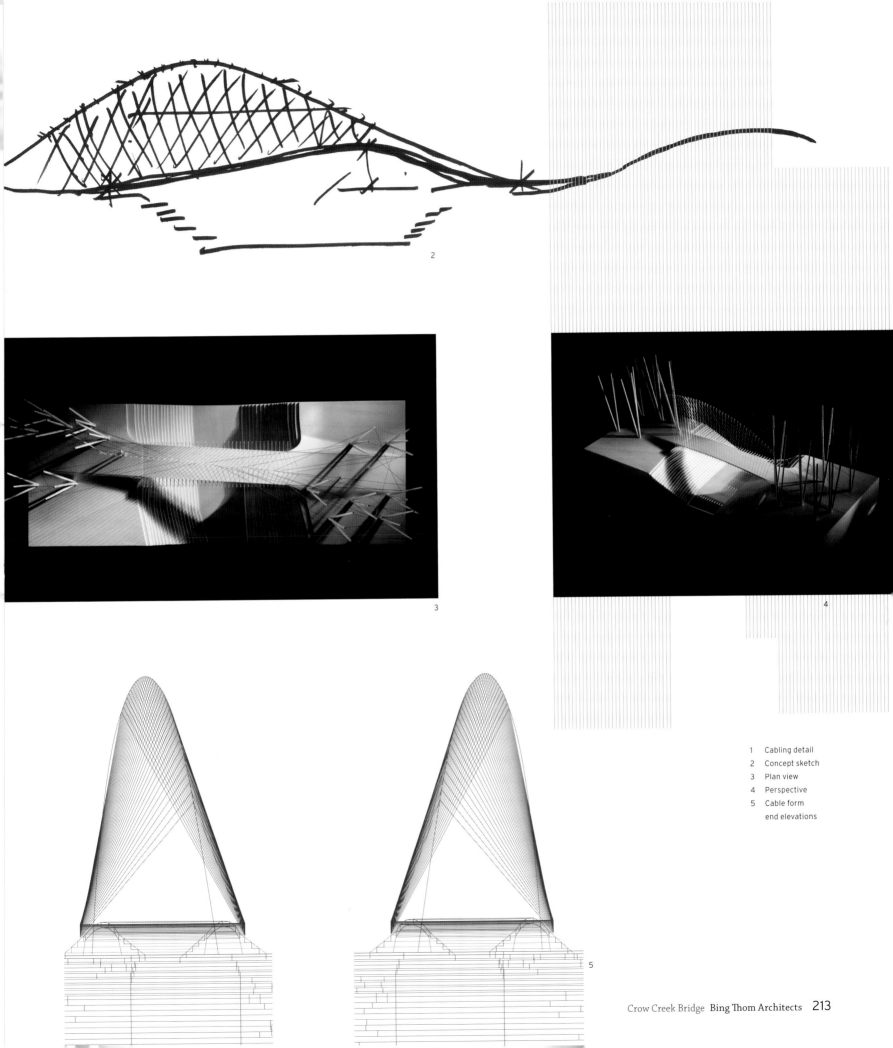

1 Cabling detail
2 Concept sketch
3 Plan view
4 Perspective
5 Cable form
end elevations

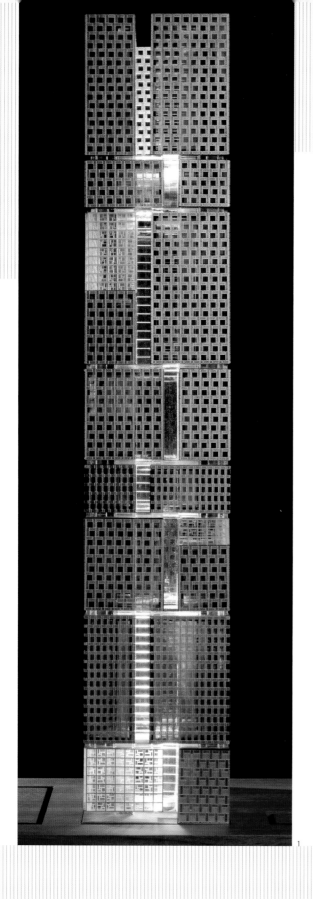

1

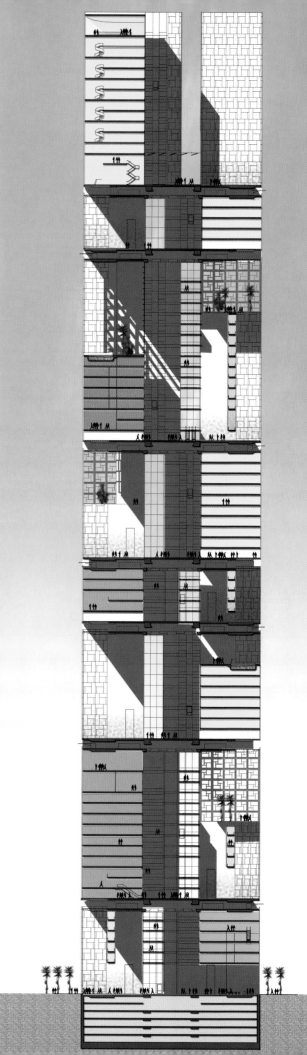

2

DUBAI TOWER, UAE

GRIMSHAW

The design concept for this 269,420 m² (2.9 million ft²) tower emerged from the need to balance three major factors: to reflect Arabic culture and the traditions of Islamic vernacular architecture; to create a building with multiple functions, including office, retail, hotel and residential areas; and to give an intelligent response to the hot, humid climate.

Reference to the architecture of the region gives insight into how to achieve the necessary level of climate control, creating comfortable internal conditions with minimal energy consumption. The Dubai Tower adapts the vernacular *mushrabiya* screen (a projecting 'window' of timber latticework) and incorporates the principle of having controlled openings and internal squares to maximize benefit from day lighting without being subject to the sun's heat.

The site's dimensions – too small for independent towers, too large for a single tower – led to a basic floor plate of four quadrants organized around a central core. The quadrants, separated by a 9-m (30-ft) gap, serve as the living/working spaces while the core functions as communal atrium, providing access to the perimeter offices or apartments. This design creates a series of vertical villages.

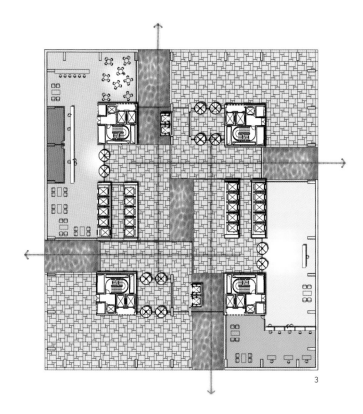

3

1 Elevation illustrating façade
2 Section
3 Ground floor plan
4 Mezzanine level plan
5 Hotel foyer plan

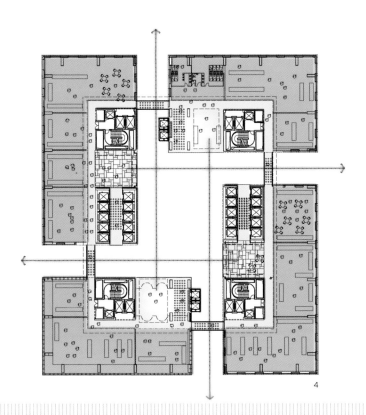

4

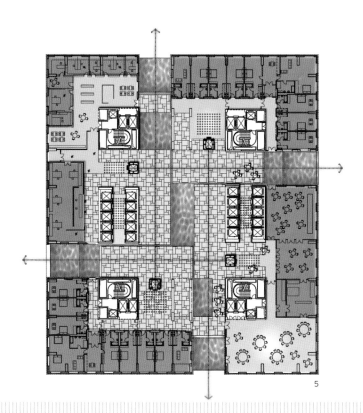

5

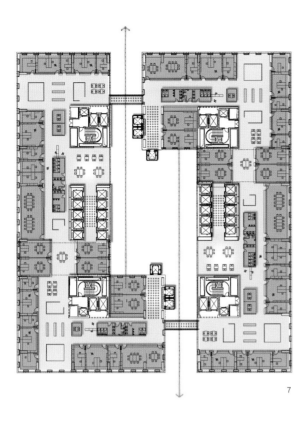

The tower is designed to accommodate eight of these villages, each comprising different numbers of floors and its own atrium. The quadrants are linked across the light slots by glazed bridges, and, should it be required, quadrants can be fused to supplement usable floor area. In the residential areas, the atrium serves as the 'village square'. The residents will access their apartments via an open balcony. All apartments have perimeter views and each village has access to an external pool.

The office spaces follow the same principles, but users enjoy dedicated lifts and 'fused' quadrants to increase usable area. In the hotel unit, the atrium houses the public facilities, including restaurants, bars, lounge areas and retail units. The upper five storeys of the entrance villages are occupied by retail space.

The core of the building is a stiff, hollow rectangular extrusion that extends throughout the structure. Continuous solid shafts at each corner accommodate stairs, fire-fighting lifts, goods lifts and service risers. With the solid shafts in the core connecting with the primary perimeter columns to carry the vertical load, the floor space in between can be completely column free, allowing for maximum flexibility.

6   Main atrium
7   Office floor plan
8   Hotel floor plan
9   Apartment
    floor plan

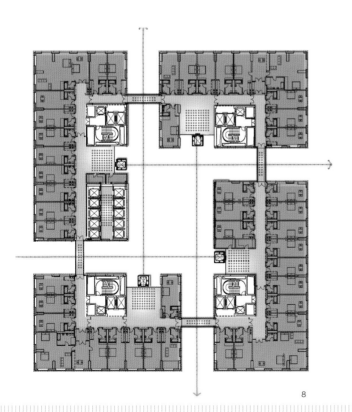

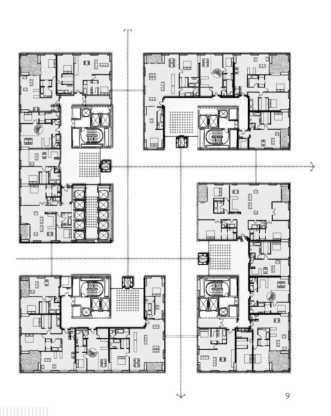

FOOTBRIDGE OVER THE SEINE, FRANCE
DIETMAR FEICHTINGER ARCHITECTES

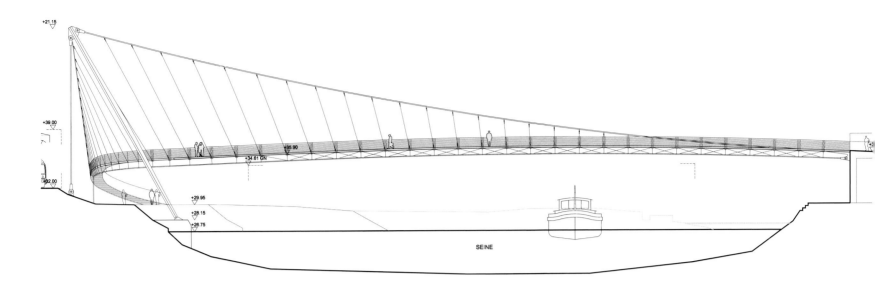

Designed to span a tributary of the Seine, between
Sèvres and Île Seguin, this exquisitely delicate footbridge performs the
purely functional role of linking the island with the mainland tram
system, ready for the construction of a new museum upon Île Seguin.

However, while function is the overriding reason for all bridges
to be built, this design by Dietmar Feichtinger Architectes carries more
than its share of aesthetic charm. The architect has designed it to integrate smoothly into the walk along the river in a way that urges those
promenading to veer across and visit the island.

From each direction along the river walk, the bridge sweeps around
in graceful arches from the land side of the walk, up and over it at a gentle
incline, to a pedestrian way over the water. However, the sublimity of the
design is almost lost on those who would use the bridge, the beauty of its
curves reserved for a bird's eye view.

1   Plan view
2   Longitudinal
    elevation
3   View from
    the island

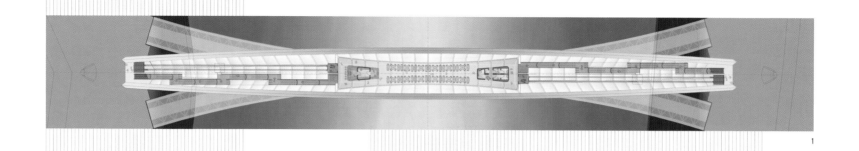

GLASGOW FOOTBRIDGE, SCOTLAND
LIFSCHUTZ DAVIDSON SANDILANDS

Hotels have bars, airports have bars, so do restaurants, art galleries, museums and even the odd office block. But a bridge with a bar, this has to be a first. This quite remarkable design for a pedestrian bridge with an observatory bar within its arch was put forward for a limited competition to provide a £25 million (US$37.2 million) landmark bridge over the River Clyde in Glasgow, Scotland.

Spanning 150 m (492 ft), the arched steel structure supports a sweeping footbridge, which is shaped like a slender X in plan. The crossroads in this X is described by architect Lifschutz Davidson Sandilands as a place to celebrate meeting in the geographical heart of the city, and take a moment to stop and dwell rather than merely striding across.

However, more dwelling would probably have been achieved at the observatory bar directly over the pedestrian walkway. Accessible via stairs or a dramatic funicular, the bar is cocooned in glass between and below two large structural steel arches. The glazed structure is V-shaped in section and graduates from a slender element at ground level to a space over a storey high at its apex in the centre of the arch.

Inside the glass construction, the bar is suspended from the steel bridge structure and can accommodate up to a hundred people at any one time. Access to it is restricted by vertically hinged entrance doors at each end of the bridge.

2

1   Plan view
2   Elevation showing
    circulation

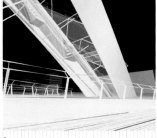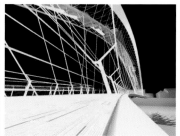

3

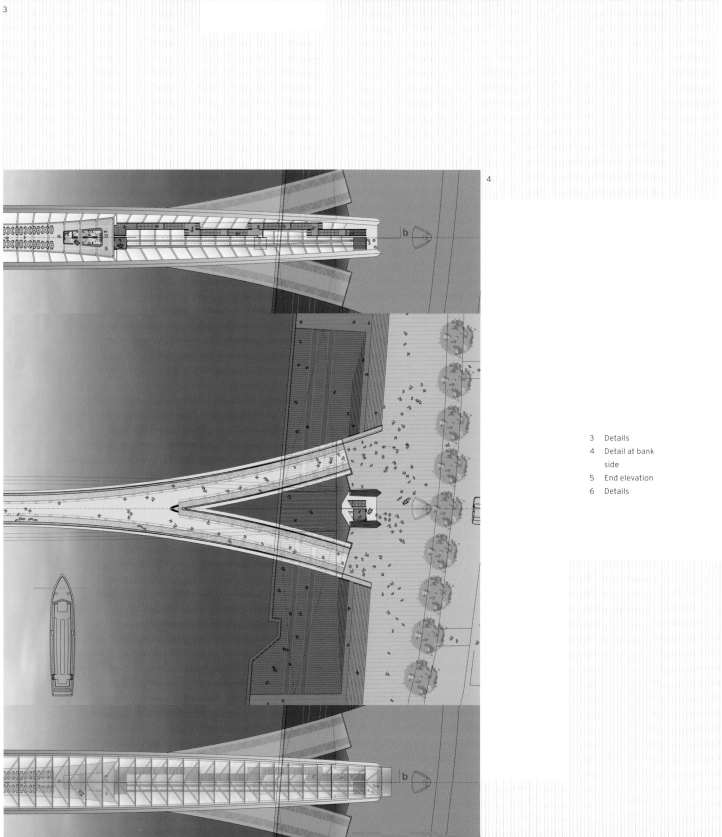

4

3 Details
4 Detail at bank side
5 End elevation
6 Details

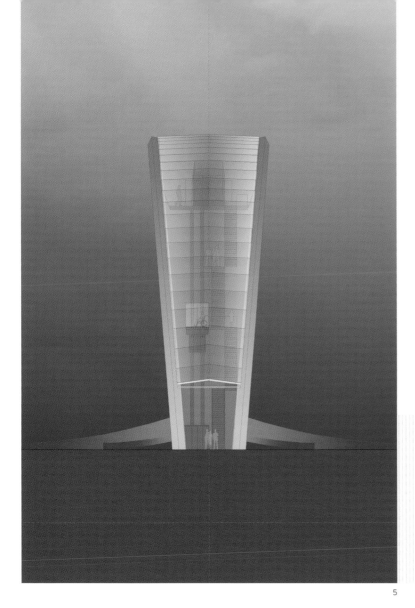

5

This combination of glass and steel responds to the local industrial vernacular of the river, which was once a thriving port for vessels from across the globe. The new bridge and bar provide views down the river Clyde and are a destination themselves, attracting visitors and creating a new crossing.

The bridge was designed as part of a regeneration initiative for two deprived areas of Glasgow. It is a fine example of exciting structural engineering and architecture combining to create a spectacle.

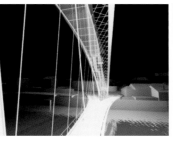

6

7

8

228 Bridges and Towers

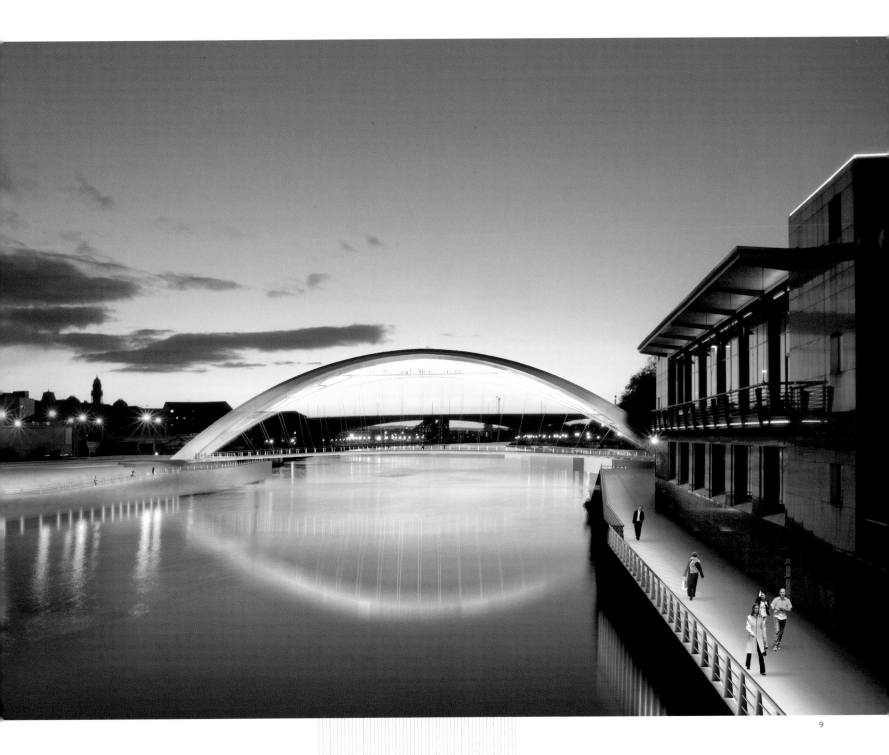

7 Pedestrian deck
8 Perspective
9 Night view from
downstream

HYPERBUILDING, THAILAND
OFFICE FOR METROPOLITAN ARCHITECTURE

STABILITY BY CONNECTIONS

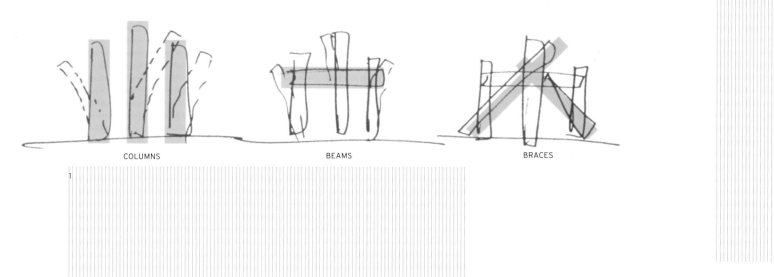

COLUMNS   BEAMS   BRACES

1

1   Concept sketches
2   Model view

Designed for Phra Pradaeng, a peninsula on the west bank of the Chao Phraya river in Bangkok, Thailand, the Hyperbuilding is a study for a 5,000,000 m² (53.8 million ft²) self-contained city for 120,000 inhabitants. It includes housing, education, culture, welfare, medical, amusement and industry resources in a gigantic and somewhat unwieldy design by Rem Koolhaas and the Office for Metropolitan Architecture (OMA).

OMA sees Bangkok as 'a city on the edge of the tolerable' – from its traffic and haphazard development, to its politics and policing. Therefore, the Hyperbuilding is designed to alleviate some of the elements that cause crisis: it reduces commuting by introducing a place where people can stay, and creates an ordered development, so potentially reducing policing issues in time.

The site selected, on Phra Pradaeng, a green reserve on the west bank of the Chao Phraya river, is close to new business development and important urban infrastructure. It is connected to the city, while being a microcosmic city in its own right.

3

3 Circulation routes
4 Model from
 ground level
5 Plan of horizontal
 circulation
6 Perspective
7 External
 elevators

4

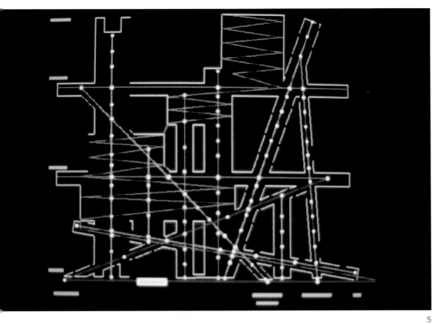

5

To achieve urban variety and complexity, OMA structures the building as a metaphor of the city: towers constitute streets, horizontal elements are parks, volumes are districts, and diagonals are boulevards.

Four boulevards with cable cars, gondolas and train elevators connect the Hyperbuilding with the city below, six streets with high- and low-speed elevators are the main vertical connections, and a walkable promenade of 12 km (7.5 mi.) goes from ground level to the top.

OMA states in its design philosophy that, 'although initially the concept of a Hyperbuilding seems irrevocably linked to societies of hyper-development, the advantages of hyper-concentrated structures and programs are more evident in societies undergoing ... modernization at full force. In other words, the Hyperbuilding may be less credible in the almost "completed" urban conditions of... Japan or America... than in a developing condition where the virtues of the hyperbuilding, the provision of an enormous controllable critical mass, could be a demonstrable advantage.'

6

7

MANHAL OASIS, UAE

ONL

ONL's Manhal Oasis master plan for a sector of the city of Abu Dhabi, in the UAE, is envisaged as a destination/experience among the surrounding urban sprawl.

The master plan seeks to integrate 2.2 billion m² (23.7 billion ft²) of new development in 58 ha. (143 acres) of land, while retaining an existing tree plantation and park over 20 ha. (49 acres). Two museums and the 'Manhal Xperience', a landmark structure and viewing tower, are planned, as is a shopping mall and wellness centre and the Manhal Downtown and Manhal Souk, featuring four sixty-storey-high twisted towers. Another 10 ha. (25 acres) of green areas will be added between the towers and the edges of the oasis, where additional trees and bushes from the plantation may be relocated.

At the edges of the oasis, evoking the canyons along the mountain *wadis*, there is a series of educational buildings and indoor sports and health facilities, integrated into the landscape. Behind these are four series of thirty-storey-high mixed-use towers, residential and offices, echoing the mountains at the horizon of the deserts and oases of the United Arab Emirates.

Manhal Downtown is formed by a double set of twin towers. The initial condition of the Manhal Oasis development is described by ONL as 'like a board game', with the two teams of players neatly arranged along the opposing long sides of the site. ONL has transformed the board game into an interwoven mixed-use urban area, where the players have made several moves and have become interlaced in a complex web of rela-

1 Aerial view
2 Main section

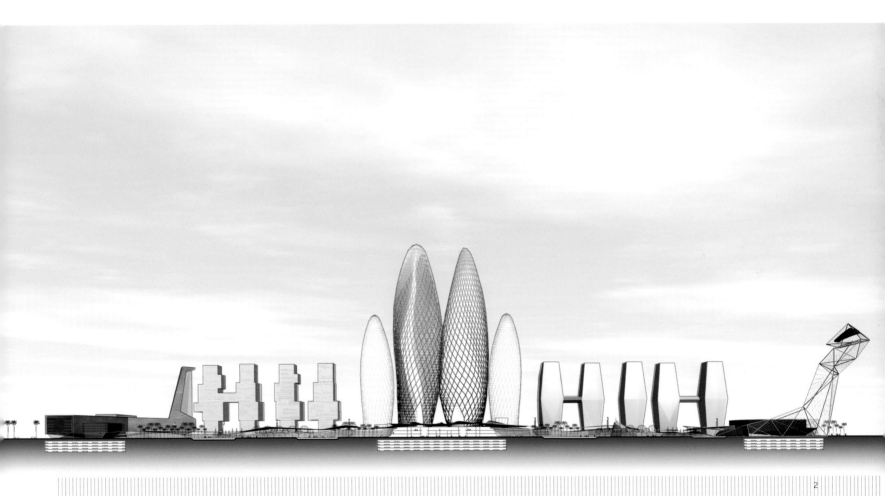

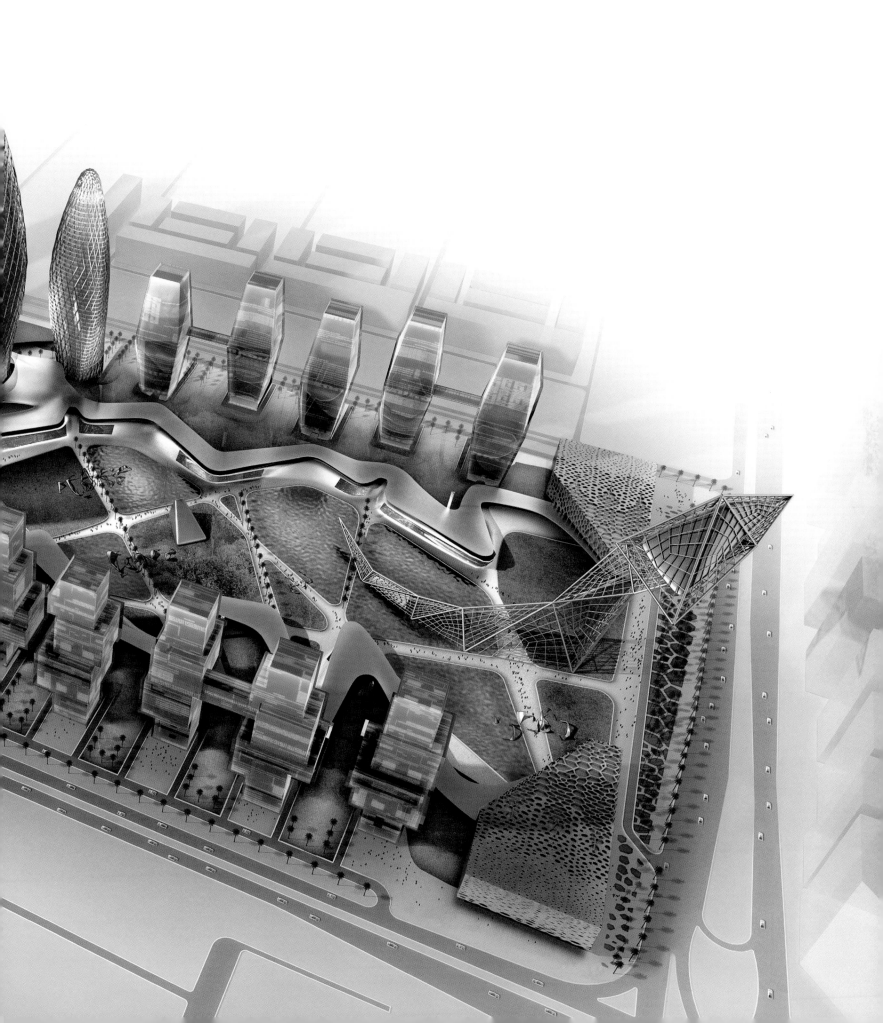

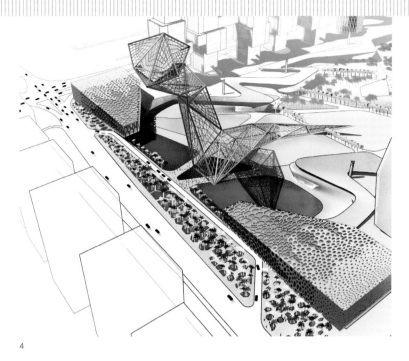

4

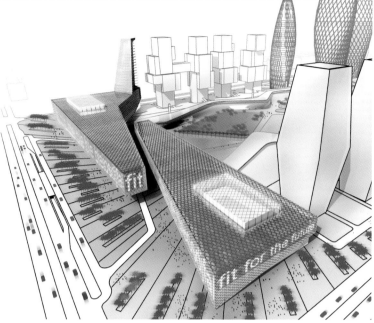

5

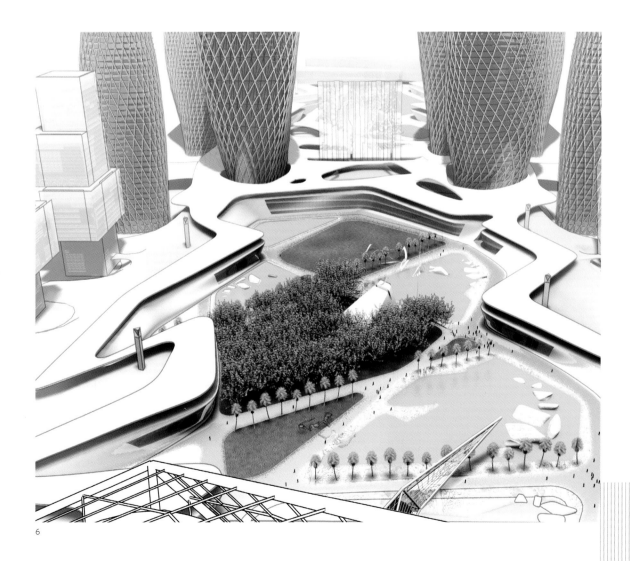

6

7

tions. The connected 300-m (984-ft) high twin towers, one pair dressed in a golden structure and greenish glass and the other pair dressed in a silver structure and bluish glass, represent the mixed-use nature of the Manhal Downtown area.

The rows of towers at either side of the central park represent the mountains at the horizon of the oasis. The golden colour represents the morning and evening sun colouring the body of the mountains, the silver colour the blistering sun at noon. The towering high-rise structures will add a dramatic new skyline to the existing contours of Abu Dhabi.

The Manhal Oasis has the ambition to be a downtown home for approximately 50,000 residents and an additional 50,000 workers, and to be the host of millions of guests each year.

SHANGHAI CENTER, CHINA
RTKL

1 Tower (left)
   in context
2 Tower base

As with many a building that is designed to go beyond the normal parameters structurally and aesthetically, the architect has to ask questions of the perceived precedents and challenge ideals. In its design for the Shanghai Center, RTKL has sought to respond to the challenge of the modern skyscraper by identifying and solving a number of existing problems in current skyscraper design. The architect sees much current tower architecture failing to engage the landscape around it, failing to recognize the scale of the surroundings and failing to create anything more than a superficial transition from the ground to the sky.

The entire physical form of this tower can be shaped from a sheet of paper, using a pair of scissors, like an origami figurine. Whether viewed from the street, straight ahead from a distance, or down from any of its sky lobbies, the Shanghai Center will always maintain its unity of expression and form. It is this purity that RTKL has attempted to bring to the manic metropolis that is Shanghai.

The architect has set about this project in a way that it says challenges the status quo of today's skyscraper as a purely iconic gesture by seeking to create a design that could more successfully respond to these shortcomings. In response to the pervasive absence of site/building integration surrounding the Shanghai Center site, the architect's design proposes an experience of transition: from passive landscape to active urban space busy with human activity, and from a dynamic multi-use programme to office space. It also instigates the movement from high-rise building to supertower – the latter rising above the city skyline, becoming 'simple, serene, void of texture, weightless and silent', as if aspiring to leave behind all reference to measured effort and demonstration of technology.

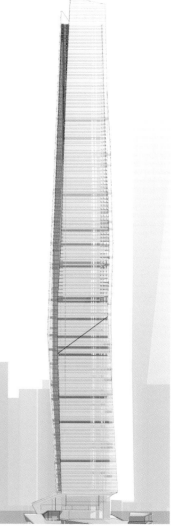

4

3   Night view
4   Elevation
5   View of skyline

RTKL has considered the moment that the building touches the earth as potentially the most important element of the design. It sees much of ground-level Shanghai as littered with structures that intrude severely into the landscape, often completely replacing it with forced footprints and mass. For the Shanghai Center, RTKL proposes an approach in which the very land on which the tower is built becomes the object of transformation.

A spectacular sky-high twisting tower, creating an iconic visitor attraction for Shanghai, in readiness for the 2010 World Expo: that was the brief for Will Alsop's Shanghai Kiss.

Alsop teamed up with engineer Arup to develop what he describes as 'an exciting alternative' to the original concept of an observation wheel. The design is inspired by the romance and passion of Shanghai. Intended to capture the essence of this magnificent city, the Kiss is a dynamic object of beauty, which engages constantly and dynamically with the cityscape. The 250-m (820-ft) tall sculptural tower rotates once every four hours, while a series of pods travel up and around the legs offering visitors unique and exciting views over the city: views which change as the Kiss rotates and as the booming city of Shanghai evolves.

Alsop sees his Shanghai Kiss as a dynamic gateway to the future and a strong icon for the area. In addition to riding in the Kiss's pods, visitors can experience the Digital Showcase City exhibition, contained within an entertainment complex beneath the dramatic structure. This will become the focus for exhibiting and experiencing new technology developed in China and from other parts of the world.

The site for this extravagant architectural gesture was a parcel of real estate alongside the Huangpu river. The central city location, on the Puxi side of the river, commands panoramic views along the river including the historic Bund and the new city developments across the river in Pudong.

1

SHANGHAI KISS, CHINA
ALSOP

Looking like a giant ribbon of sugar candy, the Kiss takes iconic gesture-led design to a new level. It is likened to the Eiffel Tower by Arup's project director, Chris Carroll, and in as much as it is for an Expo, it is similar. However, as with other bold architectural statements of the more recent past, such as Frank Gehry's Bilbao Guggenheim Museum (1997), this design was also conceived to inspire the regeneration of the surrounding areas. Its client saw it as a magnet and catalyst for economic and social investment to drive the development of the north Bund.

2

3

1   Tower on the
    cityscape
2   Pod route up
    the tower
3   Viewing pods
4   Night view

4

TENSEGRITY BRIDGE, USA

WILKINSON EYRE ARCHITECTS

Wilkinson Eyre Architects' Tensegrity Bridge is a structure to be located in the main atrium space of the National Museum of Building in Washington, DC. Connecting up the galleries on level 3, the bridge is designed both as a functional structure and as an exhibit in itself.

The scale of the principal internal space of the museum is such that an object suspended within it needs to have a certain size of its own in order not to be lost in the space. Wilkinson Eyre Architects' design, in conjunction with Cecil Balmond of Arup, proposes a three-pointed star shape (when seen in plan) conjoined with a downward pointing element to create a form derived from the tetrahedron.

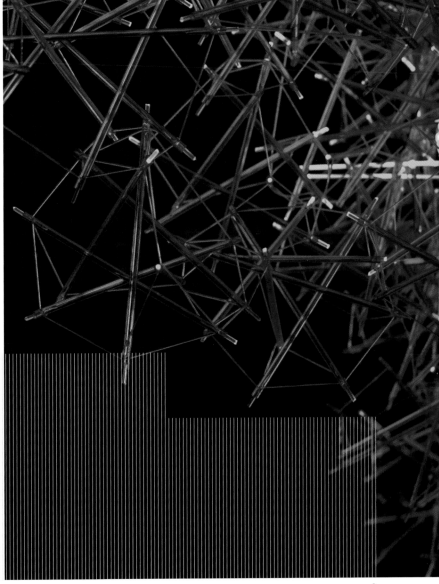

3

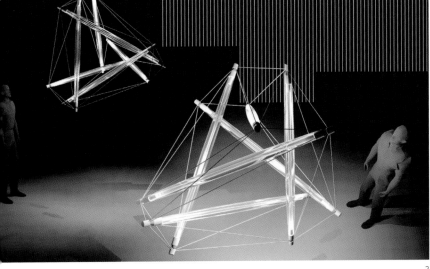

2

1   Three-pointed
     star concept
2   Illuminated
     elements
3   Random form
     detail

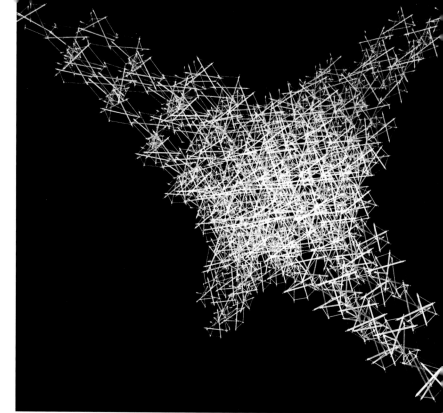

4   Plan view
5   Amidst the bridge
6   View from above

The team wanted the design to be an interactive bridge that acts as a true exhibit about the nature of materials and structural behaviour. As a structure it needed to express volume without sheer opaque mass, while also having a defined form to provide a degree of clarity and legibility.

The answer was a 'mesh' or 'network' of compressive elements of seemingly random forms working together to create a single form made up of myriad alternating compression and tension members. Interactivity comes in the form of each compressive element being electronically linked to react to the forces within by illuminating. In this way the forces acting on the structure as visitors walk across the bridge will be literally illustrated in a light display.

Detailed design saw the bridge developed from a basic elongated tetrahedral form into series of tensegrity modules, which together make up a three-dimensional grid. Within this matrix, the structural form allows for modules to be removed to create spaces and to vary the density of the members.

The structural development also informed the aesthetic concept further, as it was found that the overall form could be tilted to give a more dynamic effect, but also to allow visitors to enter the structure's spaces rather than just walk on it.

The bridge design features a transparent deck so that visitors can view the structure below and see the lighting effect of the forces interacting on it as they walk across.

THE EDGE, UNITED ARAB EMIRATES
DENTON CORKER MARSHALL

Denton Corker Marshall proposes a powerful architectural statement for this Dubai scheme: metal-clad towers set within the landscape offer a unique response to the prevailing climate. The design envisages a living and working environment that vertically layers activities in a sequence, which progresses from private living / work areas, through a privileged interactive zone, to spaces where full public accessibility is available.

The overall composition can be perceived as three distinct elements: podium, cluster office tower, residential / hotel towers. The towers, which accommodate the office, hotel and residential users, are striking complementary forms that integrate and appear to naturally grow out of the podium.

The podium is a low-level development in which five storeys of built form are covered with a skin of perforated metal facets to produce a sculptural form evocative of a sand dune or a tent. This structure blurs the landscape boundaries between inside and out, providing shade and excellent amenity for occupants.

1   Aerial view
2   External form
    perspective

2

10

Two blocks of accommodation towers contain the hotel and the serviced apartments. Emerging from the podium formation they sit beside the dominant form of the office tower and take on the appearance of a miniature downtown. Contrasted with the massive scale of the office tower, these buildings exhibit a sculptural quality which naturally integrates with the podium formation. Externally, their perforated screen façades obscure traditional floor-to-floor readings, enhancing appearance as an integral part of overall form. The perforated metal screens are a unifying element across the whole project.

The Edge Denton Corker Marshall 255

1

THE LEGS, CONFIDENTIAL LOCATION

AEDAS

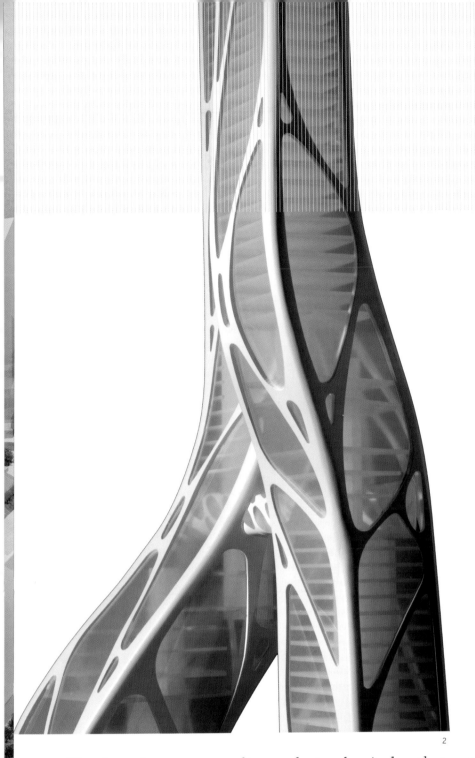

2

3

The Legs is an extraordinary design by Aedas that was conceived to challenge the convention of high-rise construction and the structural limitations which have restricted the evolution of building tall. The clients and proposed site are confidential.

The project consists of four distinct programmes: a five-star hotel, serviced apartments, residential units and offices. Aedas has sited the serviced apartments and hotel on the uppermost floors to ensure the best views. Each accommodation type is independent, but both share the intermediate lobbies as well as amenities within the sky lobbies via a bridge link located midway up these gigantic towers. The offices and residential components are seen both as the financial and posi-

tional base for the project, recouping the initial costs and occupying the lower floors.

At the core of each tower are express elevators to transport guests up to the sky lobby where they can transfer to whichever tower / amenity they require. However, as the design of the towers is not a standard stacked construction, and because they bend at the knee, so to speak, a central structural concrete or steel core is not a viable construction option. Instead, Aedas proposes an exoskeleton, which is not dependent on an internal core at all. This structural approach utilizes a strong external, tube-like component and uses the actual skin of the building as the structure, thereby negating the dependence on an internal core.

The material palette of the tower is intended to convey a unique identity within the context of La Défense. Matte-finished stainless steel is used as cladding on the structural frame. The curtain wall is designed using low iron glass with a low emissivity coating in insulating units. Extruded aluminium frames have stainless-steel caps. Back-illuminated glass at the core wall with computer-controlled colour-changing light fixtures allows for a flexible, animated lighting display at ground level. A similar effect is achieved at the top of the tower, where the stainless-steel frame is illuminated by similar light fixtures.

4   Façade structure
    and floor plans
5   Tower core and
    approach views
6   Perspective from
    main entrance

6

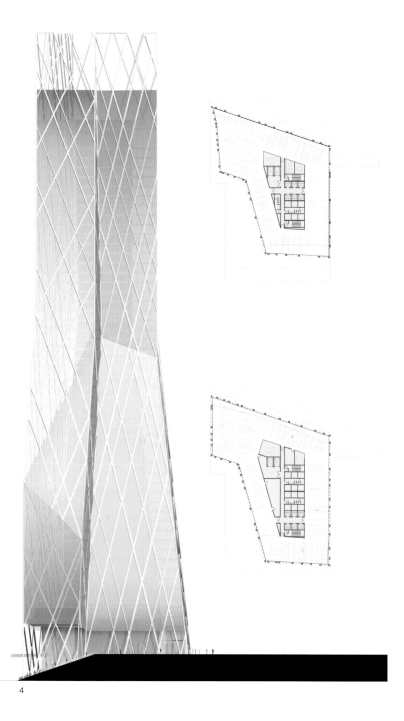

4

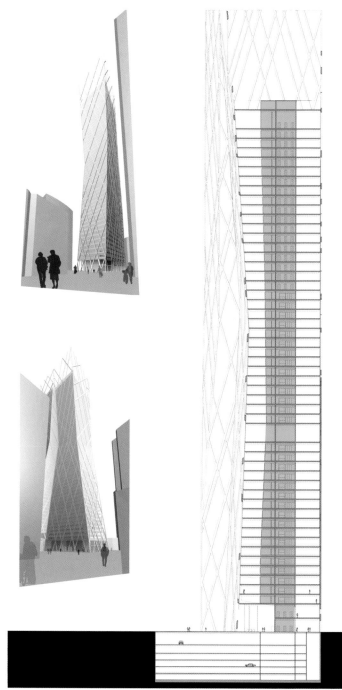

5

WORLD CULTURAL CENTER, USA

RAFAEL VIÑOLY ARCHITECTS WITH FREDERIC SCHWARTZ,
SHIGERU BAN AND KEN SMITH

REMEMBER

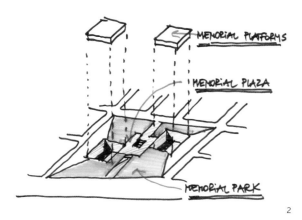

MEMORIAL PLATFORMS

MEMORIAL PLAZA

MEMORIAL PARK

2

LOWER MANHATTAN
JULY 4TH 2006

③ RENEW

3

1   Towers at night   4   Ground level
2   Memorial concept   5   Internal space
3   Renewal concept

In October 2002, following the destruction of the World Trade Center on 11 September 2001, the Lower Manhattan Development Corporation (LMDC) initiated the Innovative Design Study, a master plan competition to rebuild the Ground Zero site. The design team known as THINK, led by architects Rafael Viñoly, Frederic Schwartz, Shigeru Ban and Ken Smith, proposed the World Cultural Center, wherein the image of the World Trade Center is transformed from one of commerce and capitalism to that of a civic resource and public memorial.

Rising around and above the footprints of the two World Trade Center towers, two open latticework energy-efficient towers 'reconstruct' the iconic city skyline and create a vertical infrastructure for a memorial and cultural centre. Significantly, and ultimately costly in the design competition, the plan stipulates civic uses as the centrepiece of the development, envisioning public and cultural facilities within the towers, rather than office space, as the primary catalyst for the revitalization of downtown New York.

4

5

WORLD TRADE CENTER, USA
FOSTER & PARTNERS

1

2

'The rebuilding of the World Trade Center site is one of the most important urban planning and architectural challenges of recent times. It is about memory, but equally it is about rebirth; a demonstration to the world of the continuing strength and faith in the future that has traditionally shaped the New York skyline.'

These are the first words of Foster & Partners' description of the 'Kissing Towers', the scheme viewed by many as the rightful winner of the competition to repopulate the World Trade Center site. Following the events of 11 September 2001, the practice commissioned an expert multidisciplinary team to conduct an in-depth study into safety in tall buildings. The lessons from that study informed the Kissing Tower proposal, which celebrated New York's positive spirit with a unique twinned skyscraper, designed to be the safest, the greenest and the tallest in the world.

The tower's crystalline form is based on triangular geometries. The two parts of the tower 'kiss' at three intervals in its 500-m (1,640-ft) height, creating strategic links for escape routes in case of emergency: these also correspond with public levels containing observation decks, exhibition spaces and cafés.

The design is articulated vertically as village-like clusters, each with its own tree-filled atrium – a 'park in the sky'. The building was to be naturally ventilated through its multi-layered 'breathing façade', and the atria played an environmental role, performing as its lungs, with the trees oxygenating the circulating air.

1   Location plan
2   Night view
3   Towers 'kissing'

3

5

4 Life between
   the towers
5 At ground level
6 View towards
   the south of
   Manhattan Island
7 Memorial garden

In urban terms, the redevelopment was identified as a catalyst for the regeneration of the whole of lower Manhattan, an opportunity to repair the street pattern that was eradicated in the 1960s and to bring new life to an area suffering economic decline. In place of a barren plaza, Foster's design envisaged green parks and streets on a human scale lined with shops, restaurants and bars.

Connections further afield were strengthened by integrating the city's public transport networks in a new interchange below ground: a new gateway into Manhattan celebrated by a soaring glass canopy. The footprints of the destroyed World Trade Center towers are preserved as sanctuaries for remembrance and reflection. Gentle ramps lead visitors down into an ambulatory lining an open volume where each tower once stood. Here, the city would be hidden from view, the sky above empty.

4

6

7

While some practices approached the design of new buildings on the site of the World Trade Center in New York from a cultural perspective, Foreign Office Architects (FOA) came at it from a scientific, business-like approach.

FOA believes that if you investigate the evolution of the skyscraper type, a process is evident in which the increase in height of the structure results in a tendency to concentrate the structural section in the periphery of the plan. This is because as the lateral forces become stronger than the gravitational ones, it becomes necessary to maximize the moment of inertia of the structure.

This design process prompted the architect to use a post and beam typology, which distributes structure evenly across the plan, into different types of tubular organizations, which concentrate structure in the periphery of the plan. But, as the structure grows taller, the strength of the material is not sufficient to provide stability to lateral forces. The traditional solution is to keep increasing the depth of the plan proportionally. This leads to building types that become extremely deep, and therefore heavily dependent on artificial light and mechanically controlled ventilation.

1   Bundle formations
2   Tower form detail

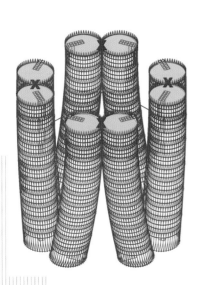

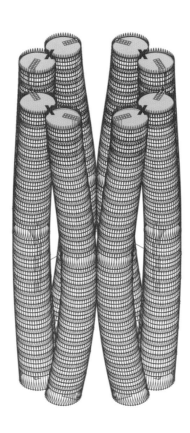

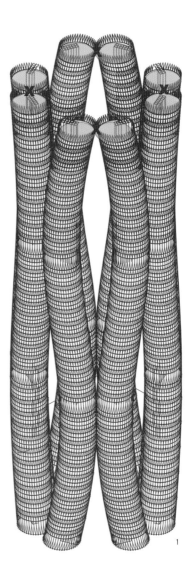

WORLD TRADE CENTER TOWER 1, USA
FOREIGN OFFICE ARCHITECTS

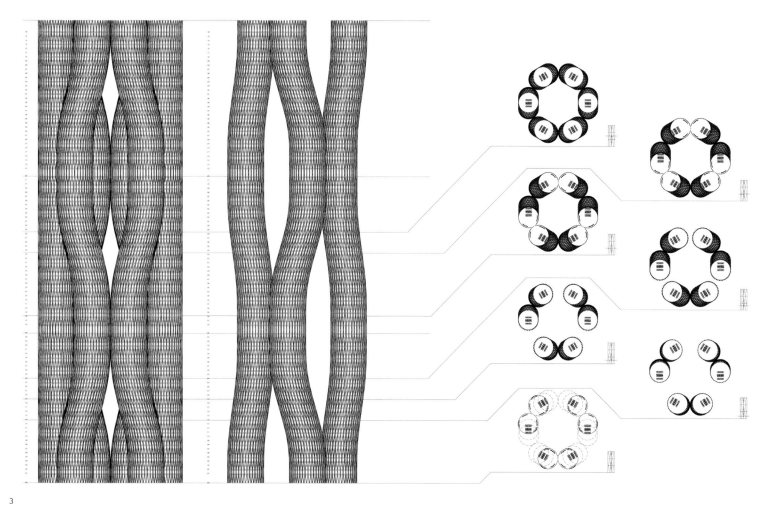

3

4

FOA has alleviated this by generating an alternative type of high rise. The practice has used building mass to create greater stability by bundling towers together. 'Instead of splitting the complex into two independent towers, like in the former WTC or the Petronas towers, to avoid excessively deep workspaces, our proposal is to maintain the physical continuity of the whole mass, and to use it as a structural advantage,' says the architect.

The proposal forms a complex bundle of interconnected towers that provide a floor area comparable to that of the original Twin Towers (884,000 m² (9.52 million ft²) on 110 floors = 8,036 m² (86,500 ft²) per floor). However, instead of spreading this between two deep-plan towers, FOA plans eight towers each of 110 floors with 1,000 m² (10,800 ft²) of space per floor.

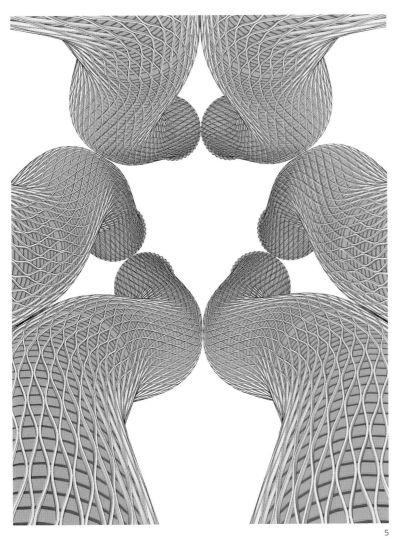

This radical departure from conventional tower design is one of the most interesting proposals for the World Trade Center site. The bundled towers buttress each other structurally, enabling the architect to increase the structural capacity without necessarily increasing the floor depth and the total area of the slender forms. This is a radically new high-rise typology; perhaps too different from the norm to win such a widely reported architectural competition.

5

3 Elevation and
  associated plans
4 Aerial view
5 View from below
6 Illustrated façade
  detail

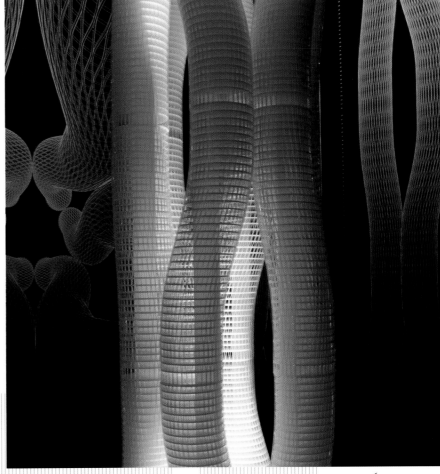

6

6.
CULTURE
AND EDUCATION

Cultural and educational building types are actually closely linked
by their goal of informing and educating the masses, whether in a formal manner or as part
of a wider visitor experience. However, their similarities stop there, as educational estab-
lishments generally fall far short of cultural buildings when it comes to money spent and
architectural design lavished upon them.

Often governed by public funds, schools and colleges have traditionally been ham-
strung when it comes to splashing out on innovative or outlandish buildings in all but a
few cases. The USA has seen a handful of exceptions, as wealthy past alumni bequeath vast
sums of money to their old university. These funds are often spent on pastiches of historic
college buildings; alternatively, a star architect – a Gehry, Predock or Libeskind – is called in
to create a signature design that serves to attract more wealthy students.

However, on the whole, advances in architecture in the education sector have come
down to reappraisals of the way the buildings operate. Historic classroom and lecture
theatre design, with a black or white board and rows of desks looking on, is now being
usurped by less rigorously controlled space. Architects are talking more and more about flexible teaching spaces that can be adapted to class sizes, lesson types and teaching methods.

The role of information technology is also playing a large part in the redesign of schools
and colleges. Distance learning is becoming common and pupils are required to communicate with teachers and contemporaries outside of the classroom. This type of education
warrants classrooms that include multiple forms of new media and the space/enclosure
to enable pupils to focus on individual learning within the group dynamic.

Environmental concerns are also having an impact on school buildings in areas as
diverse as New York and the Himalayas. The Druk White Lotus School in the remote moun-
tainous region of Ladakh, India, has been designed by Arup Associates to green guidelines
which utilize passive environmental techniques, local labour and innovative design to create
the best educational establishment in the region.

Meanwhile, US states are encouraging green building by implementing laws and ini-
tiatives on the construction of all new municipal buildings. In New York City, Local Law
86 covers all new public buildings, plus renovations and additions to existing buildings.
Architects wishing to design schools in the state now have to achieve LEED (Leadership
in Energy and Environmental Design) ratings and deliver specific energy and cost savings.

Cultural buildings in New York are also governed by this same law, but, unlike their poor educational cousins, they are already seen as environmental beacons. Governments and private organizations realize the value of ensuring that they are seen to be environmentally friendly.

In addition to this sustainable acknowledgement, the procurers of cultural buildings also want to create buildings that have architectural gravitas. They can be visitors' centres, congress buildings or religious places, a diverse range of property types, but each wants to make a mark and become the central aspect of a particular realm. As such, budgets for the design and construction of these buildings can be vast. This is fine so long as there is good leadership of the project. If this is not forthcoming then the consequences can be hugely disappointing. An apt example is the World Trade Center site. Here, culturally led designs for the new tower at Ground Zero were quietly ignored, and then Daniel Libeskind's competition-winning design for a new symbolic tower was bastardized almost beyond recognition to suit the financial ambitions of its developer.

This is one example of how it can go wrong. Conversely, the UAE is spending almost infinite amounts of money to bring culture to the desert. In Abu Dhabi, a new cultural quarter will one day be the ultimate architectural tourist destination. Four museums and performance venues, designed by Zaha Hadid, Frank Gehry, Jean Nouvel and Tadao Ando, will stand within landscaped parks and walkways looking out across the bay to the main city. The architects have been given free reign and budgets will be of little consequence in this massive undertaking. But can you buy culture, and the tourism potential that goes with it? Or should the wealthy sheikhs who fund these somewhat egotistical projects focus their attention on their own rich local culture and tradition, and the plight of those not so privileged that they live alongside?

Whether a building is part of a structured reappraisal of teaching methods or a bold statement made to attract and educate visitors on the cultural identity of a region, it must be designed to maximize its educational potential. The successful realization of such a building is something that people will witness and be inspired by: the way it performs contributes directly or indirectly to the mental stimulation of many. This is a weighty burden to put on the shoulders of an architect, but unless a building performs well, its shape and architectural drama are of little consequence.

ARCHITECTURE FOUNDATION, UK
ZAHA HADID ARCHITECTS

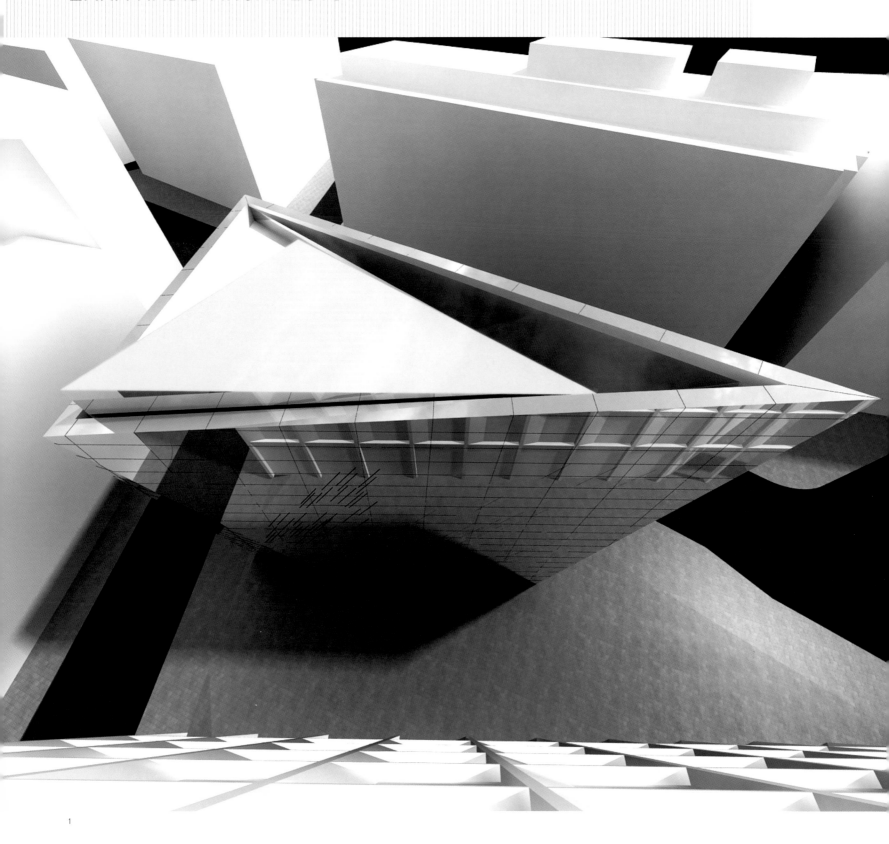

1

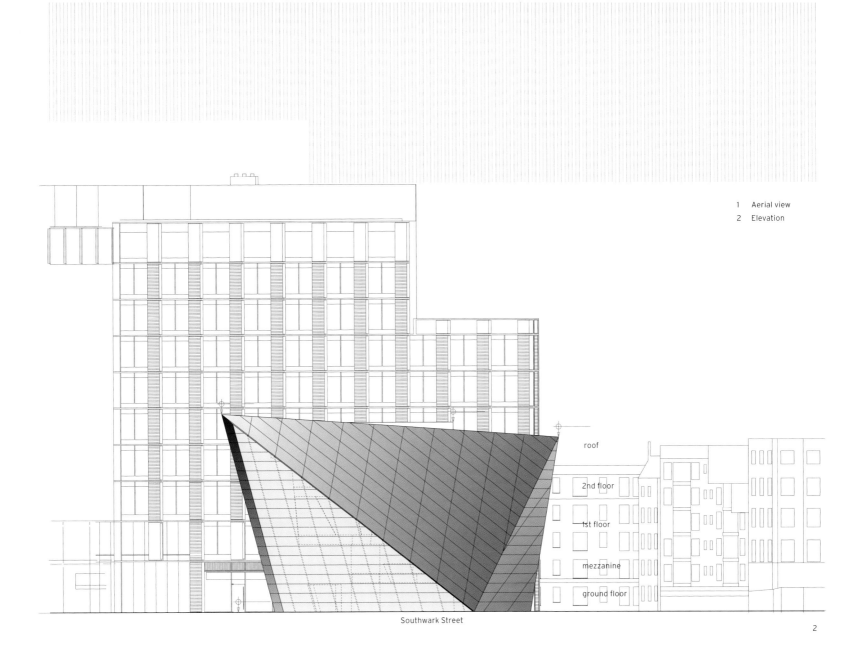

1   Aerial view
2   Elevation

roof

2nd floor

1st floor

mezzanine

ground floor

Southwark Street

2

Zaha Hadid's design for the Architecture Foundation

in London, UK, is envisioned as a sculpture: mysterious, intriguing and not referable to traditional architectural typologies. As a solid metal mirror-clad diamond the building is meant, as with all of the architect's work, to generate excitement, to be a new point of interest within its immediate surroundings.

The building is described by the architect as 'literally reflecting the city around it inwards and creating a new centre of knowledge'. Its physical presence is dematerialized with the use of a highly reflective surface, and the contrast between the powerful sculptural mass of the structure and the lightness of its reflective envelope create a bold and enigmatic statement for the heart of London.

The shape of the building is a direct consequence to the urban environment in which it sits and the relations it establishes with its surroundings. The peculiarity of the triangular corner site is transferred in the three dimensions, giving life to a rich architectural composition that is made all the more interesting by its close proximity to neighbouring buildings. This is architecture conceived as a pure design statement. The structural elements work to their full potential and are clearly used as a celebration of architectural development, alongside the flashy façade.

The 640 m^2 (6,890 ft^2) design does, however, have functional requirements. On the street level a main entrance leads to the atrium/exhibition space, which also hosts a bar. A mezzanine with balcony overlooks the atrium. On the first floor there is another exhibition space,

which can be used for lectures. Finally, the offices of the Foundation are on the second floor. The open plan arrangement of much of the building enables reconfiguration of spaces to accommodate different exhibitions, or reorganization of the Foundation over time.

The building's strategic location in the city is designed to encourage people from the nearby cultural and tourist attractions on the banks of the river Thames, including the Tate Modern and National Galleries, to explore further afield from the usual tourist areas.

3

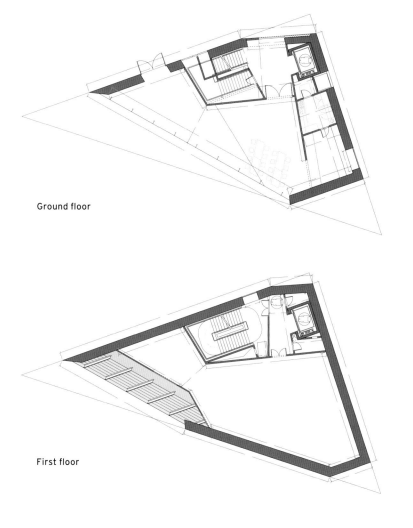

Ground floor

Mezzanine

First floor

Second floor

4

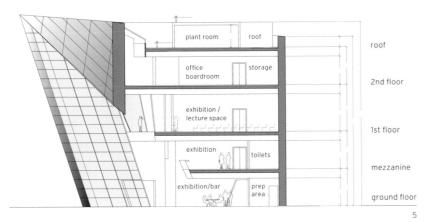

plant room	roof		roof
office boardroom	storage		2nd floor
exhibition / lecture space			1st floor
exhibition	toilets		mezzanine
exhibition/bar	prep area		ground floor

5

6

3 Perspective towards main entrance
4 Floor plans
5 Section
6 Internal exhibition / circulation space
7 Towards the main entrance

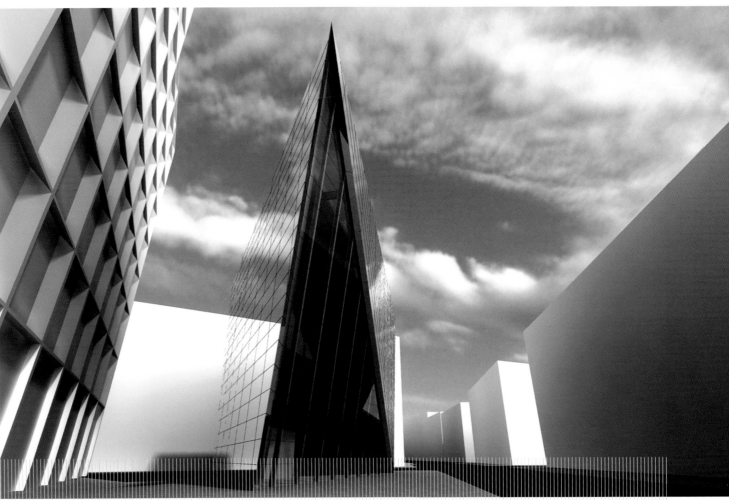

7

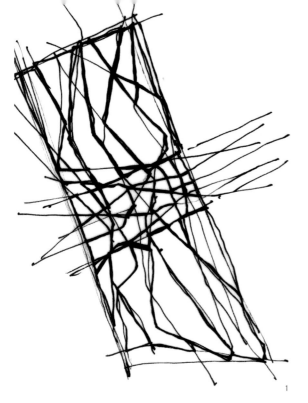

Fletcher Priest Architects' competition entry for the Bezalel Academy of Arts and Design campus is a bold and dynamic architectural response that provides a recognizable landmark for an institution renowned for innovation.

Established in 1906 as the Bezalel School of Arts and Crafts, the institution celebrated its centenary as Israel's leading academy in its field by organizing an international architectural competition for its new campus in the heart of Jerusalem. The resulting buildings will be the largest and most prominent architectural undertaking in the city in over a decade.

1

2

BEZALEL ACADEMY OF ARTS AND DESIGN, ISRAEL
MATTEO CAINER AT FLETCHER PRIEST ARCHITECTS

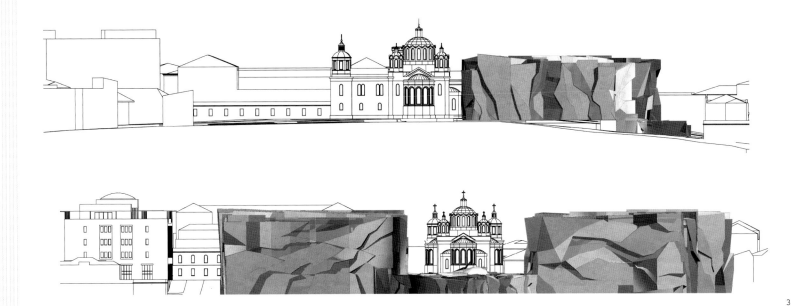

1   Concept sketch   3   Southeast (top)
2   The landscape   and northeast
    in between   façades
    schools   4   Site plan

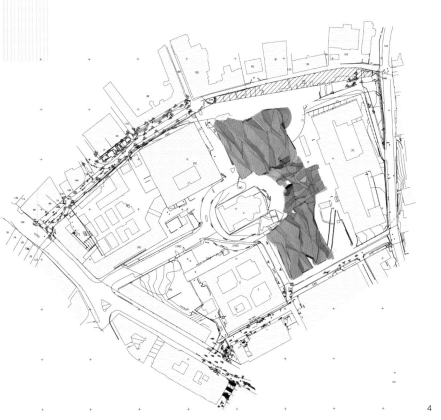

The Academy is home to 1,765 students and 400 teachers and is spread over three campuses – Mount Scopus, Jerusalem; the historic Building of Bezalel in Jerusalem city centre; and the Bezalel Gallery in Tel Aviv. Bezalel incorporates both traditional crafts and state-of-the-art technologies throughout its ten departments: fine arts, architecture, industrial design, visual communications, photography, video, animation, ceramic and glass design, jewelry and fashion, and history and theory.

This design for the new campus, by Fletcher Priest Architects, draws inspiration from the massive stone outcrops that break through Jerusalem's carpet of city streets and squares. Programmed spaces within the 36,500 m^2 (392,900 ft^2) academy are clearly organized within the dramatic architectural addition. Public and communal areas are arranged around the ground and plaza levels. The main entrance penetrates the plaza to the principal public space, which features a historic Russian church. The two Bezalel buildings can be accessed from here. Individual academic departments are arranged on the upper levels of the buildings, enjoying views across the city.

Arriving at the campus is envisioned as a singular experience, with the entrances and public spaces visible through a fractured ground plane. A protected view corridor is the generator of the form, providing select glimpses of life within the campus. The entrance way drives through the mass of stone, splitting and deforming it.

Entrances, studios and workshops appear hewn from the massive landform, and the shear stone walls of Jerusalem limestone resemble the excavated face of a quarry. Fissures allow light to penetrate deep into the structure, while glazed openings appear as mineral seams that sparkle and illuminate the rough-hewn shapes.

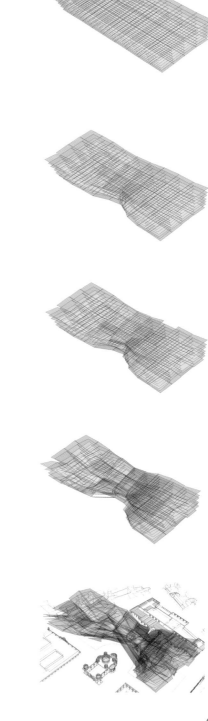

Industrial Design
MA + BA

Cinema / Visual
Communication

Fine Art MA + BA

Photography

Jewelry + Fashion

Screen based
Arts

Architecture BA

Ceramic / Glass
Design

Architecture MA

Internal Common
Space

External Common
Space

5

5 Educational
distribution
diagram

6 Deformation
of grid (top
to bottom)

7 Aerial view

8 Internal space

BICENTENARY CULTURAL CENTRE, ARGENTINA
KUWABARA PAYNE MCKENNA BLUMBERG

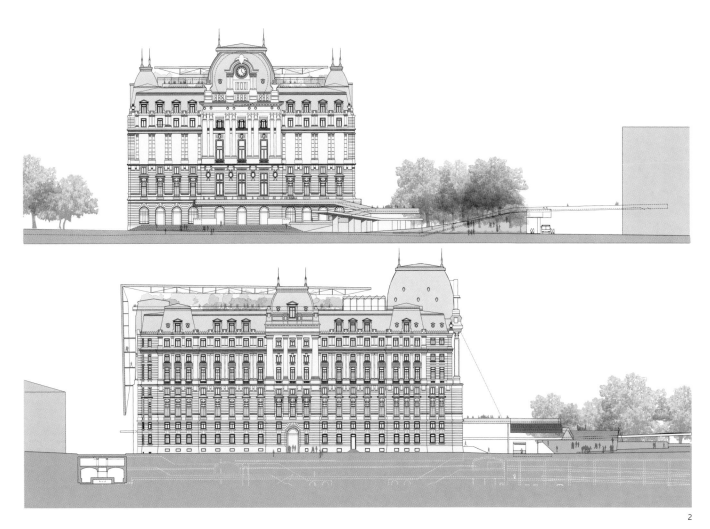

The design for the Bicentenary Cultural Centre in Buenos Aires by Kuwabara Payne McKenna Blumberg (KPMB) transforms the Palacio de Correos y Telecomunicaciones (the Buenos Aires Central Post Office), the five-block site which surrounds it, and the area just beyond into a new cultural precinct. Called the Quartier Cultural, this area is located at the heart of Argentina's most populous city and is designed to embrace all kinds of creative art form.

Five 'events' organize KPMB's scheme. Stepped garden terraces pivot around the Palacio and define a shallow green bowl on the Beaux Arts building. A grand processional stairway creates a stage, a rostrum, and a terrain for daily activities and celebratory events. A large-scaled L-shaped plane floats over the rooftop of the building and folds down

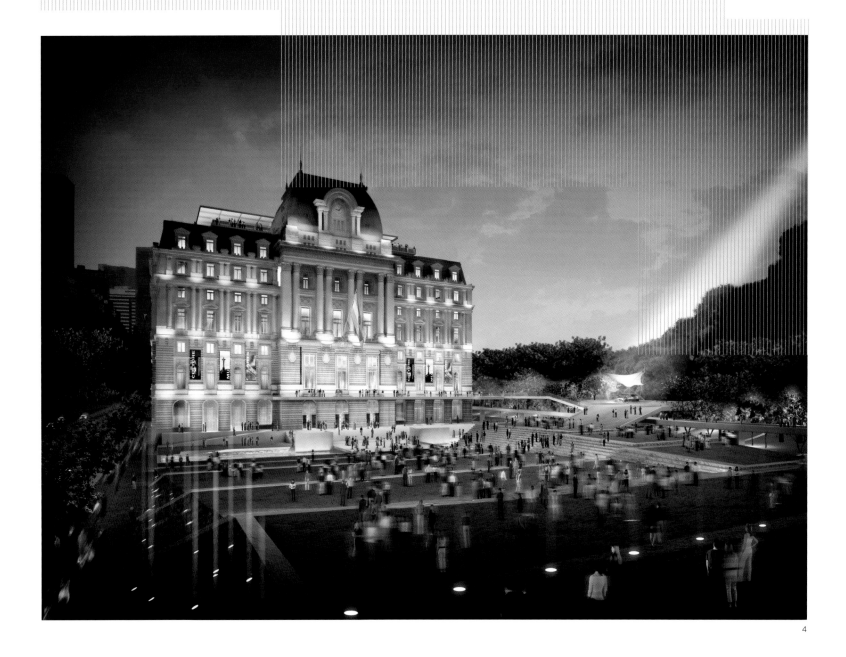

4

over the Corrientes façade. The extension of the project creates an open, public space for gathering in front of the Corrientes façade of the Palacio. And, finally, a new world of music and art is created within the Palacio: articulated as a curved volume, it contains the full programme of performance spaces, while conserving the integrity of the primary historic interiors and the Beaux Arts exterior.

The roof of the Palacio is utilized to put the building in touch with the entire city. A meeting spot and platform for sightseeing, with venues for dining or drinks, it features a large 'solar roof' of photovoltaic panels and solar thermal collectors, which floats like a screen over the centre of the building and transitions into a fritted glass scrim as it folds down over the Corrientes façade.

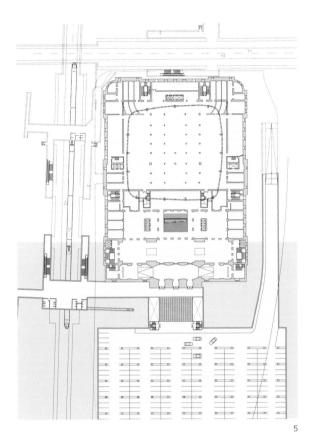

5

4 Front elevation
  and square
5 Plan view
6 Music pod wall
7 Concept sketch

6

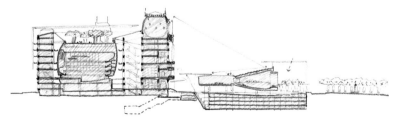

7

Internally, new rooms for music are bundled together to occupy a pod-like biomorphic form, which is inserted into the centre of what was formally the building's back-of-house. This curved volume of performance spaces that includes concert and recital halls is inserted into the orthogonal plan to generate a positive tension between old and new.

The project has an impressive array of environmental features including a rainwater recovery system, photovoltaic panels, solar thermal collectors and ground source heat pumps. Mist will be sprayed on extremely hot days to reduce localized exterior temperature by 15° C (59° F). Green roof technology supports storm water retention, and provides insulation and cooling. Fresh air is pumped from outside underground into the building and an evacuated tube system releases stored heat from radiant panels. This then allows air tower shafts to act as solar chimneys during the summer, drawing air up through the building to be released at the top.

1

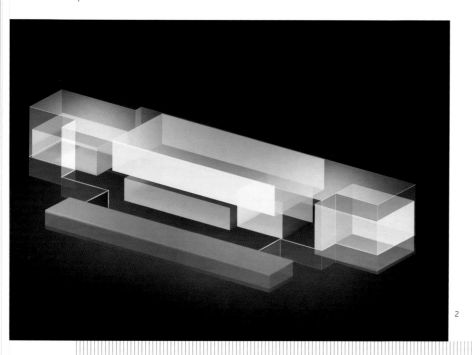

2

CENTRE FOR MUSIC, ART AND DESIGN,
UNIVERSITY OF MANITOBA, CANADA
PATKAU ARCHITECTS

The Centre for Music, Art and Design (CMAD) is an 8,900 m² (95,800 ft²) interdisciplinary facility designed for the University of Manitoba in Winnipeg, Canada. It is located to create a new interdisciplinary arts precinct, connecting an existing disengaged collection of buildings to form an 'arts courtyard', defined on three sides by buildings, and on the fourth by a proposed pedestrian passageway.

The Faculty of Architecture, the Schools of Fine Art and Music, and the integrated Architecture, Fine Art, and Music Library share CMAD. Patkau Architects examined how the schools operated and then proposed a radical shake-up of the way activities are divided up. The architect states that 'instead of a one–one correspondence between program requirements and spaces, a many–many correspondence was proposed by developing "Six Big Rooms" that would accommodate varied program activities.'

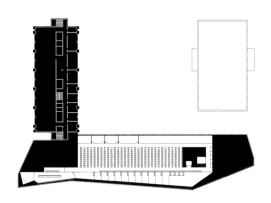

1   Longitudinal
    section
2   Activity 'cubes'
3   Main entrance
4   Plan views,
    second to ground
    floor (top to
    bottom)

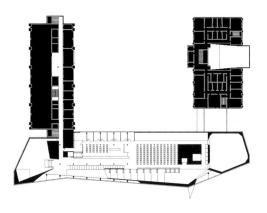

3

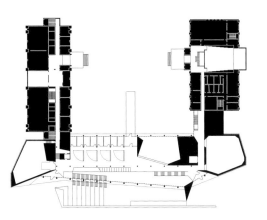

4

This functional design was conceived so that by virtue of being shared and multi-use, the Big Rooms create new opportunities for interaction between disciplines. Accompanying them are the support teaching spaces necessary to meet the exacting technical requirements of the design brief. In contrast to the structured interactivity of the Six Big Rooms, the support space is designed to no programme at all – 'Mix Space' is the name given it by Patkau. It is designed to 'support the unexpected: the serendipitous interaction essential to interdisciplinary learning and research'.

To reinforce the interdisciplinary nature of the facility, and to make the programme activities more public and accessible to the university population, the building is also sited so that it interconnects with the campus infrastructure as much as possible. Entrances are located

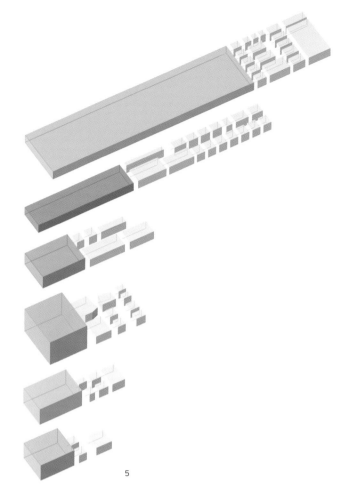

5

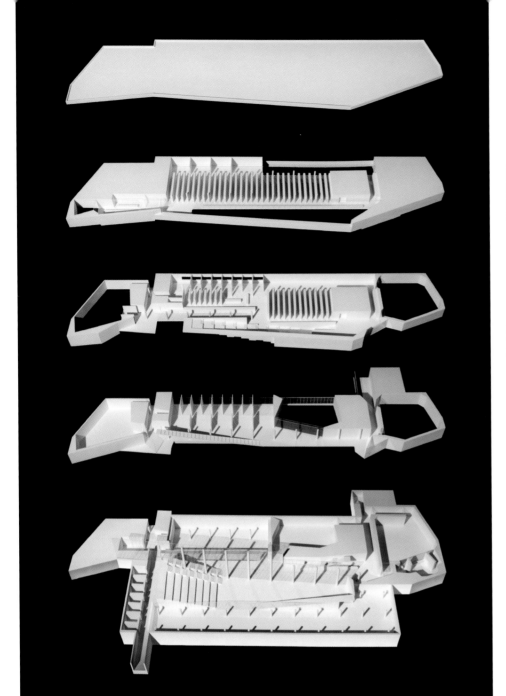

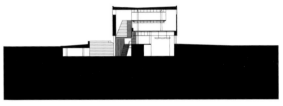

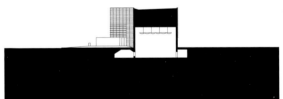

7

8

strategically to connect with existing pedestrian routes. Below ground, circulation is organized so as to significantly extend the campus tunnel network, the primary means of circulation during the Canadian winter.

The design is a left-field step for the rigorously formal environment of higher education in Canada. It is intuitive but ultimately perhaps a little too brave for the client.

CHANGSHA CULTURE PARK, CHINA
MAD

At some 60,000 m² (646,000 ft²), the Changsha Culture Park, in China's Hunan province, is a mammoth project that features three distinct internal zones separated by external promenades. This doesn't sound dissimilar to many other multi-building projects. However, the Culture Park is designed as one building, its roof undulating up and over the internal spaces and down to meet the ground and the external walkways.

In plan the building is irregular, roughly five sided; its roofscape pock-marked with circular apertures and similar decorative markings. When seen from ground level, this remarkable design is dominated by the three internal spaces – the concert hall, library and museum. Tallest is the concert hall, with a dramatic glazed façade on two elevations and the sloping roof façade draped towards the centre of the building. The largest of the internal spaces is the museum, which is not as tall as the concert hall but covering more floor area.

The lowest part of the building's undulating roof does not actually descend to ground level, it is a storey high, enabling visitor circulation under the entirety of the roofscape and covered access to all three attractions. Escalators provide access to the roof from the interior, while externally ramps ascend from ground level.

MAD, the young practice responsible for this design, sees it as creating a 'new cultural plateau for Changsha City', one which simultaneously serves as an organic link between the urban context and waterfront. The architect describes the park as having two surfaces that respond equally and articulate to the internal function. But the external environment is the more interesting of the two, a new urban space that in unashamedly of the 21st century, its materiality and form being almost impossible to construct just a few years ago. Out here, the public can promenade or enjoy external exhibitions and performances: they can wander the lower central spaces or climb the slopes to admire views from on top of the library, concert hall and museum.

1   View on approach
2   Aerial view

1

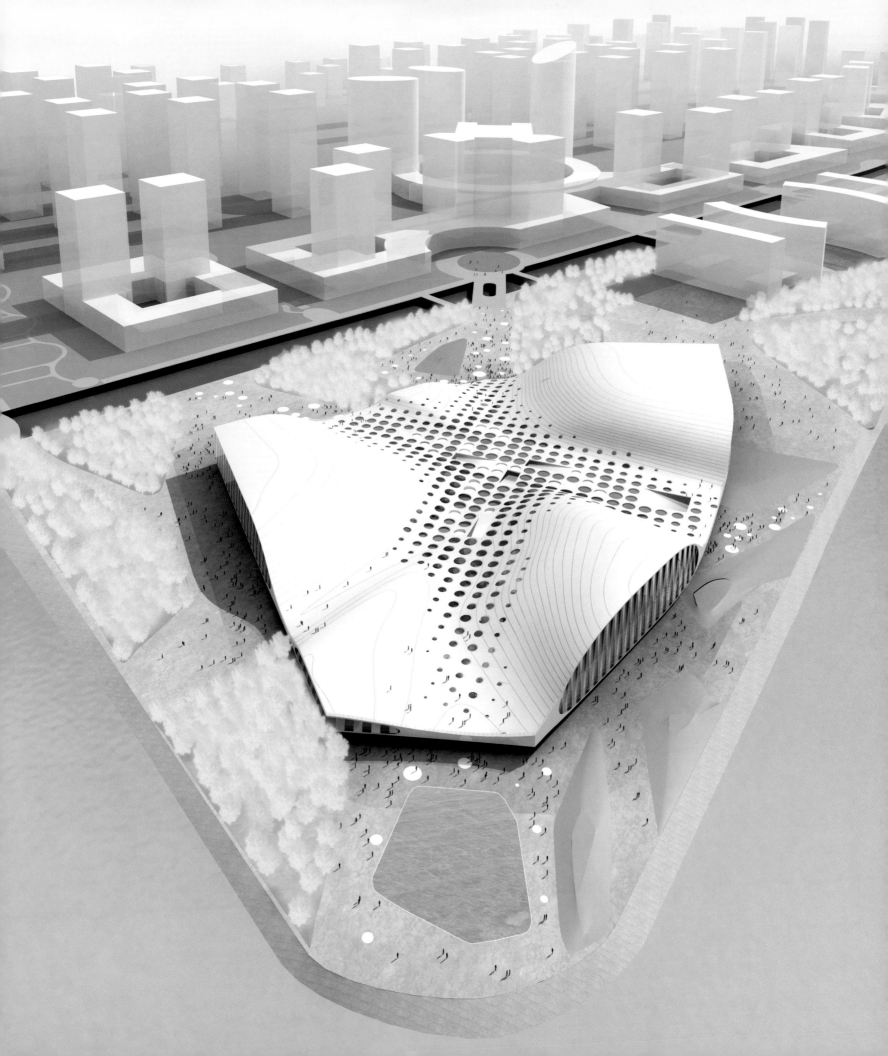

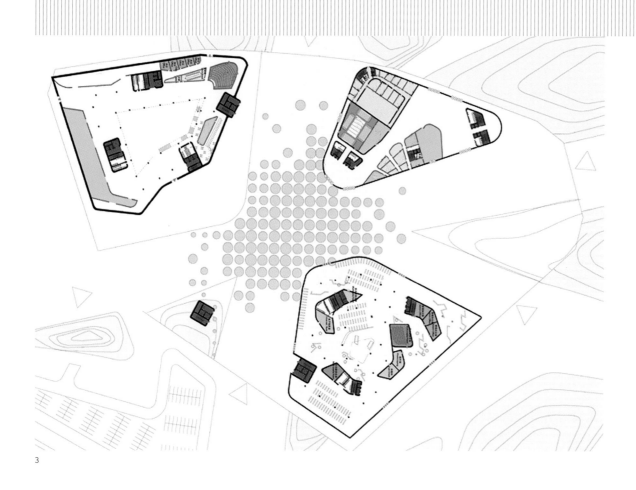

3

Like many projects in China, the client for this project was the state – Changsha Culture Government. And, like many other Chinese urban areas, this one is striving to present a new, friendly face to tourists and foreign visitors. This design presented an ideal too radical for those in authority, but then that is something that architects constantly do, and a design ethic with which MAD will hopefully persevere.

4

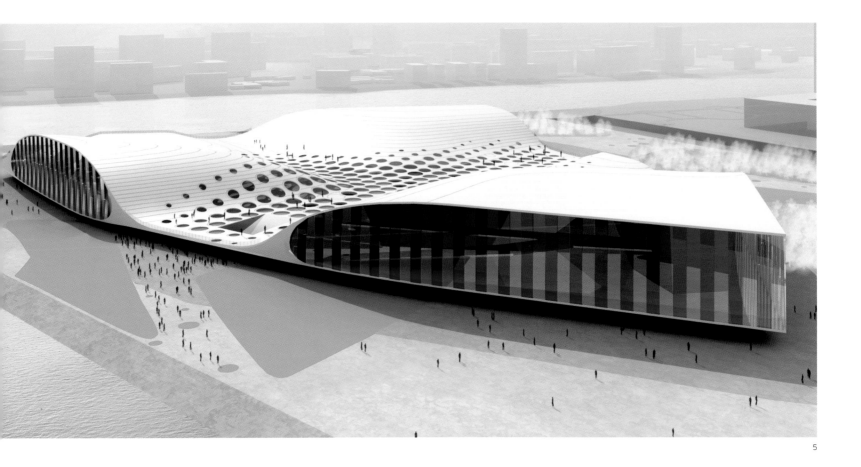

5

3 Site plan at
  ground level
4 Internal
  circulation space
5 Population of
  approach
  and roof
6 Topographical
  site plan

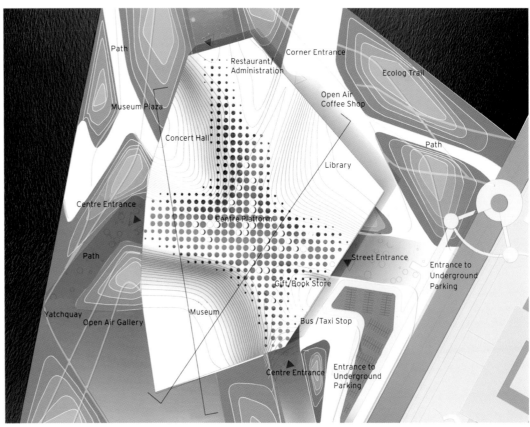

Path

Corner Entrance

Ecolog Trail

Restaurant/
Administration

Open Air
Coffee Shop

Museum Plaza

Concert Hall

Path

Library

Centre Entrance

Centre Platform

Path

Street Entrance

Entrance to
Underground
Parking

Gift/Book Store

Yatchquay

Open Air Gallery

Museum

Bus /Taxi Stop

Centre Entrance

Entrance to
Underground
Parking

6

The Connecticut Center for Science and Exploration is an exciting design for the 2004 competition held by the client of the same name. Moshe Safdie's curvaceous creation takes on the city's predominantly rectilinear architecture to make a statement on the skyline. However, it also strives to create urban connectivity, weaving together existing riverside paths and terraces, contributing to the urban whole.

The architect has had fun in this work, designing an exciting laterally biased building with a wooden structure, in contrast to the high-rise steel frames surrounding it. Its shape evokes the sciences, its geometrics reminiscent of astronomical instruments, rocket thrusters, alien craft: it challenges our curiosity, 'uplifting the spirit', says Safdie.

Safdie describes the two main elements of the design as 'nacelles', a term commonly used in aviation and spacecraft design to describe the housings for jet engines. These nacelles thrust out from the crowded cityscape into the openness of the river. They could be seen as the engines of the city, driving it into a new millennium.

The nacelles are perched atop a podium, sitting side-by-side, and are shaped as segments of two great toroids. These two dramatic halves of the centre are united by a great roof structure. Bowl-shaped like an amphitheatre, this inverted dome is clad on its south side in photovoltaic panels, a vast array of which provides some of the power for the centre. The northern half of the roof features a series of stepped gardens and between them is a void looking down to street level. The nacelles' structure is made up of a diagrid laminated wood lattice, which cloaks the surface of the nacelles in an ordered and repetitive geometry.

The 14,600 m^2 (157,150 ft^2) centre is organized into six levels in total. The first level is the entry at the street; the second, the podium; the third and fourth levels, within the nacelles, are exhibit and theatre levels; the fifth level, also within the nacelles, is the upper mezzanine; and the top level is the roof garden. Below the podium, public parking, offices and back-of-house spaces are accommodated.

CONNECTICUT CENTER FOR SCIENCE AND EXPLORATION, USA
MOSHE SAFDIE & ASSOCIATES

1 Centre in context
2 View from the
   bridge between
   the buildings
3 View up to the
   bridge
4 Aerial model view
5 Roof top at night

Safdie has linked his new addition into the existing urban fabric by creating the northern portion of the roof surface and the public space around the podium below as an extension and part of a series of linked piazzas, which also bridge to the river abutting the site.

DURA EXEMPLAR SCHOOL, UK
DRMM

1

Designed as an exemplar school for the British government's Schools for the Future programme, dRMM's Dura sets out to reappraise the 'school experience and challenge conventional educational design ethics'.

The architect's research found that despite their prominence within communities, most school buildings are routinely used for only forty per cent of their lives, and learning is generally restricted by the building arrangement to the time spent in classrooms. This lack of use makes schools expensive buildings, full of unclaimed opportunities for more learning.

dRMM's approach is to invent a classroom construction which can easily be altered, offering future adaptation, extension or even removal. In the Dura, halls are large volumes, spectacular, multifunctional and spatially connected rather than separated from the daily life of the school. One of Dura's two halls is conceived as a predominantly social space, an open forest as entry to the heart of the building, with mature trees in a temperate climate, and easy access to friends, information and food.

 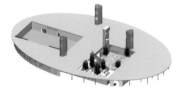  

2

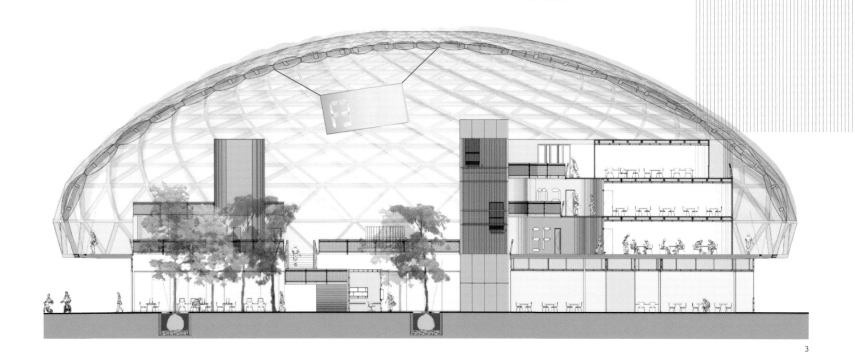

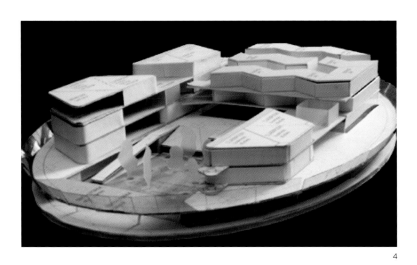

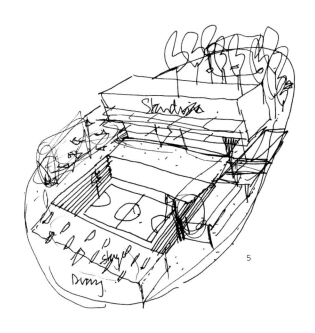

1	Populated elevation	3	Cross section
2	Building up the accommodation within the bubble	4	Massing model
		5	Concept sketch

This hyper-modern school is user-friendly. The design prioritizes space, daylight and views. An enormous, mainly transparent ETFE (ethylene tetrafluoroethylene) volume enables a variety of modular classroom types to be extensively configured and reconfigured. Classrooms have adjacent spaces to colonize and the school can extend economically. This inside/outside open space creates a generous social collective, and gives every school the right to plan and change their own departmental layouts according to pedagogy, phasing or ambition.

Passive services provide fresh cooled / heated air direct to all classrooms at little or no energy cost, without expensive plant or maintenance. Construction utilizes ecologically sound, durable materials prefabricated off-site, enabling a short and dry on-site period. Cutting-edge technologies, tested and proven on built projects have allowed this unique design development. The extensive choice offered by the design solution will internally define each Dura school, the whole composition further characterized by space, light and trees under an enveloping sky.

dRMM has developed a radical but practical school design for the 21st century, with the deliberate intent of transforming the imposed and deterministic nature of educational buildings into individualized places of learning, empowerment and variety.

6

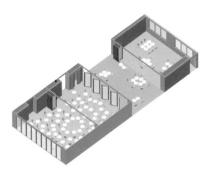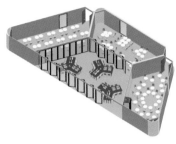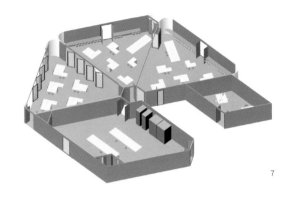

6 Typical classroom
7 Reconfiguration
of teaching space
8 Naturally lit
sports hall

EARTH CENTRE EDEN, ISRAEL
KOHN PEDERSEN FOX

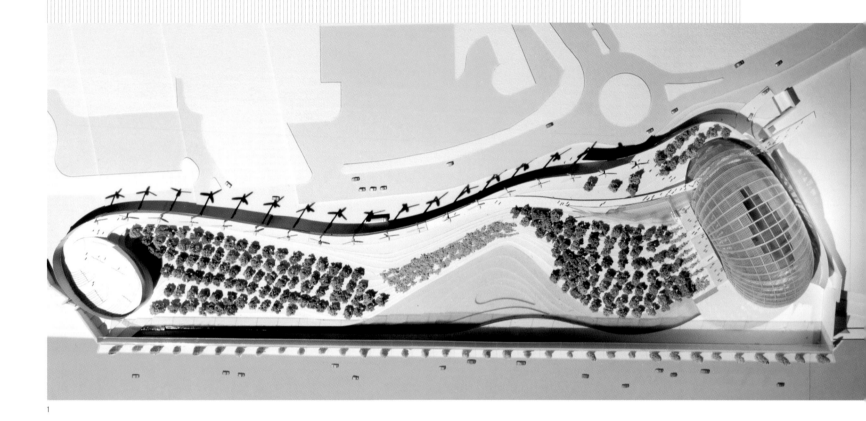

1

Tel Aviv University held a limited international competition for a new school for its Environmental Department for the study of Ecology and Nature (EDEN). Kohn Pedersen Fox's (KPF) design proposed a precinct of building and outdoor spaces in two phases, the first of 4,500 m² (48,440 ft²), and a second of 2,500 m² (26,910 ft²). Together, they act as an exhibit and tool, as well as a working department, so that all those who visit the university will go away with a deeper understanding and appreciation of the world's ecosystem.

The climatic balance of temperature is a prime focus of the architect's design. The competition-winning concept is based upon the creation of a series of microclimate buffers that reduce the wide variation of temperatures during working hours. These buffers enable the building to operate with a minimum of energy expended while remaining comfortable to work in.

Three microclimate buffers create this hierarchy of comfort. The first microclimate is the walled garden that acts as a cold air and water reservoir, trapping cool air and moisture that collects at ground level during the night and early morning. This entirely passive element has a surprisingly large cooling impact on the buildings, when compared to non-walled properties nearby.

The taurus-shaped trellis just outside the building envelope forms the second microclimate. This shell blocks direct sunlight while allowing diffused light and cooling breezes to pass by the building. Finally, the third microclimate is the internal atrium, which retains the cooler temperature from night hours, regulating heat gain throughout the day.

Within these climatic buffers, the two elliptical buildings split the university departments – ocean biology, fresh water and water resources in one dome, and eco-toxicology, physiology and biotechnology in the other.

The design proposes a strategy of incorporating sustainable remediation of material, and active power generation too. The walls and floors are made of Porocom, a recycled material made from the residue of industrial paint applications. It has a high structural strength and good acoustic absorption. On one border of the walled garden multiple wind turbines also take advantage of the windy site.

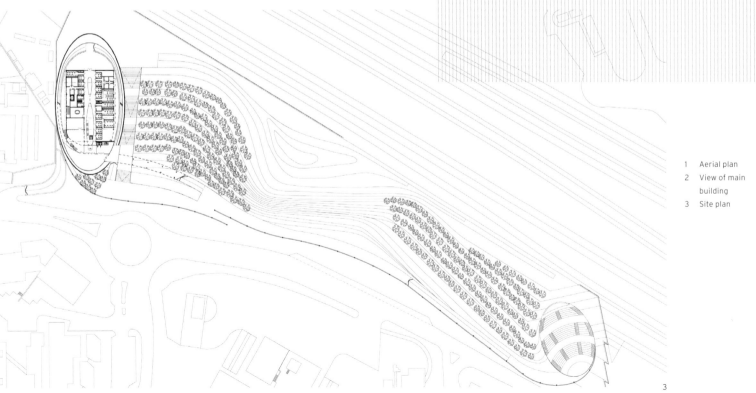

1   Aerial plan
2   View of main
    building
3   Site plan

EUROPEAN SOLIDARITY CENTRE, POLAND
PENTAGRAM DESIGN

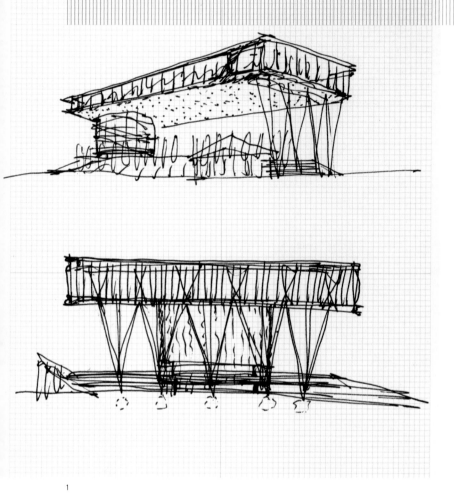

1

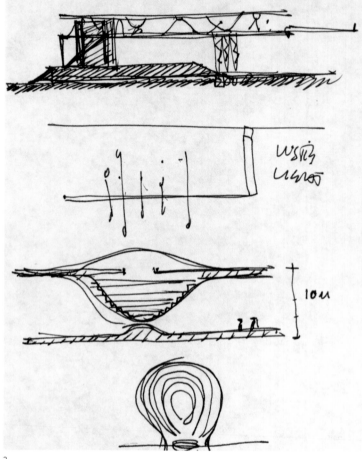

2

Pentagram Design proposed this building, called the Interrex, for an international architecture competition for a European Solidarity Centre (ESC), to be built in Gdansk, Poland. The 2007 competition called for a structure that would act as an international centre of culture, housing a museum, temporary exhibition space and academic research centre. Conceptually, the building is to memorialize Solidarity, the first non-communist trade union in a communist country, founded in Gdansk in 1980.

The proposal contains two interconnected parts: the Interrex, a dramatic structure that separates Poland's earthbound past from its reconsolidation as a free nation; and the Interregnum, an expansive horizontal representation of the breathing space created by Solidarity.

The Interregnum is an expansive space that connects to the city of Gdansk and the square's iconic monuments, while the power

of the floating Interrex above gives physical expression to the feat Solidarity accomplished by refusing to yield throughout years of repression.

The Interrex is loosely conceived of as a ship – with a hull, mast and sail – as the Solidarity Movement was founded by workers from the Gdansk Shipyard, the site of the proposed building. In consideration of this context, the Interrex has been designed to be fabricated with the skills and materials that shipyard workers uniquely possess.

The 'mast' of the Interrex is a cylindrical glass tower that contains the main vertical connections to the exhibition spaces and is wrapped in a bas-relief glass screen. The mast displays the history in the spiral cast-glass screen (viewed from a ramp within), as well as containing three floors of exhibition space, all hung within the column; archive space; and entrances to all the public rooms above.

The 'sail' that sits atop the mast slowly rotates, pausing to allow for panoramic views of the Monument to the Fallen Workers, the John Paul II Chapel, the historic gate to the shipyard entrance, and the shipyard and river beyond. The sail is coloured to abstract the national flag and is the main symbolic element of the Interrex. The red underside is lit in each of the structural dimples, giving a soft, warm glow to the spaces defined by the hovering mass.

The five supports of the sail are enclosed structural trusses, with stairs from the spaces above and mounted to the wheels below that allow the sail to move through space.

(previous pages)
1, 2 Concept sketches
3   Site rotation
      concept

4 Upper level
   floor plan
5 Night time
   perspective
6 Upper level
   interior
7 Section

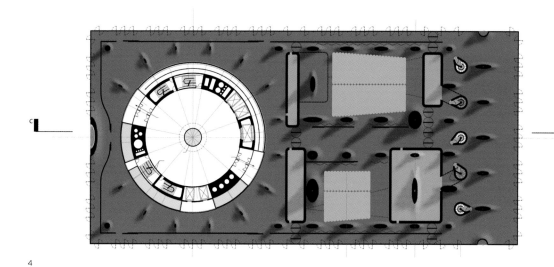

4

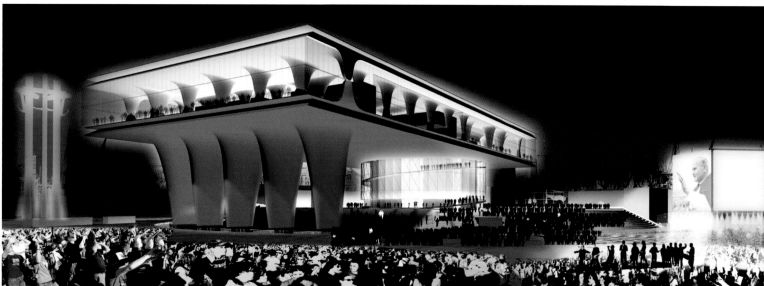

5

6

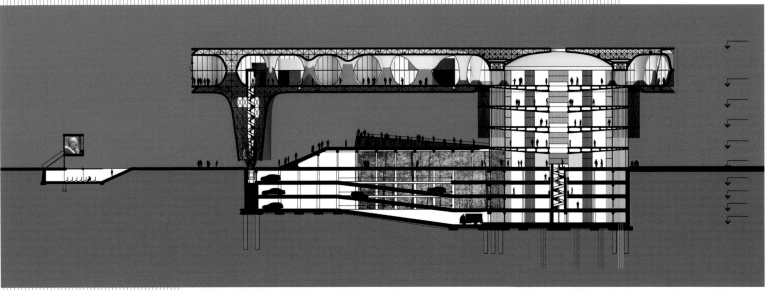

7

GRAND MOSQUE OF ALGIERS, MOROCCO
ARCHITECTURE STUDIO

This was the French practice Architecture Studio's proposal in the international competition to design a new Grand Mosque of Algiers, Morocco. At the core of a vast reorganization programme of Algiers bay, the planned mosque stands on a 20 ha. (49 acre) plateau. Its minaret rises some 300 m (984 ft) high to beckon worshippers from far and wide.

The project is both traditional and contemporary, ambitious and realistic. Architecture Studio's proposal takes its inspiration from sacred architecture and from Algerian culture. The square shape is a pragmatic architectural decision, and the decorative flower arrangements of the façades are reinterpreted in a very contemporary way. The plan is adapted to the urban context, while the rhythm of the pillars finds inspiration in the religious architecture of the region. This is characteristic of North African mosques – the rejection of more formal outlines and limitations. Historically, the design takes reference from the teaching of Islam and ancient cities such as Tlemcen, Kairouan and Cordoue.

The scale of the mosque makes it a central place of worship for the capital, and its positioning on the plateau gives it pride of place in the city. Architecture Studio's project integrates well into Algeria's cultural landscape. The gradual undulating form of the roof reminds the onlooker of features of Algerian desert landscapes, while the use of concrete is not only inexpensive but also echoes the construction some of the most prestigious buildings of the city.

The wide, sweeping roof protects the collection of buildings and the outdoor spaces in the mosque complex from the heat of summer and autumnal storms. Below it, the mosque has space for an almost unbelievable 40,000 worshippers. In addition to this, spaces for the arts, culture and education are also provided.

Architecture Studio has taken reference and been deferential to many aspects of Islam and historic mosque design, while creating a gigantic addition to Algiers that can cope with the massive numbers of worshippers and tourists in the 21st century.

1   Aerial
    perspective
2   Axonometric
3   Façade detail

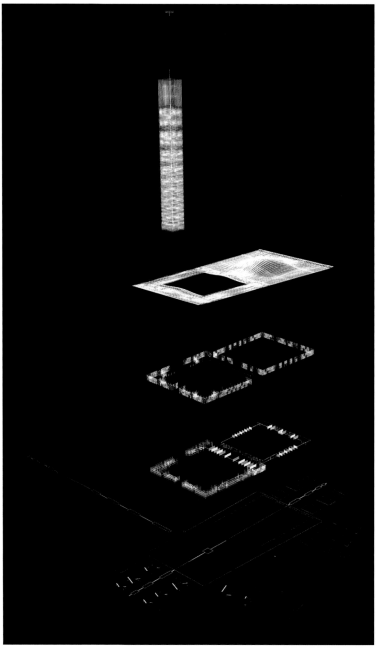

2

3

GRONINGER FORUM, THE NETHERLANDS
ERICK VAN EGERAAT ARCHITECTS

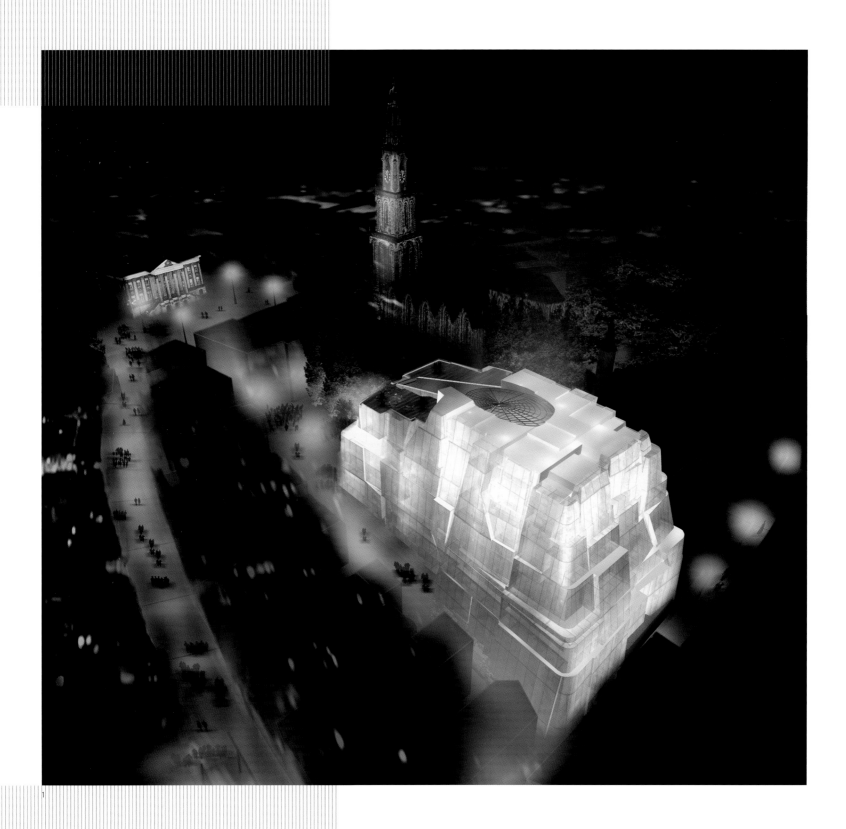

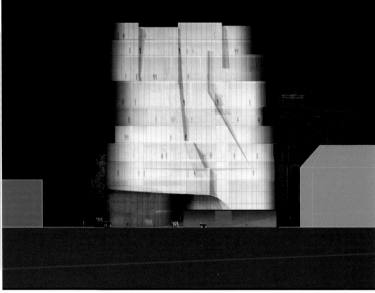

Standing on five sturdy supports or 'feet', as the architect calls them, the Groninger Forum hovers one level above the ground, facing the Grote Markt in a revitalized area of Groningen in the Netherlands. The design, by Erick van Egeraat Architects (EEA), would have made an extravagant and exciting addition to this historic Dutch city.

The building comprises 21,064 m^2 (226,730 ft^2) of space laid out over eleven levels. It houses a collection of leisure facilities, from a cinema, auditorium, library and information domains to exhibition space, a panoramic lounge, roof terrace café and a kids' play area.

The ground level almost seamlessly unites with the surrounding public square. Glass walls can be opened to create a continuous space in and outside the building, allowing visitors to wander freely. Above, the building's translucent alabaster façade gives it a semi-translucent appear-ance. At night, the building stands out as an illuminated beacon in the centre of the city.

The Forum's notched shape suggests a soft sculpted rock, which narrows towards the top and peaks with the transparent roof of the central cone. Internally, the cone transects all levels of the building. Its reddish, earthy skin evokes images of a canyon but also promotes a sense of nurture and warmth. At the same time, cuts in the façade breathe vitality and energy throughout the building by allowing shimmering natural light to penetrate deep into the core.

The main body of the building is accessed via an escalator through the cone. On the first floor escalators enable visitors to shortcut through the building and reach all areas directly. Visitors who want to explore the building can wind their way upwards around the cone via the central staircase.

1   Night view
2   Model showing
    carved-out centre
3   End elevation
4   Neighbourhood
    section

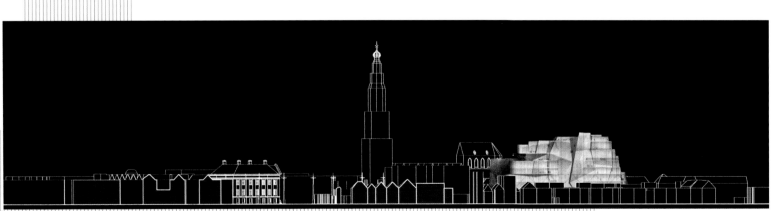

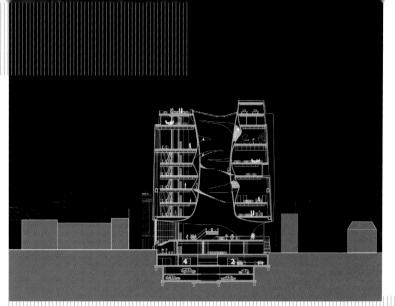

5

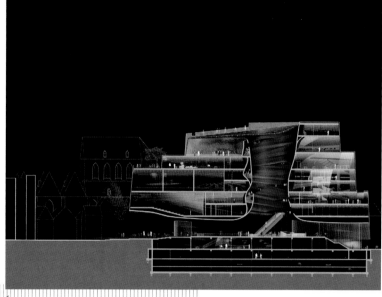

6

7

The architect uses this flexible circulation to create zones that enable parts of the building to be opened and closed without affecting the use of other areas. For instance, the cinema, the exhibition area and the rooftop café can remain open late at night or on Sundays.

8

9

10

5   End section
6   Side section
7   Site plan
8   Interior
9   View from
    approach
10 Interior

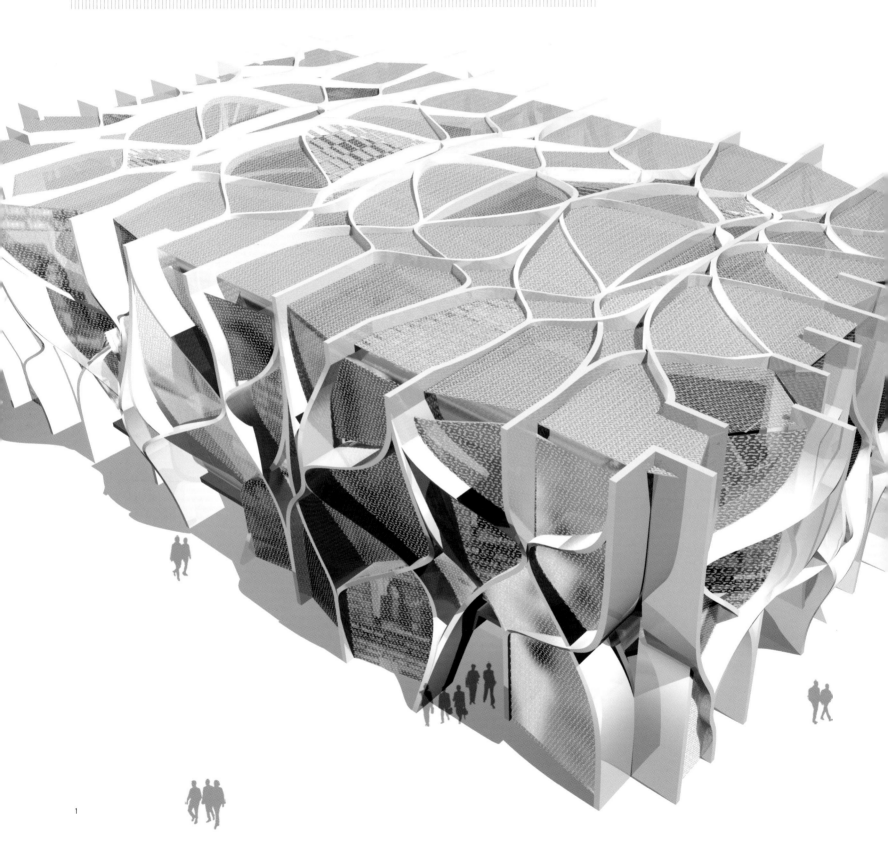

1

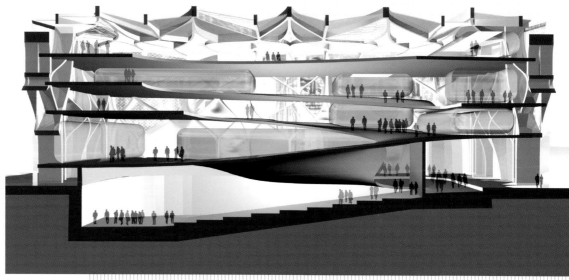

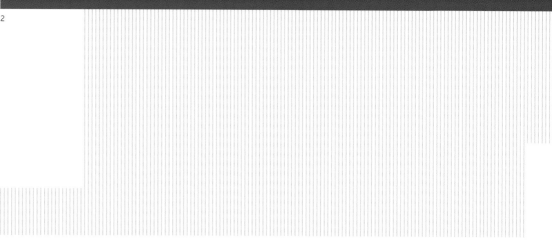

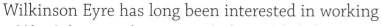

2

1   Aerial layout
2   Longitudinal
    section

Wilkinson Eyre has long been interested in working in Milan, Italy, a city with a reputation for design of the highest quality. This proposal for a new House of Human Rights Cultural Centre presented an ideal opportunity to strengthen the architect's relationship with the country and also provided a chance to work with Amnesty International.

The House of Human Rights spatial brief was at best sketchy when Wilkinson Eyre came to the project. There was no exact location and the building had to serve several functions and end users within one architectural entity. However, the architect revelled in a perceived freedom from constraint to design a building clad in a curvaceous façade that seems to dance in front of one's eyes.

The building design looks critically at the idea of boundaries and blurs them, allowing public and private spaces to fuse and intersect, thus applying the idea of inclusion throughout the centre. The accumulation and diffusion of information is another central theme, it being one of the founding principles of Amnesty International as an organization. By integrating LED technologies into the building envelope, the building itself has been transformed into a powerful medium for transmitting information.

These philosophical visions then had to be married with the more pragmatic requirement for a design solution. This accommodated many different elements, including conference and meeting space, retail, relaxation and administrative facilities. The design has to be sufficiently flexible to be applied to a number of contexts and situations.

While all of Wilkinson Eyre's designs are in essence a response to context, the use of advanced technologies and 3D software has allowed the architect to create an architecture parametrically connected to the shape of the supposed site. The building is able to adapt its shape organically to that of the site without modifying substantially its internal relationships, which are based on a continuity of space.

3

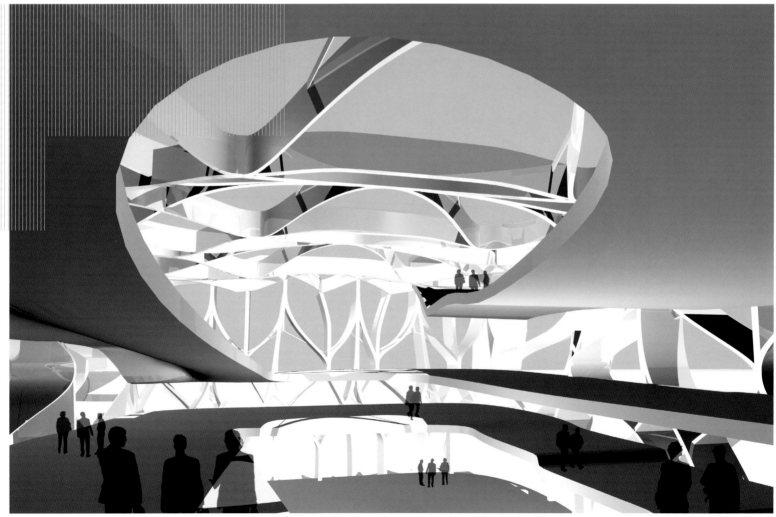

4

5

3   Structural façade
    detail
4   Interior
5   Internal
    circulation
6   End elevation

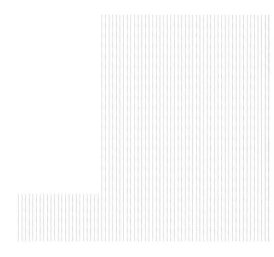

6

JOSEPH REGENSTEIN LIBRARY ADDITION, UNIVERSITY OF CHICAGO, USA

SKIDMORE, OWINGS & MERRILL

1

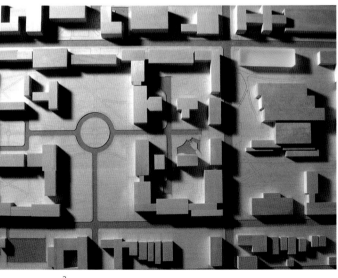

2

1 Aerial model view
2 Site within the campus
3 Façade detailing

The Joseph Regenstein Library Addition at the University of Chicago, USA, was designed by Skidmore, Owings & Merrill (SOM) to accommodate the planned expansion of the university's collections over the next twenty years. This relatively small building is a striking addition to the campus and a somewhat extravagant design for a building that essentially houses an automated storage and retrieval system.

However, SOM states that one of the primary concerns in conceiving the new structure was to create an aesthetic that would represent a new symbol for the university. The building had to stand out but also be legible as an expansion of the collegiate gothic vocabulary of the majority of the campus. Hence, the architect created a building skin that is inspired by multiple elements including the composition of the delicate tracery of cathedral stained-glass windows, the campus's gothic history,

and the microscopic texture of paper. Each strand of inspiration refers to the 'very lifeblood of the institution' and the central element to the library expansion – the book.

The façade is made up of strands or bars of differing size. The heavier elements define the load-bearing steel structure, while a finer network of mullions holds panels of ceramic frit-coated glass and photovoltaic panels. The combination of these expressed elements in the façade and the relative organic form of the structure set it well within its surroundings and create the sense that this new building is a sculptural object that belongs in the park.

The inclusion of photovoltaic panels in the building's façade aims to contribute to the lowering of its carbon footprint in accordance with the university's environmental goals.

1

The Konstantinovsky Congress Centre is a 21st century addition to Niccolo Michetti's sophisticated 18th-century scheme for the grand Konstantinovsky Palace in St Petersburg, Russia. Erick van Egeraat Architects (EEA) has adopted Michetti's principles and extended the landscape grid to the site of the new conference centre. It creates a new urban plan, which integrates the Konstantinovsky Palace, Consular Village and the new Konstantinovsky Conference Centre.

In deference to the palace, EEA conceals the scale of the new building and creates a certain harmony between old and new. All of Michetti's principal axes and lines of sight are continued in the landscaping of the

KONSTANTINOVSKY CONGRESS CENTRE, RUSSIA
ERICK VAN EGERAAT ARCHITECTS

2

1   View on approach
2   Aerial view in
     context
3   Section

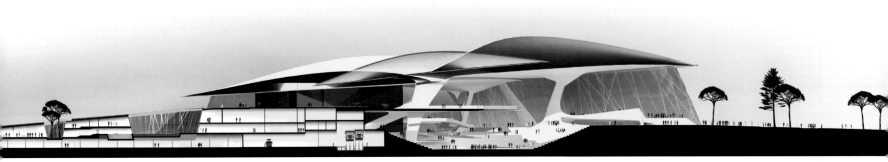

3

4

5

new plot and play a crucial role in shaping the Congress Centre. In order to conceal its large scale, parts of the new building including the spa, the business club, the conference area and the press room are embedded into a hill. Daylight for these embedded rooms is delivered via a series of glass roofed winter gardens and patios, carved out of the hill.

The centre's main functions tower above the hill and are covered by a tripartite, seemingly floating roof. Varying in size, each roof segment represents one of the three main functions – congress hall and chamber hall, both enclosed and connected by the multifunctional foyer.

The chamber hall offers outstanding acoustic conditions for musical performances. Its interior style is inspired by the classic Italian concert halls. In contrast, the big congress hall is futuristic in appearance.

6

7

4, 5 Internal
     circulation /
     exhibition spaces
6   Night view from
     the water
7   Main auditorium

It offers fully adaptable tiers and is therefore prepared to host a wide range of international events with up to 2,500 visitors.

Multiple layers and balconies allow visitors to see and to be seen. Full-height glass façades let light flood into the building and offer panoramic views to the Constantine Palace and the Gulf of Finland.

All in all, the Konstantinovsky Congress Centre is a major addition to the Strelna area, both in scale and in the prospects it offers. EEA has preserved and, if possible, reinvigorated the splendour of Niccolo Michetti's design by minimizing the visual impact of the new building and extending the existing landscape.

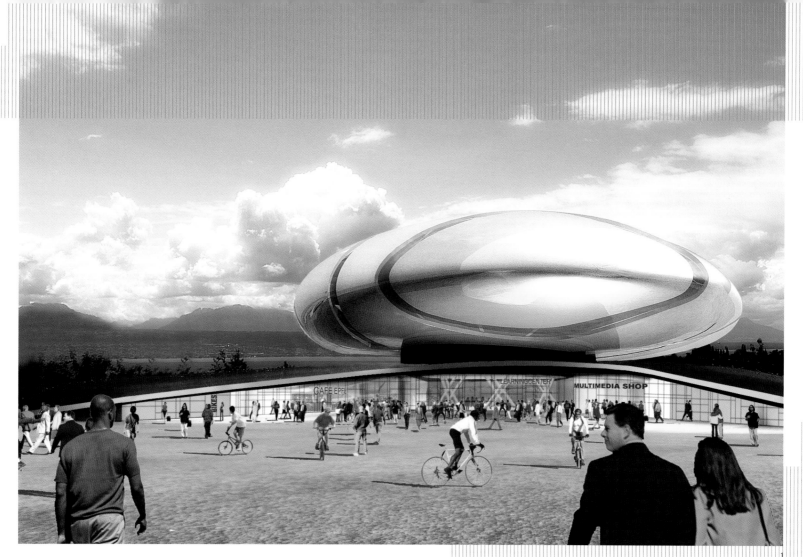

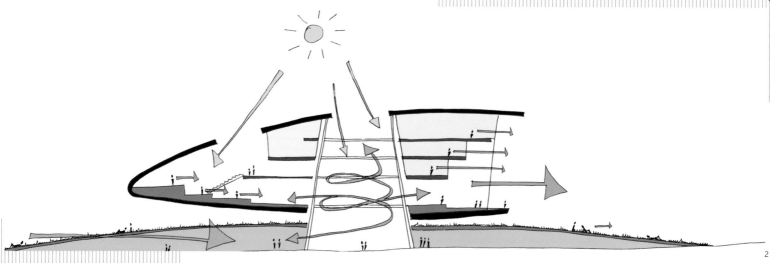

LEARNING CENTRE, ÉCOLE POLYTECHNIQUE FÉDÉRALE
DE LAUSANNE, SWITZERLAND

MECANOO

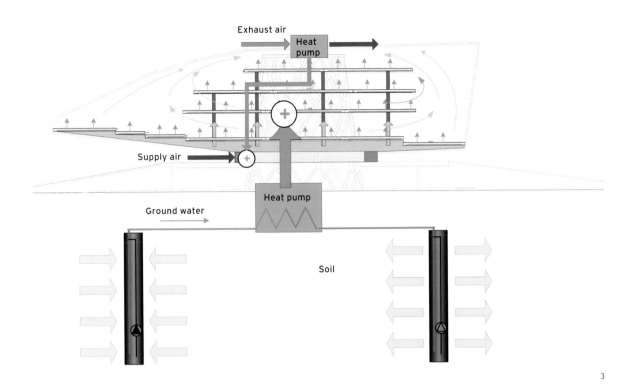

Exhaust air

Heat pump

Supply air

Heat pump

Ground water

Soil

3

The École Polytechnique Fédérale de Lausanne (EPFL) in Switzerland is designed as a centre for progressive environmental studies. It houses eductional facilities, study rooms, informal meeting spaces, archives, research library, a foyer with exhibition space and restaurant in a building totalling 15,000 m² (161,460 ft²) in area. However, Mecanoo could never make a building that straightforward.

The architect sees the polytechnic as being renowned for its lively campus, situated on the banks of Lake Geneva with the Alps as a backdrop: as a place where students and lecturers come together not only for study and research but also for social and cultural exchange. Mecanoo's design is aimed to express this strong dual identity within the building.

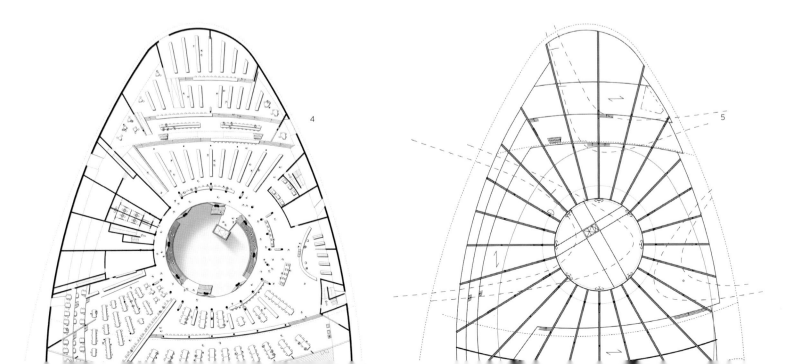

4　　　　5

6

The architect sets out to thrill and also engender environmental thinking into the design which, around a tall central hall, rotates on a ring of ball bearings at the same speed as the earth – fifteen degrees per hour. This constant movement keeps the large glazed main façade constantly ahead of the sun's path. By avoiding direct sunlight the building does not require shading, daylight can be used to the building's optimum advantage and energy consumption is kept as low as possible. The three boomerang-shaped windows in the appropriately named Wing's skin allow natural daylight to penetrate throughout the interior.

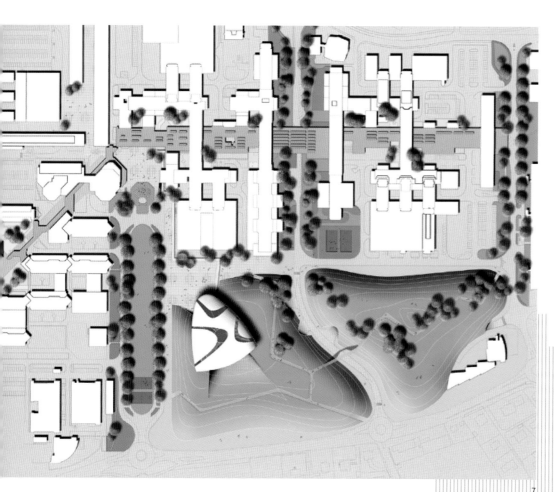

7

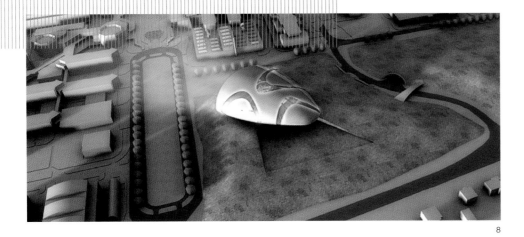

8

Above the entrance hall and the rotating mechanism, the Wing has four floors. The first of which, the piano nobile, has terraced floors that provide generous views throughout the interior. Long tables, easy chairs and smaller rooms can be used for study, reading and meetings. An atrium houses stairs that lead to seminar rooms and faculty accommodations. On the uppermost level is a restaurant with a panoramic window.

Externally, the slopes of an artificial hill form an inviting place for people to gather to study or relax. Opposite the campus's central square, a large wedge has been cut into the hill, forming a new open space ringed by a library, shops, cafés, offices for student societies and the large entrance hall for the new EPFL.

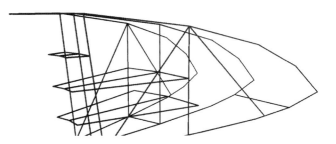

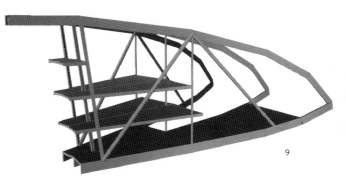

9

6 Daytime aerial view
7 Site plan
8 Aerial view at dusk
9 Structural grid
10 Night view of main elevation

10

1

Designed in 2000 for Centro Congressi Italia, the Rome Congress Centre is an award-winning project without ever being built. The design picked up a Royal Academy Summer Exhibition Gold in 2001 and a commendation in the MIPIM Future Project Awards in 2003.

This elegant design for a congress centre is, according to the architect, the result of a 'distillation of primary activity areas to define the constituent parts of the building – in particular private and public spaces'. Placing a large exhibition and conference space within an urban setting is a complex challenge: a key aspiration of the project was to avoid the pedestrian barriers and inactive frontages that can typically define the public realm.

The building was to be sited in the EUR district of Rome, which was developed during the Fascist era as an extension of the capital in a style reflecting the classical and rationalist tendencies of the period. The design placed the new complex, with its conference halls and retail, restaurant, administrative and other support spaces, beneath a great over-sailing roof, formed as a shallow vault and structurally free of supporting columns. This dramatic canopy provides a distinctive visual foil, connecting the terraced public piazza, congress square, auditorium and retail facilities, with a large multi-purpose hall placed on top.

ROME CONGRESS CENTRE, ITALY
ROGERS STIRK HARBOUR & PARTNERS

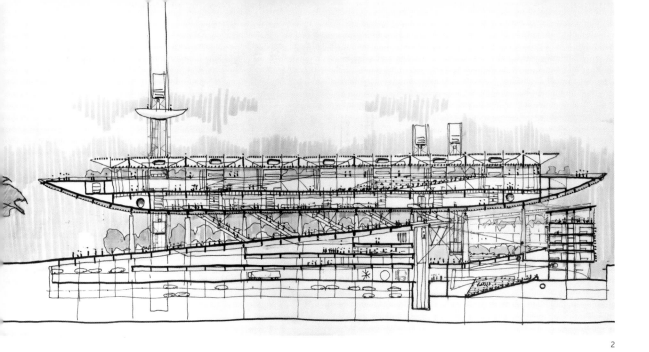

2

3

1   Concept sketch
2   Long section
    sketch
3   Section in context
4   Internal
    illustration

4

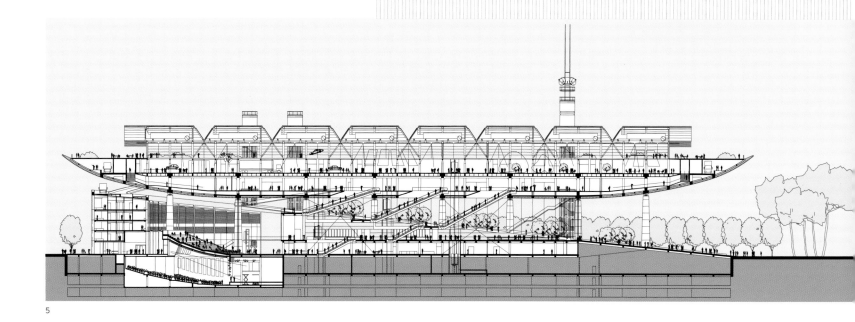

5

Sophisticated services exploit the thermal mass of the concrete underbelly as a climate moderator, optimizing the use of natural light and ventilation, while photovoltaic cells provide power.

The inclined area around the building provides generous public space, partly enclosed, partly open-air, animated by escalators and wall-climber lifts serving the conference halls above and the restaurants and retail arcades beneath.

The design was never built, as with all others in this book. However, its design aspirations can be appreciated in Rogers Stirk Harbour's completed National Assembly for Wales, which bears a striking resemblance and must be assumed to be a progression of the Rome design.

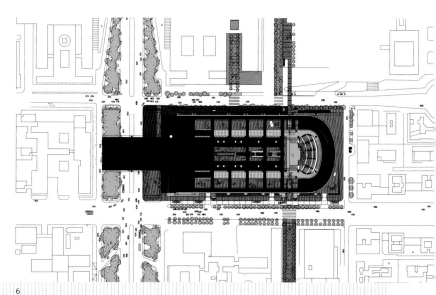

6

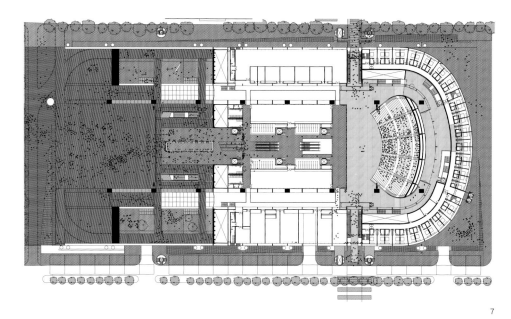

7

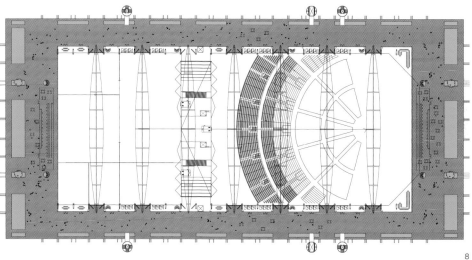

8

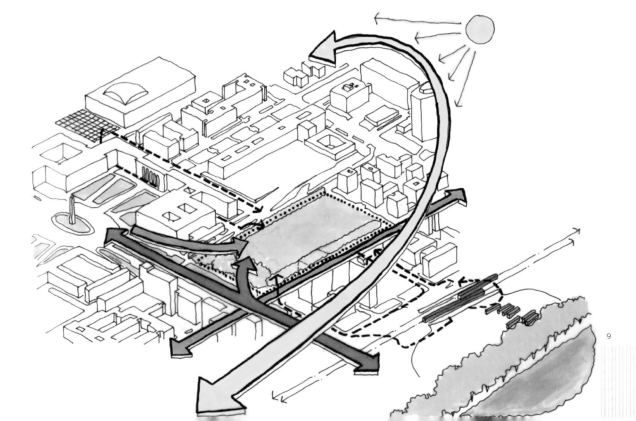

5 Longitudinal
   section
6 Ground level plan
7 First floor plan
8 Roof level
9 Ingress / solar
   path diagram

9

339

ROYAL COLLEGE OF ART BATTERSEA CAMPUS, UK
FEILDEN CLEGG BRADLEY

1

Feilden Clegg Bradley's (FCB) design for a campus for the Royal College of Art, east of Battersea Park in London, brings together sculpture with fine and applied arts in a project proposal that has a strong identity – a 'factory for the arts' as a destination in its own right.

FCB's solution perceives the scheme as a grid of space with a series of linear buildings weaving across the site: the warp and weft creates a lattice, introducing daylight into the building at many points. This idea creates a building that can accommodate the changing identity of its inhabitants, blurring separate distinctions for maximum flexibility, with an emphasis on horizontal and vertical connectivity, with external terraces on every level.

The architect's approach considers the quality of natural light as fundamental to the project. It proposed a roof allowing north light to penetrate the building in a straightforward and economic way: internally the configuration compliments this, so natural light can penetrate deep into the spaces on all levels. To achieve this, FCB suggests 'over-layering', allowing for many configurations of different-height volumes with differing daylight requirements within one overall form.

The building is low carbon with a zero carbon future, maximizing natural lighting (roof lights are twice as 'useful' as windows for day lighting buildings), natural ventilation and high levels of thermal mass. If the scheme had gone further, investigations for bore hole water would have

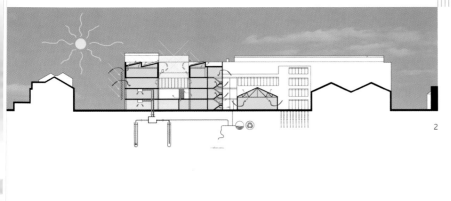

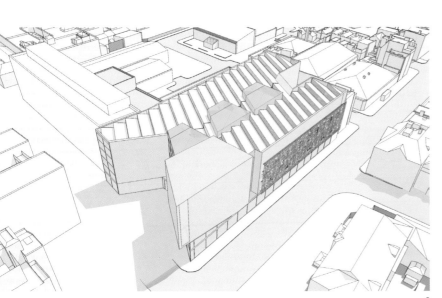

AMBIGUITY : POSITIVE VOID SPACE.

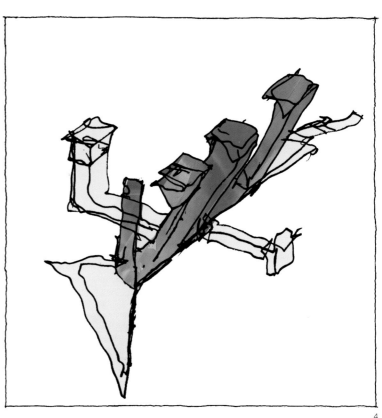

1 Evening
   perspective
2 Environmental
   diagram
3 Aerial view
   showing
   central atriums
4 Spatial
   representation
   of atriums and
   circulation

been carried out, while combined heat and power and the installation of a modular power plant / energy centre were slated to service the entire building.

The design envisages modifying the existing shed space with a lightness of touch which allows it to retain its character. Materials used are robust and low maintenance – in-situ concrete, used both externally and internally, has a valuable reflectivity and neutrality. FCB has developed processes to minimize the cement content of concrete, maintaining its positive attributes while minimizing CO_2 emissions.

The scheme provides a net floor area of up to 7,000 m^2 (75,350 ft^2). FCB introduces retail outlets on the ground floor, in addition to light industrial workshops, galleries, performance spaces, bars and a café.

1

WÜRTH CULTURE AND CONGRESS CENTRE, GERMANY
J. MAYER H. ARCHITECTS

Designed for an international competition in 2006, J. Mayer H. Architects' Würth Culture and Congress Centre in Künzelsau, Germany, is an exciting structure derived as much from the contours of its surroundings as any learned architectural style. The building is an uneven ripple, or wrinkle, in the earth's surface, pushing up to create spaces without rectilinear bearings.

Client Adolf Würth GmbH & Co.'s brief for the competition was to transform an existing manufacturing site into a lively, pivotal centre for arts that would have charisma and destination appeal. The architect's stand-alone building comprises four separate wings joined by a main internal space at the centre. It is situated on the highest point of the site, 'growing out of the landscape' and commanding unparalleled views over the surrounding countryside.

The building was to be used year round by a variety of artists, and as such the design is suitably loose, comprising a mixed-use composition of performance spaces, museum, conference facilities, library and hospitality areas. The free, open nature of the ground floor and the central part of the building is reflected in the façades, which start out transparent and become increasingly opaque as they climb upwards.

The flowing forms of the external aesthetic are continued internally: the curved surfaces that comprise the volume create a dynamic tension within the body of the building, while simultaneously framing the exterior. And this framing sets off the view out into the landscape that is very important to Mayer. He states that the building is grounded within the site by its fluid connection to the landscape, creating a venue where landscape and architecture can unite; something that so often building designs lack.

1   Ground floor plan
2   Site model

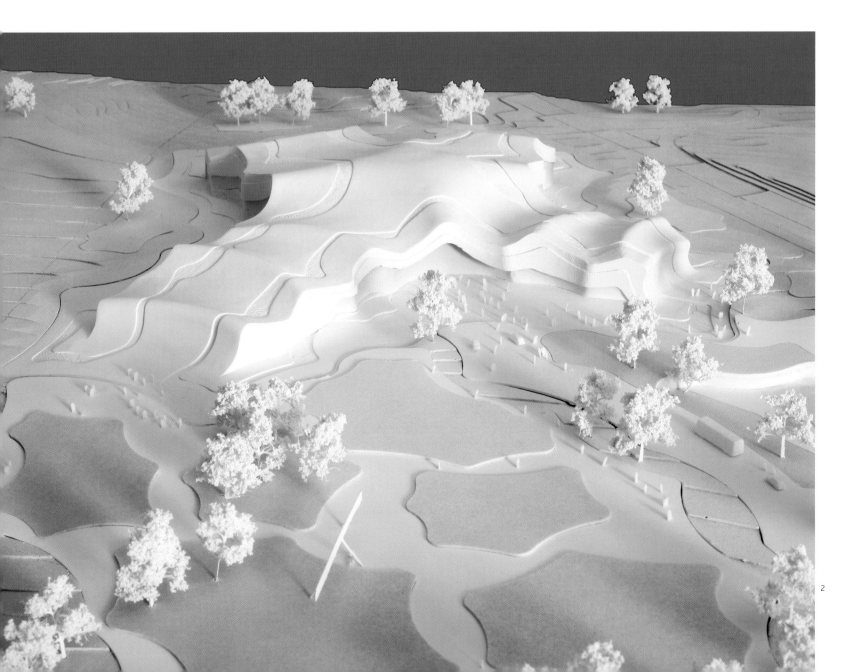

2

3

4

5

6

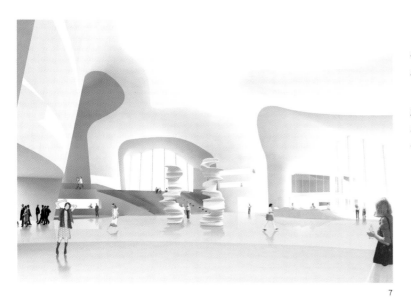

7

At a more pragmatic level, internal visitor circulation revolves around the central space, while staff and delivery entrances are easily accessible due to the radial nature of the building's design.

During the day, the building seeks to blend with its landscaped garden surrounds. At night, all this changes and instead of becoming a dark bulk, the building is lit from within, its opaque façades glowing with what the architect describes as a 'festive elegance'.

8

9

7.
WORK AND TRAVEL

Buildings that are designed for work and travel may appear to represent two entirely disparate architectural sectors. However, without highlighting the obvious – that many people are employed within the buildings that we associate with travel, and that their working lives are undoubtedly affected by the quality of those buildings – there are numerous other similarities between these building types and their histories.

In the first instance, the places in which we work and the ones we travel to and from can both be viewed as giant machines. The former is a facilitator for human action, a processor of our endeavours. The reason for which many people are employed is to make some contribution – of labour, sales, units, experience or some other quantifiable asset – before they 'clock off', often with a sigh of relief, but not so often thinking about how this input is being developed, advanced by the work machine.

The latter is more literal. A transport building, no matter what type, is designed as a human conveyor belt. Just as our bags are checked in, labelled and sent scuttling into the bowels of the airport, before almost always magically appearing on a similar conveyor at our destination, so we are processed, fed, watered and spat into an aeroplane; or refreshed, refuelled and poured back onto the motorway; sold tickets, coffee and newspapers and sent running to our seats in a train.

These functional requirements dominate the design philosophy of both building types. They inform the very shape and aesthetic of the building and chasten the designer with their rigidity, because everything must conform to rational ideals, must be logical and easily read by all. As a consequence, for many years the buildings in which many of us work were almost uniformly designed with little or no regard for architectural joy. From the industrial-age workhouse to the 1970s city centre office block, these environments have been monumentally grim. All that has altered is the freedom with which employees are allowed to leave their workstations to relieve themselves.

Conversely, transport buildings did for a long time have a romance or glamour about them, from the original Roman roadside inn, where horses were rested and men fed and watered, to Victorian-age railway stations. And from there to early airports, among the most evocative of which were Eero Saarinen's terminals at New York's Idlewild Airport (what is now JFK) and Washington Dulles International – buildings which oozed with the excitement of flight, mimicking the shape of plane wings and enchanting those lucky enough to be able to pass through them.

However, as flight and other forms of transport became more accessible to the common man, larger, more utilitarian buildings sprang up to keep pace with the demand. The airport, that symbol of the romance of travel, was forced to conform to a need for maximum throughfare, and its curves and lines were forsaken for check-in desk space and departure hall square coverage. The transport building, be it airport, rail station or motorway service station, was relegated in architectural terms to the level of functional shed.

This lack of architectural empathy has continued until very recently in both work and transport buildings. The only striking office building was a very tall one, while all that could be said for transport hubs was that they got better at becoming retailers of mediocre food and unnecessary consumer goods. However, exceptions existed and innovations were explored. In New York, the fifty-nine floor Citigroup Center on the corner of 53rd and Lexington in 1977 was one, if not the first, to feature a tuned mass damper at its top to counteract sway in excessive winds in 1977. This didn't enhance its looks, but it did advance high-rise architecture greatly. More recently, 30 St Mary Axe in London – the 'Gherkin' to friends – made architects stand back and reappraise office tower form and function, with its aerodynamic, sustainable design.

Meanwhile, travellers have witnessed a resurgence in good transport architecture, most notably in airports. Beijing now has one of the most elegant airports in the world, thanks to Foster & Partners and the incentive of hosting the 2008 Olympic Games. Madrid's new Barajas Airport terminal by Rogers Stirk Harbour & Partners opened in 2007 with a blaze of colour – a Rogers trademark – to rave reviews from architectural commentators and travellers alike. Meanwhile, the much maligned Heathrow Terminal Five is still a dramatic design statement, even if the practicalities of launching its network of commercial flights proved initially troublesome.

But these new design icons for both travel and the workplace have not happened thanks to mega-rich benefactors or design hungry clients. They are being created to meet new and differing demands within each sector. Transport and work buildings still have to perform well first; then, if that performance equates to a striking looking piece of architecture, there is a bonus for all to be had. The architect's task is a multi-faceted one, but if undertaken with inspiration and vigour the outcome can be spectacular, while still offering the performance demanded in these most prosaic of sectors.

AL RAJHI BANK HEADQUARTERS, SAUDI ARABIA
SKIDMORE, OWINGS & MERRILL

1

Commissioned by Al Rajhi bank to design its new headquarters in Riyadh, Saudi Arabia, Skidmore, Owings & Merrill (SOM) proposed a complex that is simultaneously monumental to reflect the stature of the bank, symbolic and respectful of Islamic culture, and sensitive to the surrounding desert site conditions.

The complex focuses on an iconic tower that rises from a water courtyard and is surrounded by land forms and pavilions. Limited to thirty floors by Riyadh's zoning regulation, this central tower breaks from traditional high-rise building techniques by integrating references to Islamic culture into its structure. The base of the tower's structure is four external columns that suspend each interior level within them. This square-based design reflects the square courtyards of Islamic cosmology as paradises that are marked by *iwans*, or symbolic gateways.

1   Banking floors
    between the
    great pillars
2   View up from
    the tower base

2

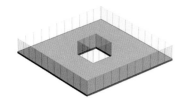

3

4

These columns are reminiscent of ancient Middle Eastern monuments and are used to suggest the importance of the bank. Their fair-faced, concrete construction allows the tower to respond to the harsh desert climate by creating an internal oasis in the central space. The project includes a banking hall, a 600-seat auditorium, offices for the bank, prayer space, a cafeteria, a roof garden and an underground parking structure for 1,100 cars.

The entrance to the bank is hidden within the columns, leading to a lobby that soars 50 m (164 ft) high and suspends the mosque on the next level. Each floor's alignment rotates in a circular pattern following the contour of the columns and providing orientation appropriate for different sections of the building: the street level faces the Riyadh city grid, the Mosque level faces Mecca, and the office levels provide maximum views of the city while shading interiors from the harsh desert sunlight.

3   Services diagram
4   Concept diagram
5   Mosque
6   Tower elevation

5

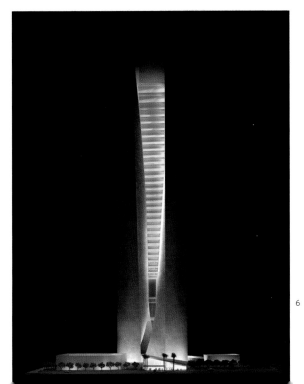

6

Al Rajhi Bank headquarters Skidmore, Owings & Merrill **357**

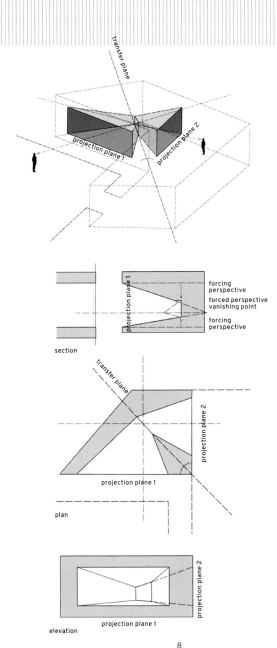

forcing
perspective

forced perspective
vanishing point

forcing
perspective

section

plan

elevation

transfer plane

projection plane 1

projection plane 2

8

9

The design carefully responds to the harsh desert environment in creative ways. First, the 'inside-out' design allows for the concrete columns to act as a barrier to the change in temperature from day to night. The columns also act as thermal storage vessels, housing built-in heat storage labyrinths which store the coolness of the desert night to reduce the intake temperature to the HVAC (heating, ventilation and air-conditioning) units.

Shading provided by the columns prevents initial sun exposure, while an intelligent façade reacts to solar movement, closing blinds automatically in response to direct sunlight and opening them when the sun moves away.

7 Periscope
  windows
8 Window diagram
9 Main lobby

5

5 Main auditorium
6 Internal work
space
7 Projecting
imagery onto
the façade

The folded loops also organize the spaces in the building. Screens are sides of the loops separating inside and outside. These opaque sides can be treated as a broadcasting device, as a piece of film capable of producing coloured, changing images.

The building's compact plan means that public areas evolve under, between and above the studio level. This produces a large open space connected to the surrounding landscape at ground level, where an art gallery, foyer for the BBC cinema, BBC shop and small café are located.

6

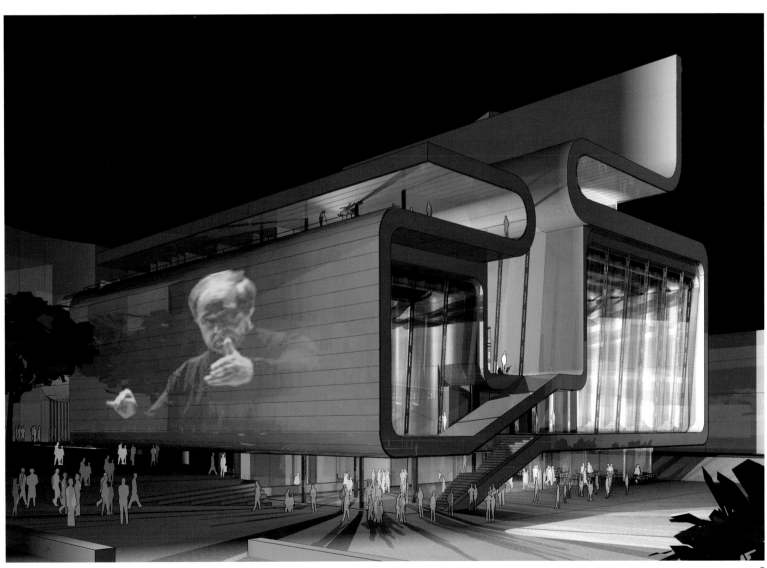

7

BMW EVENT AND DELIVERY CENTRE, GERMANY
SAUERBRUCH HUTTON

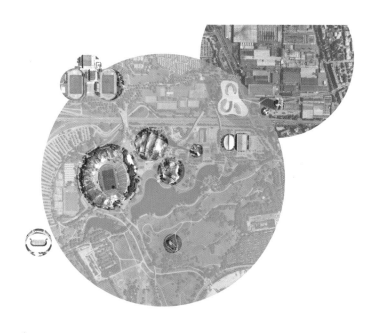

1

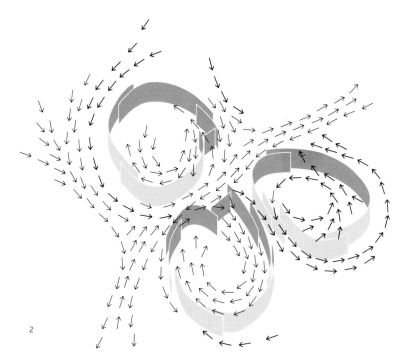

2

The BMW Event and Delivery Centre, in close proximity to the company's headquarters in Munich, was conceived as possibly one of the first 'tourist attractions' for the car-buying public. This may seem preposterous to some, but only recently the Mercedes Benz Museum, designed by UN Studio, has been completed and opened in Stuttgart.

BMW envisaged the centre as an exciting arena to display their cars to customers from around the world who wish to collect their vehicle in person. Architect Sauerbruch Hutton describes the scheme as a 'new stage for BMW', which is interpreted as a public place in Munich's Olympic Park.

Housed beneath a single organically shaped roof, the 53,800 m² (579,000 ft²) complex includes three separate glazed halls. Each is designed for a specific activity event, exhibition or performance. These three volumes are located in landscaped park-like surroundings, which flow seamlessly around the centre, under the roof canopy and between the halls.

Particular effort has been made to give the buildings a degree of permeability and perceived accessibility, via fully glazed façades and open plan spaces. The organic form of the three volumes is informed by the various streams of pedestrian movement across the site. The meandering routes of people strolling across the park, not visiting BMW, have been taken into account, and overlapped by those of the centre's visitors.

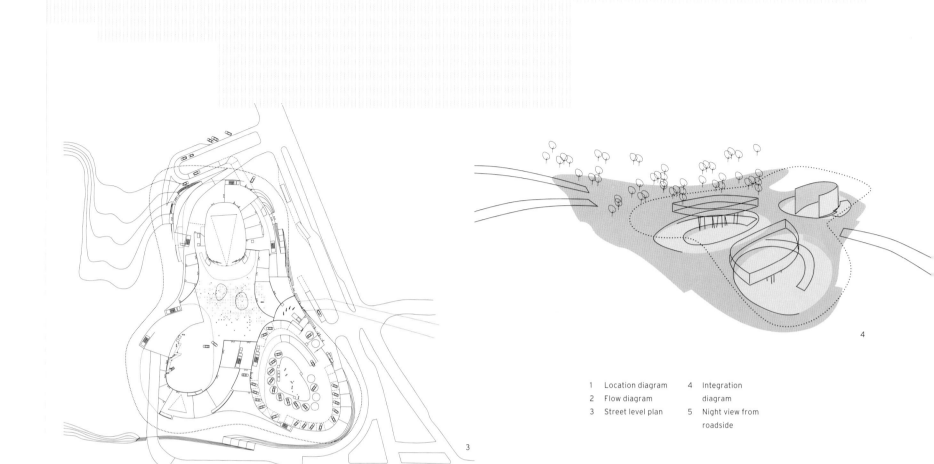

1 Location diagram
2 Flow diagram
3 Street level plan

4 Integration
   diagram
5 Night view from
   roadside

COLLINS PLACE, AUSTRALIA
WOODS BAGOT

Woods Bagot's principle objective for the design of Collins Place, Brisbane, Australia, is to 'bring together a diversity of commercial functions into one precinct linking existing infrastructure and public amenities and creating a vitality within the new public realm'.

The scheme includes a 'gateway' or 'marker' tower that defines the Grey Street multi-rise zone and a second medium rise block, between which is a new public space that is home to Collins Place Heritage Building, which has stood on the site since 1890. These pivotal elements are supplemented by a new civic space, retail outlets over two levels, commercial office space with bridge links, residential apartments, student housing and a new subway link, station ticketing and support infrastructure.

The architect's concept links both bus and rail transport to the centre of the site and creates a public gathering space around the historic brick Heritage Building. This central space provides an environmentally controlled environment. Landscaping elements such as trees and water temper the atmosphere and canopies provide filtered sunlight and protection from rain. Woods Bagot describes the area as 'a social "heart" and an environmental "lung" to the development'.

Architecturally, the design brings an international built form to the Brisbane skyline. Its overall appearance is textural and filigree through a plethora of external louvres that provide environmental comfort. Beyond the external skin various pockets of activities are visible – balconies to the residential elements and ventilated gardens to the commercial elements.

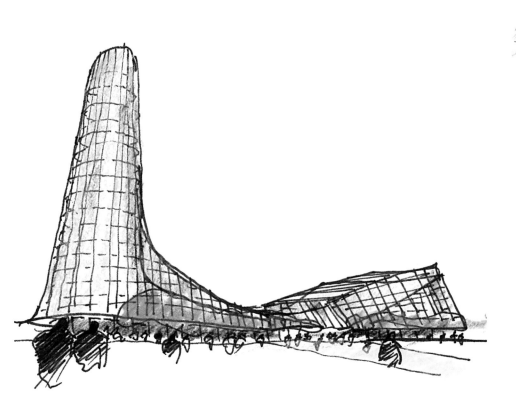

2

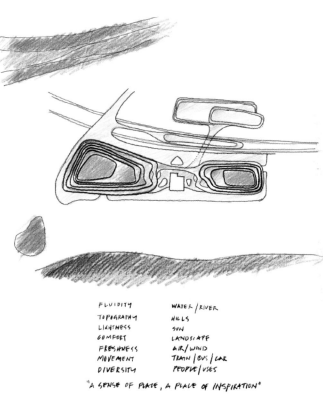

3

1   Aerial view
2   Concept sketch
3   Plan sketch

The prominent location of the site prompted the architect to propose a design of significant stature, something that created a new presence on the Brisbane skyline. However, this was not out of keeping with the city's built works. The massing of the proposal aligns itself with the constant height along Grey Street, growing into a taller component towards Vulture Street, providing a logical 'book end' and giving the site a gateway and macro identity.

4

4   View from tower
5   Tower in context
6   Tower from river
    crossing
7   Tower from
    Vulture Street

5

6

7

Collins Place Woods Bagot **371**

ELIZABETH HOUSE, UK
MAKE

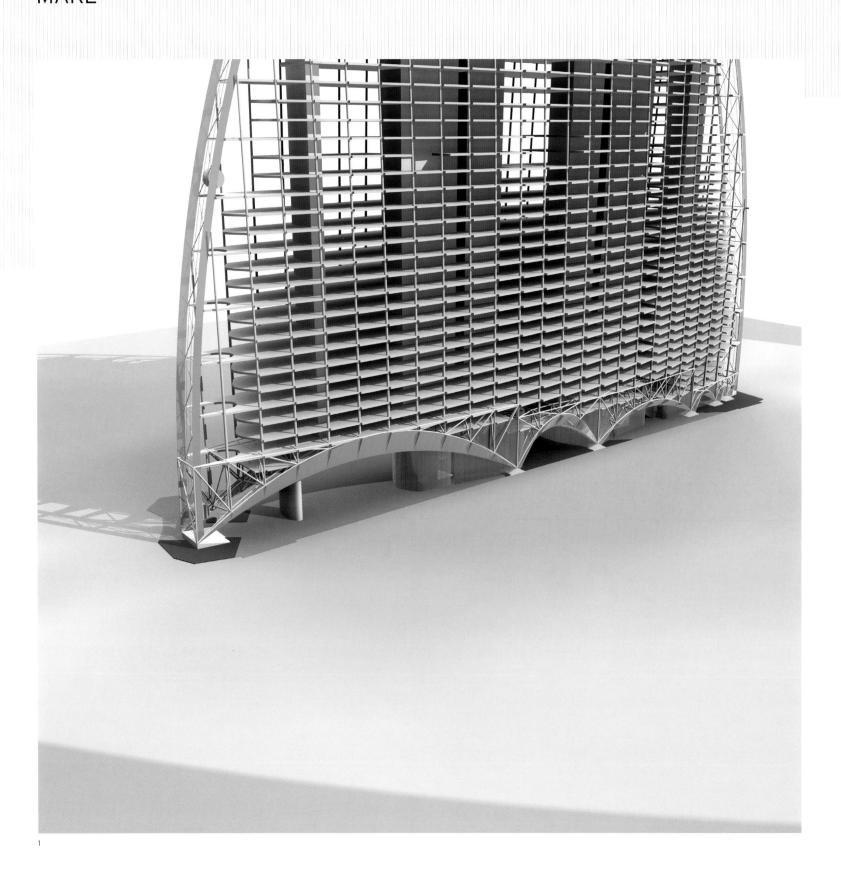

This shortlisted competition scheme for the Elizabeth House site near Waterloo, south London, proposes a mixed-use development in the form of a squat yet striking addition to the cityscape along the banks of the river Thames.

The forty-six storey building offers 159,800 m² (1.7 million ft²) of office and residential accommodation, with retail outlets located at street level. Derived from the geometric form of the torus, the profile of the building traces the curves of the river onto London's skyline. The profile also echoes the silhouette of the London Eye and provides a suitably graceful counterpoint to the vertical towers that are currently springing up along both banks of the Thames.

The arch form is as stable and efficient as it is unusual, and this innovative scheme is achieved using conventional and highly efficient construction systems. The building is elliptical in plan, tapering at either tip and measuring 31 m (102 ft) at its widest, central point. Within the structure's smooth external envelope, floors are stacked like a ziggurat to maximize daylight penetration and cross-ventilation.

A series of public gardens occupy the projecting tips of the floor plates, rising up the outer edge of the structure to offer spectacular views out across the city. The building is also designed to meet exacting standards of energy efficiency, and it incorporates three wind turbines at its apex to supplement conventional energy supplies.

2

1   Tower structure
2   Concept sketch
3   End elevation

3

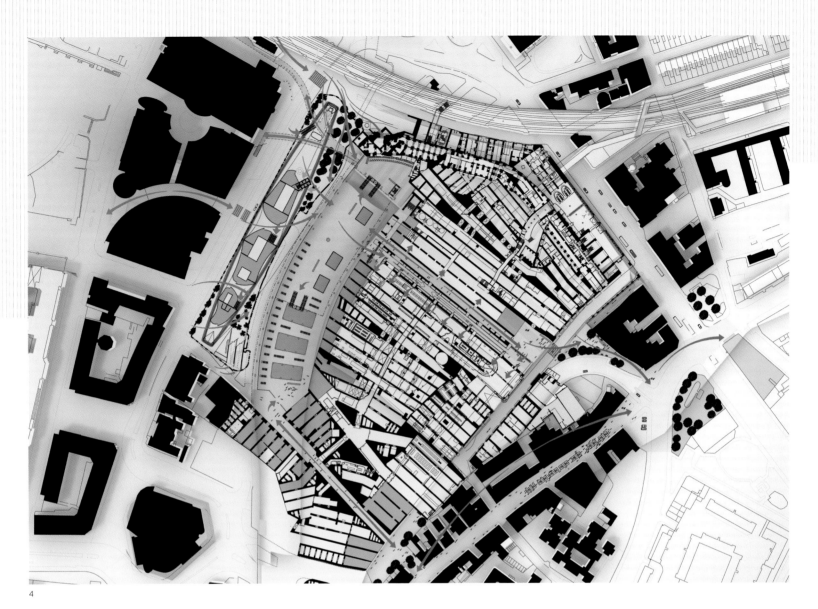

4

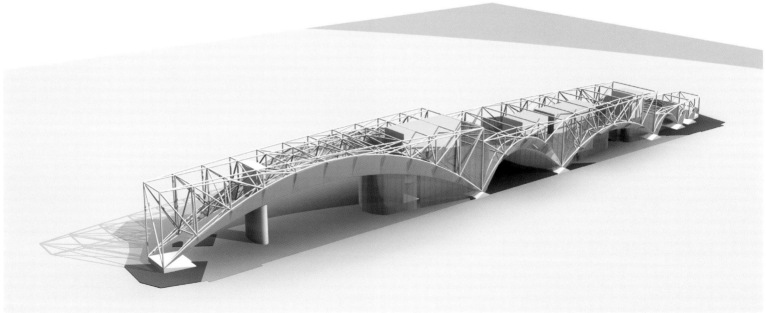

5

Lying immediately above the dense network of London Underground tunnels leading to Waterloo, the site posed significant building constraints. The arch form plays a key role in distributing loads to those areas where the ground is capable of accommodating them. In addition, the lower levels of the structure are asymmetrically modelled to assist the transfer of loads while ensuring that the building sits lightly and sensitively within its context.

The scheme also incorporates considerable improvements to the public realm at street level. Roads are rationalized and re-routed around the site to create a pedestrian oasis, and the whole development creates a new gateway to Waterloo station.

4   Site plan
5   Structural
    supports
6   Cross section

6

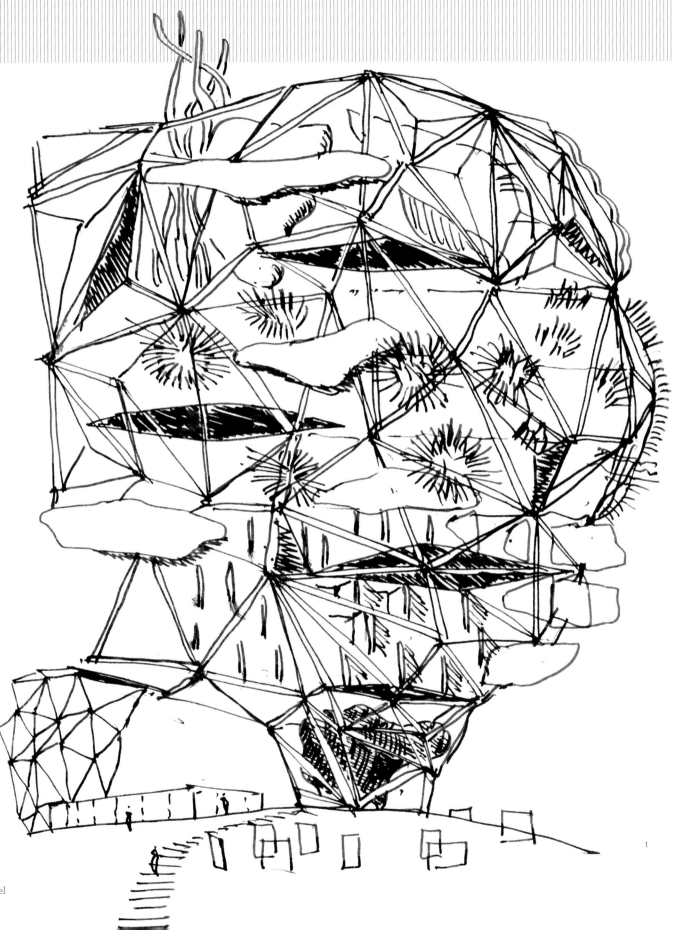

2

1   Concept sketch
2   Concept model

A consortium led by Alsop Architects won a competition to design the Fourth Grace, a new landmark development for the waterfront in Liverpool, UK. The Alsop consortium beat off stiff competition from teams led by Norman Foster, Richard Rogers and Edward Cullinan.

The Fourth Grace is intended to create a 21st-century icon for Liverpool with a series of spectacular new buildings that threaded along an illuminated waterfront. Comprising a mix of exhibition, retail, residential, community and commercial space, the proposal sits alongside the Three Graces, a trio of now famous buildings built one hundred years ago.

The project looks extremely challenging, but stripped down to its component parts the Fourth Grace is deceptively simple and, according to the architect, 'totally practical, using tried and tested financial and structural solutions'. Three main structures, the Hill, the Cloud and the Living, integrate with new pedestrian walkways, enlivened by new public spaces connected back to the city.

The Hill is a landscape from which to view the river, a permanent exhibition space, a 500-seat auditorium, a multi-purpose venue, plus shops, bars and restaurants. The Cloud – the central icon of Fourth Grace – is decorated with representations of Liverpool's eight hundred years of history. Visually changing as you move around it, the building features three nebulous rings of accommodation stacked on top of each other. Ten floors give the impression of constant rotation; while a circling route takes visitors from the heart of the hill to the top of the Cloud, to the public viewing gallery. The Living is a bold residential building with sky-high apartments, combined with retail and restaurants at lower levels.

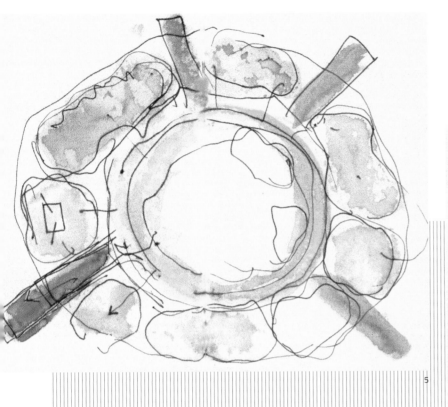

5

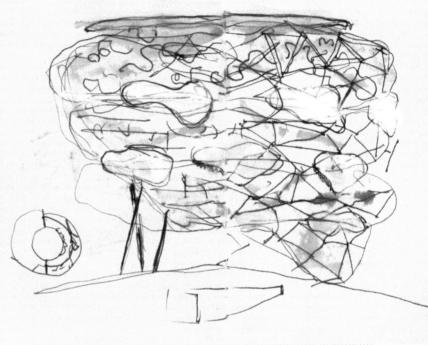

6

7

3 Perspective from
   pier head
4 Section through
   site
5 Cloud plan
   concept
6 Cloud elevation
   concept
7 Visitor pavilion
   during
   construction

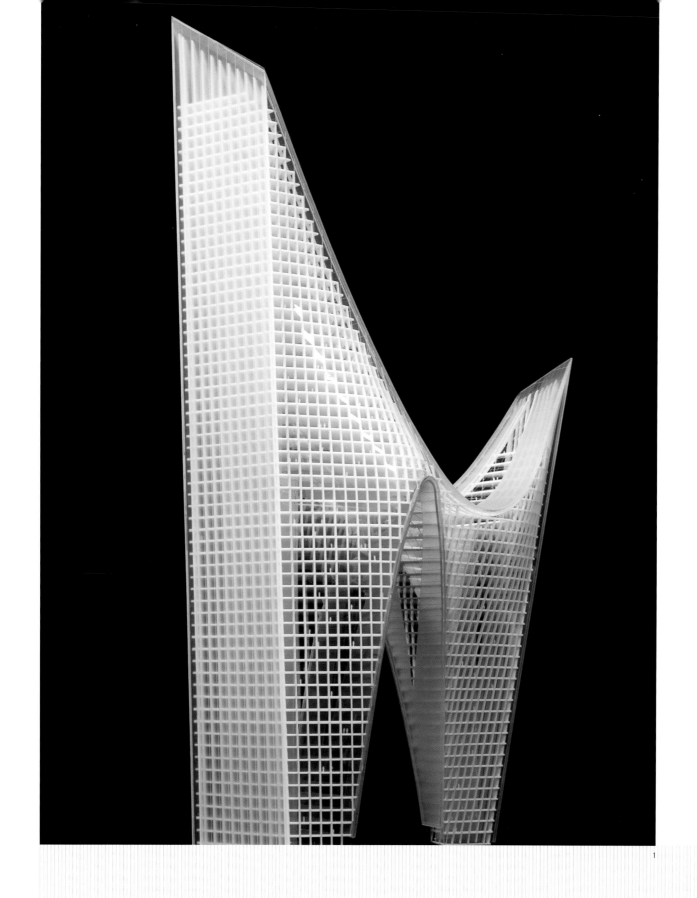

GAZPROM HEADQUARTERS, RUSSIA

STUDIO DANIEL LIBESKIND

1   Tower model
2   Elevation
3   Supporting 'leg'

St Petersburg is a city of elegant spires. When Libeskind conceived a design for the Gazprom competition, he thought of what he could do to complement those spires. 'What building could arise that would contribute to the skyline and urban fabric of the city?,' he asked. 'Should another spire dot the horizon and imprint a massive footprint and base upon the city?' Libeskind decided not, and embarked on another architectural approach – a building as an arch or gateway and symbol for St Petersburg.

The resulting design distributes the building mass within two small towers, with a huge public park in between. The main entrance is at the centre of the building, where users are able to access the two cores to the north and south. These two independent building wings emerge from the ground and come together in the sky, arching across the site, north–south, at the sky lobby where common functions such as restaurants, cafés, conferencing centre and library are located.

Above, a second arch in the sky splits the form again where the two wings re-emerge as independent structures. The south tower is topped with an observation deck offering unprecedented vistas of greater St Petersburg. The north tower continues to provide additional office space for the upper management and executive offices. At its apex, overseeing the Gazprom complex and the city as a whole, is the executive boardroom.

Internally, at the mid sections of the building where the floor plates are deeper, a large atrium space is carved out. The atrium gives the internal office space the character of a courtyard building, creating a unique atmosphere for the occupants while bringing natural light into the centre. This light-filled space runs through the body of the building, connecting several floors via communicating stairs and sky bridges.

4

4   Tower at night
5   Long section
6   Land use plan

For a new building of this scale, which is the headquarters of an energy company, responsible use of natural resources is paramount. The project minimizes land use and maximizes green space around it. Energy is generated in the most efficient way – on-site at a co-generation plant, which makes use of the heat that is generated in the process of producing electricity. High performance glazing saves energy for heating in winter and for cooling in summer, while daylight use and natural ventilation are also optimized.

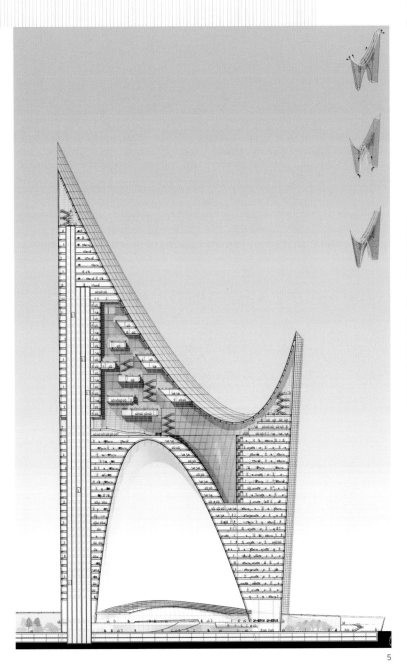

5

6

HALLEY VI RESEARCH STATION, ANTARCTICA
MAKE

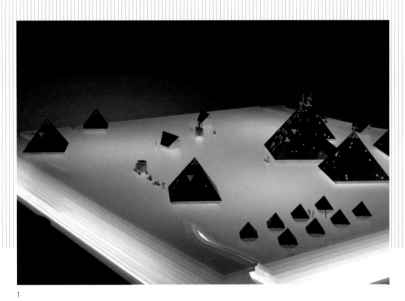

1

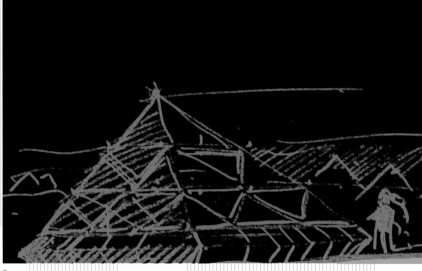

2

3

One of the designs shortlisted in the competition for a new research station for the British Antarctic Survey, this project addresses the exceptional technical challenges of designing for the harshest of climates.

The structure, designed by Make, consists of a village of lightweight pyramids, each of which deploys hover-barge technology in order to be fully mobile. So, as the ice shelf moves slowly towards the Antarctic Ocean and eventually crumbles into the sea, the research station is able to simply move itself to a safer location.

Drawing inspiration from the strategies adopted by communities reliant on a nomadic existence in harsh climates, the research station relies on an efficient use of materials and the lightest possible structural form. The pyramid offers a structurally efficient and stable form with a surface-to-volume ratio that assists insulation and a low aerodynamic profile that minimizes snow build up. The form also recalls the traditional polar tent which is still in use today.

Laboratory spaces and private living areas are distributed in ancillary pyramids, with the central structure forming the hub of the community and functioning as an emblem of the British Antarctic Survey's presence on the continent. In addition to communal facilities such as dining and kitchen areas, the main pyramid contains a hydroponic garden as the focal point of the internal space. Protected from

the midnight sun by a light filtering system, this garden provides fresh fruit or vegetables for the station's occupants. It creates humidity, which improves air quality and introduces a welcome diurnal cycle to the twenty-four hour day or night of the Antarctic summer and winter.

The hydroponic garden at the heart of the scheme also serves as a grey water filtration and recycling system, which assists the station in achieving a fifty per cent reduction in water consumption. An array of wind turbines enables the station to generate its own electricity, while natural ventilation is used as much as possible throughout.

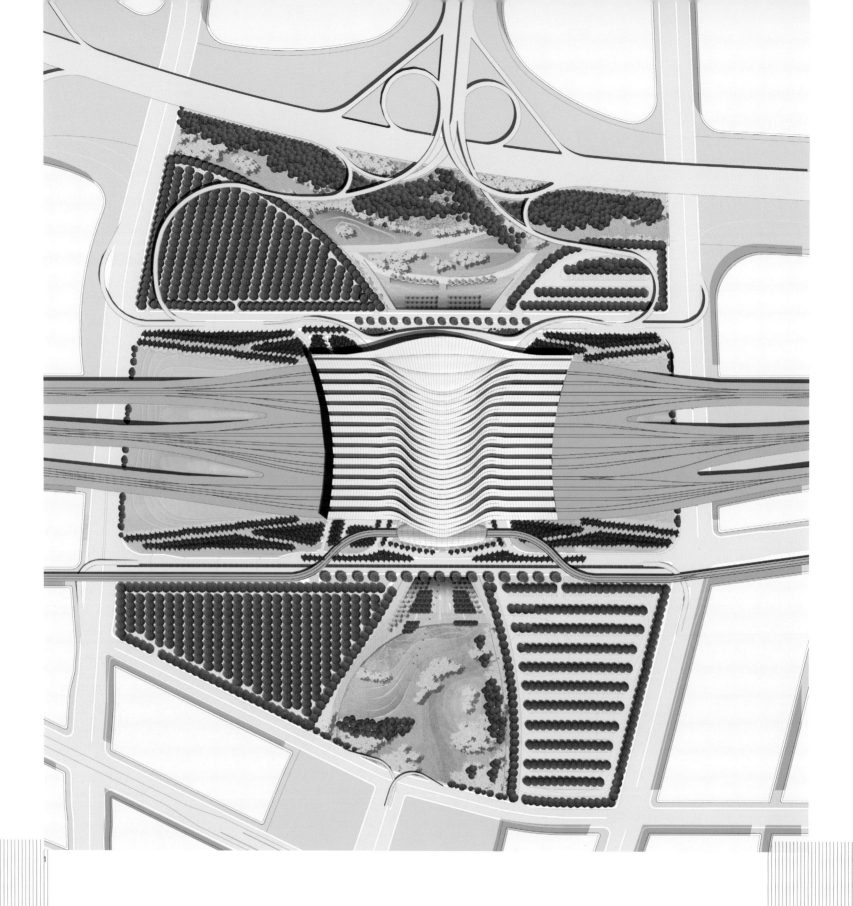

NANJING SOUTH RAIL STATION, CHINA

KOHN PEDERSEN FOX

A competition finalist for the new rail station in Nanjing, China, Kohn Pedersen Fox's (KPF) design is but one of many parts of a major expansion of China's high-speed and regular service train lines: a massive undertaking, which mimics the explosion of development throughout the country.

The new 93,339 m² (over 1 million ft²) station, designed for the Ministry of Railroads, is sited in a slight valley and bisected through its centre by a 'green corridor' which connects major parks that border the rail tracks. Inside the station, the green corridor transforms into an airy intermodal hall which is open at either end and around which the arrival hall is located. On top of this vast public space run the station's platforms and departure lounges. And finally, above these elevated lounges, a large sweeping roof protects passengers from rain, sun and wind.

The roof is the main architectural statement of the station. It is the metaphorical and physical centrepiece of the project, something which the Chinese insist on and are ambitiously excited about on all public transport buildings. Using generative component technology, KPF's initial designs for the station's roof were tested and then manipulated for their performance and optimization of certain environmental parameters such as day lighting, wind, rainwater collection, natural ventilation and ease of construction.

By designing parametrically, within the clearly set constraints of the programme brief – set platform widths, column locations and roof coverage – the design team generated a form which was the absolute product of the technology from which it was imaged and fine-tuned. This may sound somewhat calculated and devoid of inspiration; however, the result is a rippling form that flows with the movement of the trains and presents a stunning spectacle from the air.

Through all stages of design – from the initial site analysis to the structural detailing – parametric modelling was used to help build, test and improve the design team's assumptions. This is becoming ever more common in the architectural world; and far from standardizing the project, the technique produces exciting results that may not have been formulated using traditional techniques.

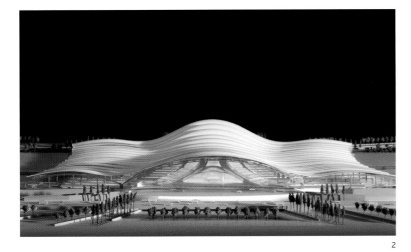

2

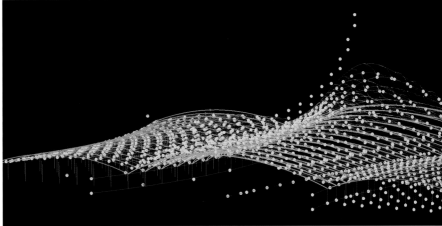

3

1   Site plan
2   Main entrance
3   Form generation
4   View from
    approach

4

5

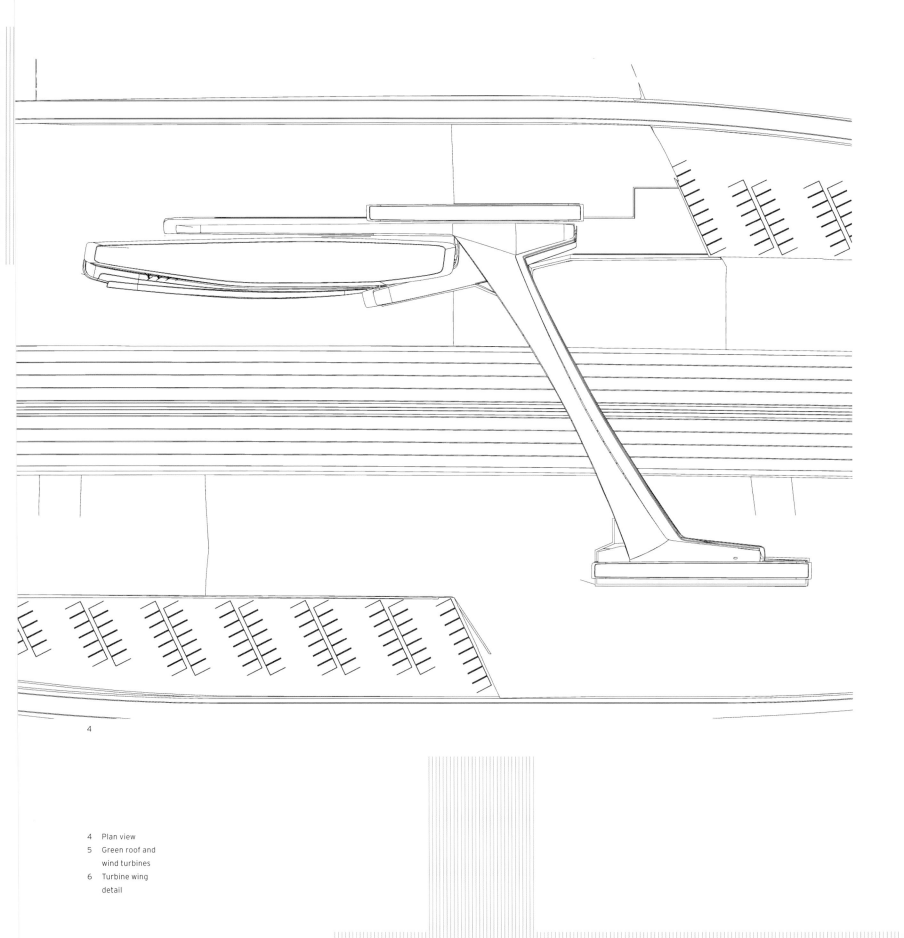

4   Plan view
5   Green roof and
     wind turbines
6   Turbine wing
     detail

5

6

The main building is set into a grass topped embankment of recycled tyres, providing thermal mass insulation. The building's shell comprises areas of transparent polycarbonate and a lightweight reinforced polymer skin over a carbon fibre frame; while the bridge is a stressed ribbon, formed by tensile cables anchored in the roadside embankments.

To limit the impact of the building on the surrounding landscape the superstructure is recessed into the roadside escarpment and roof surfaces are planted with wild grasses. The building forms an acoustic buffer between the carriageway and landscaped gardens to the rear.

Internally, multi-use cabins provide space for travellers to shower, sleep and work, while there is an open environment to eat and shop. Interior air supplemented with oxygen, the byproduct of the hydrogen processing, creates a relaxing and yet reinvigorating atmosphere; while running water routed from the reservoir is used in fountains and aqueducts.

Located in the City of Kelowna in British Columbia, Canada, the 19.4 ha. (48 acre) property of the new Tantalus Winery is characterized by gentle sloping vineyards divided by a steep tree-filled ravine and breathtaking views of Okanagan Lake. The design for a new estate production plant, by Bing Thom Architects, looks to these rolling hills and also to the gently rippling waters of the lake for its aesthetic inspiration.

Designed to support the owner's desire to produce exceptional wine in small volumes, the facility will house a gravity flow system of winemaking, a tasting bar, an event room and an art gallery that doubles as an educational and recreational resource for the public. It is part of a new generation of winery that realizes the importance of attracting visitors and providing extra revenue streams as part of a fully rounded business strategy.

Prominent in this plan is the creation of a visually striking building that will interest in its own right. The client requested a building that created a visual icon, or a contemporary architectural statement, of timeless quality, in keeping with its goal of producing high-quality wines.

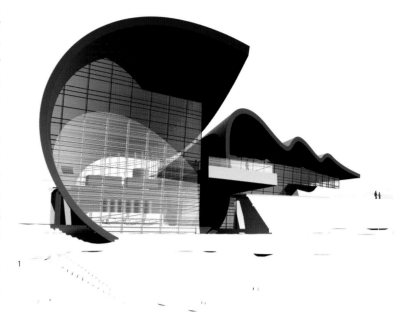

1

2

TANTALUS WINERY, CANADA
BING THOM ARCHITECTS

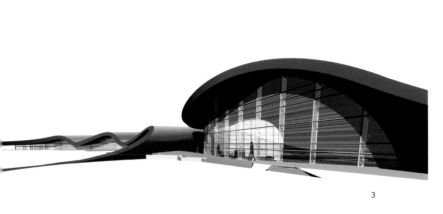

Unravelling gracefully to become the roof of the wine-tasting room and art gallery, the sculptural gesture of Bing Thom's barrel-like form engages the public with the rolling vineyards and lake beyond. The passages through the winery have been very carefully choreographed so that the visitor becomes engaged in the wine-making process through a series of carefully crafted and sequenced views of the vineyard, wine-making, storage and tasting facilities.

The initial roll in this wave-like structure and largest element of the building houses the main production facility, where the wine is processed and stored in giant stainless-steel vats. Below ground are controlled temperature storage areas, while above the visitor spaces feature large glazed façades that look out over the vineyards.

The design is adventurous and exciting, similar in intent to built projects by Santiago Calatrava in Spain and Frank Gehry in California. Where once wine production was a closed, almost secretive occupation, now visitor centres are a must, and spectacular buildings set within idyllic surroundings are ever more common.

3

1   End elevation
2   Aerial
     perspective
3   Main viewing deck
4   Transparent
     perspective

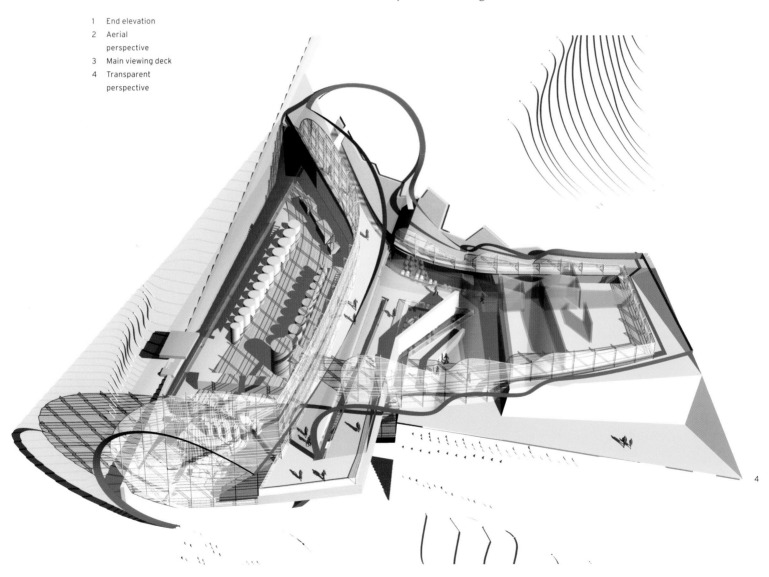

4

PROJECT CREDITS

1. ARTS AND ENTERTAINMENT

Arabian Performance Venue
Aedas

Birnbeck Island
Matteo Cainer at Fletcher Priest Architects:
Architect - Matteo Cainer
Architectural assistants - Avigael Perez,
Sergey Kudryashev

Ciudad del Motor
UN Studio:
Ben van Berkel, Tobias Wallisser with René
Wysk, Hamit Kaplan and Moritz Reichartz,
Elena Machin, Diogo Aguiar, Marc Herschel,
Timothy Mitanidis, Adolfo Nadal, Sebastian
Schott, Altan Arslanoglu

Crystal Palace
Wilkinson Eyre Architects

Musik Theater
Odile Decq Benoît Cornette Architectes
Urbanistes - Thomas Series

National Portrait Gallery
Sean Godsell Architects in association
with Peddle Thorp Architects

New Orleans Jazz Center and Park
Morphosis Architects:
Project manager - Tim Christ
Project designer - Andrew Batay-Csorba
Project team - Hunter Knight, Aleksander
Tamm-Seitz, Go-Woon Seo
Model production - Patrick Dunn-Baker
with Brock Hinze, Joe Justice, Duly Lee,
Hugo Martinez, Barbra Moss, Greg Neudorf,
Ben Smith
Structural engineer - Thornton Tomasetti
Group
Theatre consultant - Auerbach Pollack
Friedlander
Cost estimator - Davis Langdon

Performing Arts Centre
Ateliers Jean Nouvel

Qintai Art and Cultural Centre
Arup Associates

Sarajevo National Concert Hall
Urban Future Organization

Senscity Paradise Universe
Client - WCP Group
Architect and general planner - Behnisch
Architekten
Environmental consultancy - Transsolar Klima
Engineering

Sherwood Forest Visitors' Centre
Make

Stonehenge Visitors' Centre
Denton Corker Marshall

Taichung Metropolitan Opera House
Zaha Hadid Architects:
Design - Zaha Hadid and Patrik Schumacher
Project leader - Dillon Lin
Project team - Yiching Liu, Christine Chow,
Ceyhun Baskin, Inanc Eray, Lourdes Sanchez,
Jens Borstelmann, Patrik McClellan, Komal
Talreja
Structural engineering - Adams Kara Taylor
M&E Engineering - Max Fordham LLP
Acoustic consultants - Marshall Day
Acoustics
Cost estimation - IDOM UK
Presentation model - A-Models

2. ACCOMMODATION

Battersea West Hotel
Arup Associates

Bluewater
Taylor Smyth Architects:
Partner-in-charge - Michael Taylor Support
Partner - Robert Smyth
Project team - Aaron Finbow, Greg Adams,
Mike Lafreniere, Deny Faunt, Sandra Erazo
Jara, Sean Maclean

Doha Villa
Ushida Findlay

Factory 798
Bernard Tschumi Architects

Freight Ship Conversion
Ivan Kroupa Architects

Hotel Pushkin
Jan Störmer & Partners GMBH

House in the Andes
Chetwoods Architects

Maison d'Algerie
Estudio Carme Pinós

Moscow Avant Garde
(EEA) Erick van Egeraat Associated Architects

Pizota Hotel
Estudio Carme Pinós

Prince Mansour Centre
Friis & Moltke Danish Architects

Sentosa Island
Tange Associates

Southern Sudan Palace
Jan Störmer & Partners GMBH

Urban Oasis
UN Studio:
Ben van Berkel, Caroline Bos, Astrid Piber
with Ger Gijzen, Mirko Bergmann, Sebastian
Schott and Gary Freedman, Hamit Kaplan,

Margherita del Grosso, Elena Machin,
Albert Gnodde, Colette Parras, Adolfo Nadal,
Elva Magnusdottir, Simon Kortemeier,
Altan Arslanoglu

W Hotel
Ateliers Jean Nouvel

3. MASTER PLANS

Aktau City Expansion
Koetter Kim & Associates:
Key architects - Fred Koetter, Susie Kim

Battersea Power Station
Arup AGU:
Design AGU - Cecil Balmond, Charles Walker,
Carol Patterson, Allan Bell, Francis Archer,
Daniel Bosia, Lip Chiong, Annie Chung,
Toby Clark, Jarek Kubik, Rob Liedgens,
Veronika Schmid, Elisa Simonetti

Daejeon Urban Renaissance
Moxon Architects

Heart of the Forest
Edward Cullinan Architects

Murjan City
Henning Larsen Architects

New York 2012 Olympic Village
Zaha Hadid Architects:
Architectural design - Zaha Hadid with Patrik
Schumacher
Project manager - Markus Dochantschi,
Studio MDA, NY
Project architect - Tiago Correia
Design team - Ana Cajiao, Daniel Baerlecken,
Judith Reitz, Simon Kim, Dillon Lin, Yosuke,
Hayano, Ergian Alberg, Yael Brosilovski,
Daniel Li, Yang Jing Wen, Li Zou, Laura
Aquili, Jens Borstelmann, Juan Aranguren
Urban strategy - Lawrence Barth
Landscape architecture - GrossMax
Lighting design - L'Observatoire International
Engineering - Arup (structure, infrastructure,
transportation, building services, fire,
facade, materials)
Construction Cost Planning and Management
- Davis Langdon Adamson

Sewoon District Urban Redevelopment
Koetter Kim & Associates Master Planning
& Architecture:
Key architects - Susie Kim, Fred Koetter

Shenzhen Cultural Centre
LAB Architecture Studio

West Kowloon Cultural District
Aedas and Richard Rogers Partnership

West Kowloon Culture Park
Moshe Safdie & Associates

4. MUSEUMS

Canadian Museum for Human Rights
Antoine Predock Architect PC

*Civilisation Museum of Europe and the
Mediterranean*
Tod Williams Billie Tsien Architects:
Partners - Tod Williams, Billie Tsien
Project architect - Paul Schulhof
Staff - Joe Boyette, Phil Goodfellow,
Susan Son
Associate architect - Imrey Culbert LLP
Partners - Tim Culbert, Celia Imrey
Staff - Sidney Blank, Annabel Fraser

Estonian National Museum
Gianni Botsford Architects

Eyebeam Museum of Art and Technology
Diller Scofidio + Renfro:
Principals - Elizabeth Diller, Ricardo Scofidio,
Charles Renfro
Project leaders - Deane Simpson, Dirk Hebel
Structural + MEP engineering - Ove Arup,
NY (Markus Schulte, Mahadev Ramen, Nigel
Tonks)
Animation - Matthew Johnson with dbox,
James Gibbs, Eric Schuldenfrei
Associate architects - Helfland Myerberg
Guggenheimer
Media consultants - Ben Rubin, Tom Igoe,
Joe Paradiso
Geo-technical engineering - Mueser Rutledge

Guggenheim Museum
Asymptote:
Hani Rashid + Lise Anne Couture

Guggenheim Museum
Ateliers Jean Nouvel

Liannig Collection Museum
Odile Decq Benoît Cornette Architectes
Urbanistes - Thomas Series

Moesgaard Museum
Tod Williams Billie Tsien Architects:
Partners - Tod Williams, Billie Tsien
Project architect - Paul Schulhof
Staff - Joe Boyette, Phil Goodfellow, Susan Son
Associate architect - Imrey Culbert LLP
Partners - Tim Culbert, Celia Imrey
Staff - Sidney Blank, Annabel Fraser

*Museum of Contemporary Art and a Moving Image
Centre*
Sauerbruch Hutton:
Matthias Sauerbruch, Louisa Hutton, Juan
Lucas Young
Project architect - Jan Liesegang
Project team - Lara Eichwede, Andrea
Frensch, Tom Geister, Frauke Gerstenberg,
Vera Hartmann, Sven Holzgreve, Marcus
Hsu, Mareike Lamm, Isabel von Fournier,
Andreas Weber, Marijn Bokhorst, Thomas
Bzowka, Nicolas Capillon, Daria Grouhi, Katrin
Hass, Norbert Kazmeier, Emiel Koole, Miriam
Kramp, Christian Lange, Simon Schneider,
Pieter van den Dorpe

Structure and services – Ove Arup & Partners
Landscape architect – Gustafson Porter

Museum of Contemporary Art Warsaw
White Arkitekter AB

Sheikh Zayed National Museum
Moriyama & Teshima Architects
Sheikh Zayed National Museum
Shigeru Ban Architects

Victoria & Albert Museum Extension
Studio Daniel Libeskind

World Mammoth and Permafrost Museum
Antoine Predock Architect PC

5. BRIDGES AND TOWERS

Allegro Altura Tower
Tange Associates

Crow Creek Bridge
Bing Thom Architects

Dubai Tower
Grimshaw:
Architects – Neven Sidor, Enzo Cocomero,
Kai Flender, Paul McGill, Miguel Woodhead
Structural engineer – Whitby and Bird
Services engineer – Whitby and Bird
Model – Network Modelmakers

Footbridge over the Seine
Dietmar Feichtinger Architectes

Glasgow footbridge
Lifschutz Davidson Sandilands:
Smoothe

Hyperbuilding
Office for Metropolitan Architecture:
Partner-in-charge – Rem Koolhaas
Team – Yo Yamagata, with Xavier Calderon,
Donald van Dansik, Luc Lévesque, Kohei
Kashimoto
Structure, Services – Arup

Manhal Oasis
ONL [Oosterhuis_Lenard]:
Project architect – Prof ir. Kas Oosterhuis
Design team: Kas Oosterhuis, Ilona Lénárd,
Tomasz Jaskiewicz, Gijs Joosen, Rafael
Seemann, Michael Gorzynscki, Barbara
Janssen, Rena Logara, Lidia Badarnah,
Jan Gasparik, Tomasz Sachanowicz,
Satish Kumar, Dimitar Karanikolov
General consultants – Anita Mehra
Homayoun, Amir Mehra
Engineering consultant – Arup
Hotel design consultant
– Mahmoudiehconcepts

Shanghai Center
RTKL Associates Inc

Shanghai Kiss
SMC Alsop

Tensegrity Bridge
Wilkinson Eyre Architects

The Edge
Denton Corker Marshall

The Legs
Aedas

Tour M
Skidmore, Owings & Merrill LLP

World Cultural Center
Rafael Viñoly Architects, Shigeru Ban
Architects & Dean Maltz, Frederic Schwartz
Architects, Ken Smith (Landscape Architect)
Structural engineers – ARUP, Schlaich
Bergermann und Partner
Sustainability design – Buro Happold
Retail Design Rockwell Group

World Trade Center
Foster & Partners

World Trade Center Tower 1
Foreign Office Architects:
Farshid Moussavi and Alejandro Zaera-Polo
with Daniel Lopez-Perez, Erhard An-He
Kinzelbach

6. CULTURE AND EDUCATION

Architecture Foundation
Zaha Hadid Architects:
Design – Zaha Hadid and Patrik Schumacher
Project architects – Viviana Muscettola,
Michele Pasca di Magliano
Project director – Christos Passas
Structural engineer – Adams Kara Taylor
M&E Engineer – Max Fordham
Quantity surveyor – Davis Langdon

Belazel Academy of Arts and Design
Matteo Cainer at Fletcher Priest Architects:
Architect – Matteo Cainer
Architectural assistant – Yo Murata

Bicentenary Cultural Centre
KPMB Architects

Brown University Campus
Venturi, Scott Brown & Associates Inc

*Centre for Music, Art and Design, University
of Manitoba*
Patkau Architects

Changsha Culture Park
MAD

Connecticut Center for Science and Exploration
Moshe Safdie & Associates

Dura Exemplar School
dRMM

Earth Centre EDEN
Kohn Pedersen Fox

European Solidarity Centre
Pentagram Design:
Pentagram architects – James Biber,
Principal-in-charge – Michael Zweck-Bronner,
Aleksandr Mergold, Dan Maxfield,
James Bowman

Grand Mosque of Algiers
Architecture Studio

Groninger Forum
(EEA) Erick van Egeraat Associated Architects

House of Human Rights Cultural Centre
Wilkinson Eyre Architects

*Joseph Regenstein Library Addition, University
of Chicago*
Skidmore, Owings & Merrill LLP

Konstantinovsky Congress Centre
(EEA) Erick van Egeraat Associated Architects

*Learning Centre, École Polytechnique Fédérale
de Lausanne*
Mecanoo

Rome Congress Centre
Rogers Stirk Harbour & Partners

Royal Collge of Art Battersea Campus
Feilden Clegg Bradley:
Feilden Clegg Bradley Studios,
Adams Kara Taylor

School of Design
UN Studio:
Ben van Berkel, Astrid Piber with Adolfo
Nadal, Mieneke Dijkema and Juergen Heinzel,
Hanka Drdlova, Yu-Chen Li, Margherita del
Grosso, Christian Schmit
Ronald Lu & Partners – Executive Architect
Ove Arup & Partners
Landscape consultant – EDAW

Würth Culture and Congress Centre
J. Mayer H. Architects:
Client – Adolf Würth GmbH & Co
Architect – J. Mayer H. Architects
Structural engineers – Krebs und Kiefer,
Karlsruhe
Kitchen engineers – Martin Scherer,
Darmstadt
Landscape architect – Klaus Wiederkehr,
Nürtingen
Building physics – Nek Ingenieur Gruppe
GmbH, Berlin
Museum consultant – Andres Lepik, Berlin

7. WORK AND TRAVEL

Al Rajhi Bank headquarters
Skidmore, Owings & Merrill LLP

BBC White City Music Centre
Foreign Office Architects

BMW Event and Delivery Centre
Sauerbruch Hutton:
Matthias Sauerbruch, Louisa Hutton,
Juan Lucas Young
Project architect – Tom Geister
Project team – Jennifer Hauger, Jan
Liesegang, Claus Marquart, Marc
Schwabedissen, Stefan Bömelburg,
Robert Bourke, Matthew Butcher, Katrin
Hass, Marcello Mazzei, Thomas Müller,
Annika Schulz
Structural engineering
– Ove Arup & Partners
Environmental engineering
– Ove Arup & Partners
Landscape architect – Bureau B+B

Collins Place
Woods Bagot

Elizabeth House
Make

Fourth Grace
SMC Alsop

Gazprom headquarters
Studio Daniel Libeskind

Halley VI Research Station
Make

Nanjing South Rail Station
Kohn Pedersen Fox

Sustainable Service Station
Moxon Architects

Tantalus Winery
Bing Thom Architects

PICTURE CREDITS

1. ARTS AND ENTERTAINMENT

Arabian Performance Venue
Aedas

Birnbeck Island
Fletcher Priest Architects

Cuidad del Motor
Ben van Berkel / UN Studio

Crystal Palace
Wilkinson Eyre Architects

Musik Theater
Odile Decq Benoît Cornette
Architectes Urbanistes - Thomas Series

National Portrait Gallery
Sean Godsell Architects in association
with Peddle Thorp Architects

New Orleans Jazz Center and Park
Morphosis Architects

Performing Arts Centre
Ateliers Jean Nouvel

Qintai Art and Cultural Centre
© Arup Associates

Sarajevo National Concert Hall
Urban Future Organization

Senscity Paradise Universe
Behnisch Architekten

Sherwood Forest Visitors' Centre
Make Architects and Ken Shuttleworth

Stonehenge Visitors' Centre
Denton Corker Marshall

Taichung Metropolitan Opera House
© Zaha Hadid Architects

2. ACCOMMODATION

Battersea West Hotel
© Arup Associates

Bluewater
All renderings, sketches, and drawings
are produced by Taylor Smyth Architects

Doha Villa
Ushida Findlay and David Churchill
(photography)

Factory 798
© Bernard Tschumi Architects

Conversion of Freight Ship
Ivan Kroupa Architects

Hotel Pushkin
Jan Störmer & Partners GMBH

House in the Andes
Chetwoods Architects and
Andrew Putler (photography)

Maison d'Algérie
Estudio Carme Pinós

Moscow Avant Garde
(EEA) Erick van Egeraat
Associated Architects

Pizota Hotel
Estudio Carme Pinós

Prince Mansour Centre
Friis & Moltke Danish Architects

Sentosa Island
Tange Associates

Southern Sudan Palace
Jan Störmer and Partners GMBH

Urban Oasis
Ben van Berkel / UN Studio

W Hotel
Ateliers Jean Nouvel

3. MASTER PLANS

Aktau City Expansion
Koetter Kim & Associates

Battersea Power Station
Arup AGU © Cecil Balmond

Daejeon Urban Renaissance
Moxon Architects

Heart of the Forest
Images on behalf of
Edward Cullinan Architects

Murjan City
Henning Larsen Architects

New York 2012 Olympic Village
© Zaha Hadid Architects

Sewoon District Urban Redevelopment
Koetter Kim & Associates

Shenzhen Cultural Centre
Images courtesy of LAB
Architecture Studio

West Kowloon
Aedas

West Kowloon Culture Park
Moshe Safdie & Associates

4. MUSEUMS

Canadian Museum for Human Rights
Antoine Predock Architect PC

*Civilization Museum of Europe
and the Mediterranean*
Tod Williams Billie Tsien Architects

Estonian National Museum
© Gianni Botsford Architects

Eyebeam Museum of Art and Technology
Courtesy of Diller Scofidio + Renfro

Guggenheim Museum
Asymptote
Hani Rashid + Lise Anne Couture

Guggenheim Museum
Ateliers Jean Nouvel

Liaunig Collection Museum
Odile Decq Benoît Cornette Architectes
Urbanistes - Thomas Series

Moesgaard Museum
Tod Williams Billie Tsien Architects
and Michael Moran Photography

Museum of Contemporary Art
Sauerbruch Hutton

Museum Contemporary Art Warsaw
White Arkitekter AB

Sheikh Zayed National Museum
Moriyama & Teshima Architects

Sheikh Zayed National Museum
Shigeru Ban Architects

Victoria & Albert Museum Extension
Studio Daniel Libeskind

World Mammoth and Permafrost Museum
Antoine Predock Architect PC

5. BRIDGES AND TOWERS

Allegro Altura Tower
Tange Associates

Crow Creek Bridge
Bing Thom Architects

Dubai Tower
Grimshaw, Adam Parker

Footbridge over the Seine
Dietmar Feichtinger Architectes

Glasgow footbridge
© Smoothe

Hyperbuilding
Office for Metropolitan Architects
© All rights reserved

Manhal Oasis
ONL [Oosterhuis_Lenard]

Shanghai Center
RTKL Associates Inc

Shanghai Kiss
SMC Alsop
Tensegrity Bridge
Wilkinson Eyre Architects

The Edge
Denton Corker Marshall

The Legs
Aedas

Tour M
Skidmore, Owings & Merrill LLP

World Cultural Center
Rafael Viñoly Architects

World Trade Center
Foster & Partners

World Trade Centre Tower 1
Courtesy of FOA

Groninger Forum
(EEA) Erick van Egeraat Associated Architects

House of Human Rights Cultural Centre
Wilkinson Eyre Architects

Joesph Regenstein Library
Skidmore, Owings & Merrill LLP

Konstantinovsky Congress Centre
(EEA) Erick van Egeraat Associated Architects

Learning Centre, École Polytechnique
Fédérale de Lausanne
Mecanoo Architecture

Rome Congress Centre
Rogers Stirk Harbour & Partners,
Eamonn O'Mahony

Royal College of Art Battersea Campus
Feilden Clegg Bradley Studios

School of Design
Ben van Berkel / UN Studio

Würth Culture and Congress Centre
J. Mayer H. Architects

6. CULTURE AND EDUCATION

Architecture Foundation
© Zaha Hadid Architects

Belazel Academy of Arts and Design
Fletcher Priest Architects

Bicentenary Cultural Centre
KPMB Architects, Norm Li AG+I, Q Studio

Brown University Campus
Courtesy of Venturi, Scott Brown
& Associates Inc

Centre for Music, Art and Design,
University of Manitoba
Patkau Architects

Changsha Culture Park
MAD

Connecticut Centre for Science
and Exploration
Moshe Safdie & Associates

Dura Exemplar School
Architect: dRMM

Earth Centre EDEN
Kohn Pedersen Fox Associates
and Eamonn O'Mahony

European Solidarity Center
Courtesy of Pentagram Architects

Grand Mosque of Algiers
Architecture Studio

7. WORK AND TRAVEL

Al Rajhi Bank headquarters
Skidmore, Owings & Merrill LLP

BBC White City Music Centre
Courtesy of FOA

BMW Event and Delivery Centre
Sauerbruch Hutton

Collins Place
© Woods Bagot

Elizabeth House
Make Architects and Ken Shuttleworth

Fourth Grace
SMC Alsop

Gazprom headquarters
Studio Daniel Libeskind

Halley VI Research station
Make Architects and Ken Shuttleworth

Nanjing South Rail Station
Kohn Pedersen Fox Associates and Superview

Sustainable Service Station
Moxon Architects

Tantalus Winery
Bing Thom Architects

INDEX